Registered Land – The New Law

A Guide to the Land Registration Act 2002

Registered Land – The New Law

A Guide to the Land Registration Act 2002

Charles Harpum MA, LLB(Cantab)

*Barrister and Bencher, Lincoln's Inn; Sometime Law Commissioner;
Emeritus Fellow, Downing College, Cambridge*

Janet Bignell MA(Cantab), BCL(Oxon)

Barrister, Lincoln's Inn

JORDANS

2002

Published by
Jordan Publishing Limited
21 St Thomas Street
Bristol BS1 6JS

British Library Cataloguing-in-Publication Data

A catalogue record for this book is available from the British Library.

ISBN 0 85308 759 8

Typeset by Jordan Publishing Limited
Printed by MPG Books Limited, Bodmin, Cornwall

PREFACE

Conveyancing will never be quite the same again. The Land Registration Act 2002, which was introduced into Parliament on 21 June 2001, the day after the Queen's Speech, received Royal Assent on 26 February 2002 and is likely to be brought into force in October 2003. The Bill's remarkably speedy and untroubled passage through Parliament should not obscure the fact that it makes fundamental changes to the principles of real property and conveyancing in England and Wales. It has attracted attention primarily because it creates the framework for the introduction of an entirely electronic system of conveyancing to replace the present paper-based one. However, while electronic conveyancing still lies a few years off, the other major changes made by the Act do not. There is a great deal of new law that practitioners must grasp by October 2003 because it will affect what they do from the moment that the Act comes into force. In the course of the Second Reading debate on the Bill in the House of Lords, Lord Goodhart, with characteristic style, drew attention to one such change:

> 'Under the existing system various mechanisms are in place for limiting the powers of a registered owner to deal with the land. These are variously cautions, notices, restrictions and inhibitions. The new Bill simplifies these. It keeps notices and restrictions, but throws caution to the winds and abandons all inhibitions. Does this mean that, when the Bill is enacted, there will be Bacchanalian riots in the Land Registry – and can I have an invitation?'

The celebrations in HM Land Registry were, we understand, more decorous. However, the profound change to which Lord Goodhart referred is just one of many that is found in the Act. The Land Registration Act 2002 is not some tidying-up measure that merely re-enacts the substance of what was there before. It embodies a complete rethink of how a registered conveyancing system should work and, for example, introduces a completely different system of adverse possession for registered land. In this, as in other matters, it takes a leaf out of the book of many other Commonwealth countries. Land registration as we have known it in this country since 1875 has been a rather half-hearted affair. Registration has been widely perceived as a bureaucratic imposition, and its logic has never really been appreciated. This is rather puzzling. A system of title registration should be comprehensive and principled and the new Act seeks to make it so. A lawyer coming from a Torrens system of title registration might find it surprising that, in England and Wales, it has taken us so long to enact a genuine system of title registration of the kind that has operated so successfully in many Commonwealth countries for well over a century.

The new Act is only part of the story. A completely new set of draft Land Registration Rules will be issued for consultation by HM Land Registry very shortly. If that consultation is to be effective, the profession must come to terms with the new Act. This book is intended to assist practitioners to do that. It is a detailed examination of the Act. While it is not as extensive or technically detailed as the final report that was written by one of us and published in 2001 by the Law Commission and HM Land Registry with the draft Bill (Law Com No 271), it is, we hope, more approachable.

Charles Harpum *&* Janet Bignell
Falcon Chambers
June 2002

CONTENTS

TABLE OF CASES

TABLE OF STATUTES

TABLE OF STATUTORY INSTRUMENTS AND CONVENTIONS

TABLE OF ABBREVIATIONS

AEA 1925	Administration of Estates Act 1925
ATJA 1999	Access to Justice Act 1999
CLSA 1990	Courts and Legal Services Act 1990
CPR 1998	Civil Procedure Rules 1998
CRA 1965	Commons Registration Act 1965
ECA 2000	Electronic Communications Act 2000
FIA 2000	Freedom of Information Act 2000
GLAA 1999	Greater London Authority Act 1999
HA 1985	Housing Act 1985
IA 1986	Insolvency Act 1986
LA 1980	Limitation Act 1980
LCA 1925	Land Charges Act 1925
LCA 1972	Land Charges Act 1972
LPA 1925	Law of Property Act 1925
LPA 1969	Law of Property Act 1969
LP(MP)A 1989	Law of Property (Miscellaneous Provisions) Act 1989
LP(MP)A 1994	Law of Property (Miscellaneous Provisions) Act 1994
LRA 1925	Land Registration Act 1925
LRA 1986	Land Registration Act 1986
LRA 1988	Land Registration Act 1988
LRA 1997	Land Registration Act 1997
LRA 2002	Land Registration Act 2002
LRORR 1991	Land Registration (Open Register) Rules 1991
LROSR 1993	Land Registration (Official Searches) Rules 1993
LRR 1925	Land Registration Rules 1925
MCA 1980	Magistrates' Courts Act 1980
NLIS	National Land Information Service
SCA 1981	Supreme Court Act 1981
SCS	Standard Conditions of Sale (3rd edn)
SLA 1925	Settled Land Act 1925
TA 1925	Trustee Act 1925
TLATA 1996	Trusts of Land and Appointment of Trustees Act 1996

CHAPTER 1

BACKGROUND

LAND REGISTRATION IN ENGLAND AND WALES

1.1   The Land Registration Act 2002 (LRA 2002) is the culmination of a legislative process that began with the Land Registry Act 1862.[1] The essentials of the scheme of title registration that was adopted in England and Wales were first put forward in 1844.[2] However, it was not until 1875 that that scheme was implemented by the Land Transfer Act.[3] It was that Act that founded the Land Registry and the modern system of title registration. Further significant changes were made to the law by the Land Transfer Act 1897, the Law of Property Act 1922 and the Law of Property (Amendment) Act 1924 before the law was consolidated in the Land Registration Act 1925 (LRA 1925). That Act has itself been significantly amended over the years, most recently by the Land Registration Acts of 1986, 1988 and 1997.

1.2   The LRA 1925 has always been seen as the poor relation amongst the six great statutes that made up Lord Birkenhead's reforms of 1925.[4] It has been the subject of judicial and academic criticism.[5] Although it has been made to work comparatively well thanks to the ingenuity and enterprise of HM Land Registry, its replacement was inevitable. The appreciation that dealings with land, like most other forms of commerce, would have to change from a paper-based system to an electronic one, provided the catalyst for that replacement.

---

[1]   The Land Registry Act 1862 remains on the statute book, although it will be finally repealed when the LRA 2002 is brought into force: see LRA 2002, s 122.

[2]   By Robert Wilson, a solicitor. See J Stuart Anderson, *Lawyers and the Making of English Land Law 1832–1940* (1992), pp 58, 63 et seq.

[3]   It differed significantly from the system of title registration introduced by the Land Registry Act 1862.

[4]   The Acts were the Trustee Act 1925 (TA 1925), Law of Property Act 1925 (LPA 1925), LRA 1925, Land Charges Act 1925 (LCA 1925) (now replaced by Land Charges Act 1972 (LCA 1972)) and Administration of Estates Act 1925 (AEA 1925).

[5]   See, eg, Harpum, *Megarry & Wade's Law of Real Property* (Sweet & Maxwell, 5th edn, 1984), p 196: 'legislation of exceptionally low quality, which is in need of a thorough overhaul'; a comment cited and endorsed by Nourse LJ in *Clark v Chief Land Registrar* [1994] Ch 370, at p 382.

THE GENESIS OF THE LAND REGISTRATION ACT 2002

1.3   The LRA 2002, which is the most significant change to property law since Lord Birkenhead's reforms, received Royal Assent on 26 February 2002 and is likely to be brought into force in the second half of 2003.[1] When that happens, the Act will replace all existing legislation on land registration.[2] The reason why it is so significant is that it will introduce a completely new system of conveyancing within a comparatively short time. The present paper-based system will be replaced by a wholly electronic one. The Act is also designed to change the perception of registration. It creates a system whereby it will be the fact of registration that confers title rather than merely recording a title that has already been created.

The three joint Reports of the Law Commission and HM Land Registry

1.4   The LRA 2002 was the outcome of a joint project between HM Land Registry and the Law Commission which had begun in 1995. In the course of the project, the Registry and the Commission published three joint Reports.[3]

1.5   The first and shortest Report was intended to deal with certain pressing matters.[4] The draft Bill that was attached to that Report was enacted with minor changes as the Land Registration Act 1997 (LRA 1997).[5] The principal objective of that Act was to increase the speed at which unregistered land was brought on to the register. To achieve this goal the Act substantially increased the number of dispositions of unregistered land that triggered compulsory registration.[6] It also made it possible for the Lord Chancellor to introduce differential fees to encourage voluntary first registration.[7] In addition to these two

---

[1]   Some provisions of the LRA 2002 are likely to be brought into force before then to ensure that the many rules that will be required under the Act can be made.

[2]   See Sch 13 to the LRA 2002.

[3]   The Law Commission had previously published two Reports on Land Registration, proposing the replacement of the LRA 1925: see (1987) Law Com No 158 and (1988) Law Com No 173. These Reports were not written jointly with HM Land Registry and neither was accepted by the Government of the day.

[4]   (1995) Law Com No 235.

[5]   Although it was introduced as a Private Peer's Bill by Lord Browne-Wilkinson, it had Government support.

[6]   See LRA 1925, ss 123, 123A, as substituted and inserted by LRA 1997.

[7]   See LRA 1925, s 145(3), (3A), as substituted and inserted by LRA 1997.

measures, the Act also reformed the provisions of the LRA 1925 governing indemnity.[1]

1.6 The second Report, *Land Registration for the Twenty-First Century,*[2] took the form of a very substantial consultative document. Views were sought on wide-ranging proposals to replace the existing legislation on land registration with a new and very different Act. At the core of the proposals were two themes. The first was that registered conveyancing should move from a paper-based system to an entirely electronic one. The second was that the principles of registered land should be developed according to the logic and potential of a registered system (especially an electronic registered system), even though there would in consequence be marked differences as a matter of substantive law between registered and unregistered land. One striking illustration of the second theme was the proposal that the law of adverse possession as it applied to registered land should be recast so as to reflect the fact that the basis of registered title was registration and not possession (as it is in relation to unregistered land).[3] The second Report provoked a good deal of comment and debate. However, the great majority of the proposals in it were accepted on consultation and the responses formed the basis upon which Parliamentary Counsel at the Law Commission drafted a new Land Registration Bill. There was further consultation during the course of the drafting process with the Crown in relation to the registration of Crown land,[4] with the lending industry as regards further advances,[5] and generally, on the development of electronic conveyancing.[6]

1.7 The third joint Report, *Land Registration for the Twenty-First Century: A Conveyancing Revolution,*[7] comprised the draft Land Registration Bill together with a detailed commentary on the Bill running to some 370 pages and explanatory notes.[8] According to the Report:

---

1   See LRA 1925, s 83, as substituted by LRA 1997.
2   (1998) Law Com No 254.
3   This distinction has long been recognised by many Commonwealth countries that have Torrens systems of title registration.
4   See para **2.61**.
5   See para **4.12**.
6   See para **7.8**.
7   (2001) Law Com No 271. It was published on 10 July 2001 – after the Bill had been introduced into Parliament.
8   A separate set of explanatory notes was published with the Bill when it was introduced into Parliament. These notes were drafted by the Lord Chancellor's Department rather than by the Law Commission.

'The fundamental objective of the Bill is that, under the system of electronic dealing with land that it seeks to create, the register should be a complete and accurate reflection of the state of the title of the land at any given time, so that it is possible to investigate title to land on line, with the absolute minimum of additional enquiries and inspections.'[1]

In other words, the aim was for the first time to create a conclusive register, so far as it was possible. This would facilitate conveyancing by significantly reducing the enquiries that would have to be made. It would also necessarily make title more secure.

1.8   The Report accepted that the aim of a conclusive register could only be achieved by rethinking the way in which conveyancing was undertaken. At present, there is necessarily a period of time between the making of a disposition of registered land and its subsequent registration. This is because the disposition has to be submitted to HM Land Registry for registration, which inevitably takes some time. It follows that that register *cannot* at present reflect the true state of the title at any given moment. The Report acknowledged that the only way in which this goal could be achieved was if dispositions of registered land were simultaneously registered. To make that possible, not only would there have to be an electronic conveyancing system, but also the process of registration would have to be initiated by practitioners rather than by the Registry.[2] The Report also accepted that the other obvious consequence of the fundamental objective was the elimination of overriding interests – unregistered interests that bind a registered proprietor on first registration or on the making of a registered disposition – so far as this could be done.[3] The Bill reflected these aspirations. The Bill also contained provisions to implement a new system of adverse possession for registered land along the lines proposed in the second Report.

1.9   Although this third and final Report recommended certain extensions to compulsory first registration (that are reflected in the Act), it did not propose any mechanisms to compel the registration of the remaining unregistered land in England and Wales. This was so even though the Law Commission and HM Land Registry considered that all such remaining land *should* be registered as quickly as possible. The Report did, however, recommend that, 5 years after the Bill was

---

[1]   (2001) Law Com No 271, para 1.5.
[2]   Ibid, para 1.7.
[3]   Ibid, para 1.8.

brought into force, consideration should be given as to how all the remaining unregistered land might be brought on to the register.[1] There were three reasons for the delay. The first was that the effects of the changes made by the LRA 1997 and the Bill itself to compel or encourage first registration should be given an opportunity to work. Secondly, it was not easy to devise mechanisms for bringing the remaining titles on to the register that were proportionate to the intended goal.[2] Thirdly, the changes that the Bill would bring about were such as to stretch the resources of both the Land Registry and the legal profession for the next few years.[3]

THE LAND REGISTRATION BILL IN PARLIAMENT

1.10 The Land Registration Bill was introduced into the House of Lords on 21 June 2001, the day after the Queen's Speech following the General Election.[4] It had its Second Reading on 3 July 2001.[5] In terms of the Bill's policy, there were no significant changes to it during its passage through Parliament.[6] The only successful amendments were Government amendments, although a number of these were prompted by points raised in debate by the Opposition parties.[7] Those parties

---

[1] (2001) Law Com No 271, paras 2.9–2.13.

[2] The underlying problem is the cost of deducing title to such land to enable it to be registered. Even if there were no fee for registration, those conveyancing costs would have to be incurred.

[3] When the Bill was in Committee in the House of Commons, there was a lively debate, triggered by Mr Adrian Saunders MP (Liberal Democrat) about the need to compel the registration of all land in England and Wales.

[4] In that Speech, Her Majesty stated that 'Legislation will be introduced to reform the system of land registration to promote greater electronic conveyancing'. The proposals for the reform of land registration were in the Labour Party manifesto for the Election ('We will develop a modern basis for land registration to make conveyancing faster and cheaper') and were, accordingly, part of the Government's programme for the 2001–2 Session of Parliament.

[5] *Hansard* (HL), vol 626, col 726. The timetable (with references to debates where relevant) was thereafter as follows: Committee (House of Lords), 17 and 19 July 2001 (*Hansard* (HL), vol 626, cols 1384 and 1600); Report (House of Lords), 30 October 2001 (*Hansard* (HL), vol 627, col 1301); Third Reading (House of Lords), 8 November 2001 (*Hansard* (HL), vol 628, col 307); Introduction and First Reading (House of Commons), 8 November 2001; Second Reading Committee (House of Commons), 29 November 2001 (*Hansard* (HC), Session 2001–2, Standing Committee Debates, Standing Committee D), Second Reading, 3 December 2001; Committee, 11 and 13 December 2001 (*Hansard* (HC), Session 2001–2, Standing Committee Debates, Standing Committee D; Report and Third Reading, 11 February 2002 (*Hansard* (HC), vol 380, col 23); Consideration of Commons' Amendments, 26 February 2002 (*Hansard* (HL), vol 631, col 1322); Royal Assent, 26 February 2002.

[6] The Opposition did force a number of divisions, but none was successful.

[7] The Conservative Party enlisted the services of certain members of the Chancery Bar to assist it. The Liberal Democrats did not require such assistance. Their spokesman in the House of Lords was Lord Goodhart.

broadly welcomed the Bill and the debates were, in general, on points of detail, not principle.[1]

1.11 The main changes that are made by the LRA 2002 are summarised at the beginning of each chapter.

---

[1]   There was, however, the interesting spectacle of the Conservative Party apparently opposing the much tougher provisions on adverse possession: see *Hansard* (HL), vol 627, col 1376.

CHAPTER 2

FIRST REGISTRATION

THE MAIN CHANGES AT A GLANCE

2.1   Part 2 of the LRA 2002, which is concerned with the first registration of title, makes provision for the following matters:

- voluntary first registration;
- compulsory first registration;
- the effect of first registration; and
- cautions against first registration.[1]

In respect of each of these matters, the LRA 2002 makes significant changes to the law. Certain other matters are also explained in this chapter, namely the provisions found in Part 6 of the Act concerning the upgrading of titles and those in Part 7 which deal with voluntary and compulsory first registration of Crown land.

2.2   The main changes made by the LRA 2002 are as follows.

Voluntary registration

- The voluntary registration of *profits à prendre* in gross and franchises with their own titles is permitted for the first time.
- It is no longer possible to register a manor.

Compulsory registration

- Leases granted for more than 7 years become subject to compulsory registration.
- All leases granted to take effect in possession more than 3 months in advance are made subject to compulsory registration whatever their length.

---

1   See (2001) Law Com No 271, Part III.

Classes of title

– The range of persons who can apply for the upgrading of a title is extended to include persons who are entitled to be registered, chargees and persons (such as tenants) who are interested in a derivative estate.

Effect of first registration

– By way of an exception to the general rule that first registration merely reflects priorities that have already been determined according to the principles of unregistered conveyancing, the estate is held subject to interests acquired by adverse possession under the Limitation Act 1980 (LA 1980) only if the first registered proprietor has notice of them.
– The range of unregistered interests that can override first registration is cut back and provision is made for the phasing out of the overriding status of five categories of such interests 10 years after the LRA 2002 comes into force.

Cautions against first registration

– A cautions register is created to record the details of cautions against first registration.
– A person may no longer lodge a caution against the first registration of his own estate where that estate is one that he could have registered.

Crown land

– The Crown is given power to grant to itself a fee simple out of land held in demesne in order to register the title to it. In this way demesne land becomes registrable for the first time.

VOLUNTARY FIRST REGISTRATION

Introduction

2.3   Section 3 of the LRA 2002 sets out the circumstances in which a person may apply to the registrar[1] to be registered as the proprietor of an unregistered estate. The types of interest which may be the subject of voluntary first registration are:

---

[1]   That is, the Chief Land Registrar: LRA 2002, s 132(1).

(a)   an estate in land;

(b)   a rentcharge;

(c)   a franchise; and

(d)   a *profit à prendre* in gross.[1]

Who may apply for voluntary first registration?

2.4   A person may apply to be registered as first registered proprietor in two situations.[2] The first is where the applicant is the owner of an unregistered legal estate.[3] This is subject to one qualification. A legal mortgagee may not apply to be registered as the proprietor of a leasehold estate vested in him where there is a subsisting right of redemption.[4] The second situation in which a person may apply to be registered is where he is entitled to have an unregistered legal estate vested in him. This proposition is also qualified. A person may not apply to be registered if his entitlement arises under a contract to buy the land.[5] It follows that if A holds the unregistered legal estate on a bare trust for B as her nominee, B may apply for first registration. However, that will not be the case where the bare trust arises out of a contract by A to sell the land to B and B has paid the whole purchase price.[6] Were it not for this exception, it would be possible for a buyer of unregistered land to apply for voluntary first registration without first obtaining a conveyance of the legal estate to himself. This could have a number of undesirable consequences.[7] These provisions are not

---

[1]   LRA 2002, s 3(1).

[2]   Ibid, s 3(2).

[3]   'Legal estate' has the same meaning as in the LPA 1925: LRA 2002, s 132(1). The relevant provision of LPA 1925 is s 1, a provision that requires close attention.

[4]   LRA 2002, s 3(5). A mortgagee can therefore apply to be registered as proprietor of the legal estate previously held by the mortgagor where the latter can no longer redeem the mortgage. This will be so where the mortgagee has (i) obtained an order for foreclosure; or (ii) barred the rights of the mortgagor under the LA 1980, s 16 (by which an action for redemption may not be brought where the mortgagee has been in possession for 12 years).

[5]   LRA 2002, s 3(6).

[6]   It is well established that, where a buyer of land pays the entire purchase price, the seller holds the legal estate on a bare trust for him: see *Rose v Watson* (1864) 33 LJ Ch 385 (HL); *Chattey v Farndale Holdings Inc* [1997] 1 EGLR 153. See also *Bridges v Mees* [1957] Ch 475.

[7]   These include (i) the uncertain effect on priorities in relation to interests that would have been defeated had there been a conveyance of the legal estate; and (ii) the status of the contractual obligations of the parties that would otherwise have been merged in a conveyance of the legal estate. It would also provide a means of avoiding both stamp duty and the higher Land Registry fees that apply to compulsory (as opposed to voluntary) first registration. Notwithstanding these points, an Opposition amendment was tabled in the House of Lords by Baroness Buscombe, that would have enabled a buyer of unregistered legal estate who had paid the purchase price to apply to be registered in the absence of a conveyance of the legal estate: *Hansard* (HL), vol 627, col 1304. The amendment, which was prompted by The Law Society, was unsurprisingly withdrawn.

new but replicate the effect of the equivalent sections of the LRA 1925.[1]

The estates and interests that may be voluntarily registered

Registrable estates

2.5   As now, a fee simple absolute in possession may be registered.[2] A lease that has more than 7 years unexpired[3] at the time of application may also be voluntarily registered.[4] This is subject to two exceptions. First, a discontinuous lease of *any* duration may be registered.[5] As its name suggests, a discontinuous lease is a grant for a series of discontinuous periods of time, such as 2 weeks in any given calendar year for a total of 20 weeks.[6] Discontinuous leases are, in practice, rare, although they are sometimes used for time-share arrangements.[7] Secondly, what is called a 'PPP lease' cannot be voluntarily registered.[8] Provision is made in the GLAA 1999[9] for the grant of PPP leases as part of the proposed arrangements for the future of transport in London.[10] That Act empowers London Regional Transport, Transport for London and any of the subsidiaries of either body to enter into public–private partnership agreements for the provision, construction, renewal or improvement of a railway or proposed railway.[11] A PPP lease may be granted of any land comprised in any such PPP agreement and such land might include underground railway lines, stations and other installations. The reasons for excluding PPP leases from the registered system are practical and lie principally in the difficulties of mapping them.[12] It remains to be seen whether any such leases are ever granted.

---

1   See LRA 1925, ss 4, 8(1).
2   LRA 2002, s 3(1)(a).
3   For the power to reduce this period, see para **2.22**.
4   LRA 2002, s 3(3). In computing the length of the lease for these purposes, if the tenant holds a lease in possession and another in reversion that will take effect on, or within a month of, the end of the lease in possession, they are to be treated as one continuous term, provided that they relate to the same land: LRA 2002, s 3(7). This provision is not new, but replicates the Land Registration Rules 1925 (LRR 1925), SR&O 1925/1093, r 47.
5   LRA 2002, s 3(4).
6   Which means that the period during which the lease will in fact run is 10 years.
7   Cf *Cottage Holiday Associates Ltd v Customs and Excise Commissioners* [1983] QB 735.
8   LRA 2002, s 90(1). This replicates the effect of the Greater London Authority Act 1999 (GLAA 1999), s 219. It is anticipated that any PPP leases will be for a term of 30 years.
9   Part 4, chapter 7, which is concerned with Public–Private Partnership Agreements.
10   See (2001) Law Com No 271, para 8.11.
11   GLAA 1999, s 210.
12   See (2001) Law Com No 271, para 8.13.

2.6 The provisions of the LRA 2002 relating to leases significantly change the law. Under the LRA 1925, only leases with a term of more than 21 years still to run can be registered, whether the term is continuous or discontinuous.[1] The reduction in the length of leases that may be registered is connected with the changes to the circumstances in which leases are made subject to compulsory registration by the Act and the reasons for it are explained in that context.[2] There is a power for the Lord Chancellor to reduce the period still further by statutory instrument.[3]

Registrable interests

2.7 Under the LRA 2002, a number of incorporeal rights may be voluntarily registered with their own title.[4] These are:

(a) a rentcharge that is either perpetual or for a term of years of which more than 7 years are unexpired;

(b) a *profit à prendre* in gross which had been granted for an interest equivalent to a fee simple absolute in possession or for a term of years of which more than 7 years are unexpired; and

(c) a franchise which had been granted for an interest equivalent to a fee simple absolute in possession or for a term of years of which more than 7 years are unexpired.

2.8 Although under the LRA 1925 rentcharges were registrable with their own titles,[5] *profits à prendre* in gross and franchises were not. The Act provides that such profits and franchises may be voluntarily registered with their own titles. This gives effect to the outcome of consultation by the Law Commission and Land Registry on whether they should be so registrable.[6] Both *profits à prendre* in gross (such as fishing rights) and franchises (typically to hold a market) can be very valuable property rights. They may be (and in practice are) bought and sold. There is, therefore, every reason to make them registrable so that they can be dealt with as registered estates with the advantages that that brings.

2.9 One form of incorporeal right that was registrable under the

---

[1] LRA 1925, s 8(1).
[2] See paras **2.16**, **2.17**.
[3] LRA 2002, s 118(1). The power can only be exercised after prior consultation: s 118(3).
[4] Ibid, s 3(1)–(3).
[5] LRA 1925, ss 2(1), 3(xi).
[6] See (1998) Law Com No 254, paras 3.17–3.19; (2001) Law Com No 271, paras 3.19–3.20.

LRA 1925 ceases to be so under the Act. The Act contains no provision for the registration of a manor.[1] Indeed it contains provisions which enable the registered proprietor of a manor to apply to the registrar to have the title to the manor removed from the register.[2] The lordship of a manor is not an incumbrance on the land in any real sense.[3] It follows that the registration of manors offers few, if any, advantages and is, in practice, the cause of some difficulties.[4]

COMPULSORY FIRST REGISTRATION

Introduction

2.10 The number of dispositions of unregistered land that trigger compulsory registration of title was considerably extended by the LRA 1997.[5] The LRA 2002 broadly replicates the provisions of the LRA 1997, but adds a number of new triggers to compulsory registration.[6] These extensions proved to be amongst the most controversial provisions of the Act during its passage through Parliament. The reasons for the extensions are explained in paras **2.16** and **2.17**.

2.11 Compulsory registration of title may be triggered either by the transfer of a legal estate in unregistered land, or by the creation or grant of a legal estate. Some of the dispositions that trigger first registration are of what the Act calls 'a qualifying estate'. Others relate to specific types of transaction. For the purpose of the provisions on compulsory first registration, 'a qualifying estate' means an unregistered legal estate which is either a freehold estate in land or a leasehold estate in land for a term which, at the time of the transfer, grant or creation, has more than 7 years to run.[7] Dispositions of mines and minerals held apart from the surface are expressly excluded from the provisions on compulsory registration,[8] as they were under the LRA 1925.[9] However, there is no longer an express exclusion (as there was under the LRA 1925) for land which is part of a manor and which is included with the

---

[1]   In other words, the lordship of the manor.
[2]   LRA 2002, s 119.
[3]   The nature of a manor and the rights that it confers are very clearly set out by Lord Denning MR in *Corpus Christi College, Oxford v Gloucestershire County Council* [1983] QB 360, at p 365.
[4]   See (1998) Law Com No 254, para 3.20; (2001) Law Com No 271, para 3.21.
[5]   Replacing LRA 1925, s 123 and inserting a new s 123A.
[6]   LRA 2002, s 4.
[7]   Ibid, s 4(2).
[8]   Ibid, s 4(9).
[9]   LRA 1925, s 123(3)(b).

sale of the manor itself.[1] A disposition of such land will therefore be subject to the provisions of the Act on compulsory registration.

Dispositions of unregistered land that must be completed by registration

Transfers of a qualifying estate

2.12 Under s 4 of the LRA 2002, the following transfers of 'a qualifying estate' are required to be registered.

(1) A transfer for valuable or other consideration.[2] If the estate transferred has a negative value, so that the transferor pays the transferee to take the transfer, this is still to be regarded as a transfer for valuable or other consideration.[3]

(2) A transfer by way of gift.[4] A gift expressly includes the following situations:

    (a) where land is transferred by the owner to trustees in order to constitute a trust, except where that trust is a bare trust for the benefit of that owner;[5]

    (b) where a transfer of land is made to a beneficiary under a trust who is absolutely entitled to the land. It will not, however, be a gift if the beneficiary in question is the original settlor and the land is held on a bare trust for him.[6]

(3) A transfer in pursuance of an order of the court.[7] An example would be where, on divorce, a court ordered one spouse to transfer the matrimonial home to the other by way of a property adjustment order and the title to the home had not previously been registered.

(4) A transfer by means of an assent, including a vesting assent.[8] If, for example, executors assent to the vesting of an unregistered freehold

---

[1]   LRA 1925, s 123(3)(c). The reason for this rather curious exception was as follows. Where both the manor (that is, the lordship of the manor) and the lands of the manor are held by the same person and have not been severed, the lands are regarded as being appurtenant to the manor. As a manor was not subject to compulsory registration, it was thought that the sale of the lands appurtenant to it should not be either: see (1998) Law Com No 254, para 3.23. There can be practical difficulties in identifying the land which is appurtenant to the lordship of the manor, as where it includes grass verges and the like.

[2]   LRA 2002, s 4(1)(a)(i).

[3]   Ibid, s 4(6). The example that is given in (2001) Law Com No 271, para 3.26, is of a lease under which the rent payable exceeds the market rental, eg because of the operation of a rent review clause or as a result of onerous repairing obligations under the lease.

[4]   LRA 2002, s 4(1)(a)(i).

[5]   Ibid, s 4(7)(a).

[6]   Ibid, s 4(7)(b).

[7]   Ibid, s 4(1)(a)(i).

[8]   Ibid, s 4(1)(a)(ii).

estate in a person who is entitled to it under the deceased landowner's will, that assent triggers the requirement of compulsory registration. Similarly, where unregistered freehold land is held on the trusts of a Settled Land Act settlement, the life tenant dies and the land remains settled, the vesting assent in favour of the new tenant for life[1] will have to be completed by registration.

2.13 It will be clear from this list that not all transfers of a qualifying estate will trigger compulsory registration (or the Act would have said so). Among the transfers that will not are:

(a)   a transfer by a landowner to a nominee to hold on a bare trust for him;

(b)   a transfer by a nominee to the beneficiary for whom she holds on bare trust; and

(c)   where unregistered land is held in trust, the vesting of the legal estate in a new trustee.[2]

Furthermore, certain transfers are expressly excluded from the provisions explained in para **2.12**. First, a transfer by operation of law is not a 'transfer' for the purposes of those provisions.[3] If, for example, an unregistered freehold estate vests in the deceased owner's executors, that transfer does not trigger compulsory first registration. Secondly, the provisions do not apply either to the assignment of a mortgage term[4] or to the assignment or surrender of a lease to the owner of the immediate reversion where the term is to merge in the reversion.[5] Thirdly, transfers of PPP leases[6] will not be registrable.[7]

Transfers to which s 171A of the Housing Act 1985 applies

2.14 The LRA 2002 replicates the provision, formerly found in the

---

[1]   When the tenant for life dies and the land remains settled, the legal estate vests in the deceased life tenant's special personal representatives who will be the trustees of the settlement: see AEA 1925, s 22(1); Supreme Court Act 1981 (SCA 1981), s 116(1). It will be they (and not the tenant for life's general personal representatives) who will execute the vesting assent in favour of the next tenant for life: AEA 1925, s 24(1).

[2]   In consequence of the express or implied vesting declaration in the deed of appointment: TA 1925, s 40.

[3]   LRA 2002, s 4(3), replicating the effect of LRA 1925, s 123(6)(b), (c).

[4]   Ibid, s 4(4)(a). As mortgages by demise are seldom if ever created, mortgage terms are, in practice, rare.

[5]   Ibid, s 4(4)(b).

[6]   See para **2.5**. Even if PPP leases are created, the circumstances in which they will be transferable and the bodies to which they may be transferred will be very limited: GLAA 1999, s 217.

[7]   LRA 2002, s 90(2).

Housing Act 1985 (HA 1985),[1] by which certain transfers of an unregistered reversionary estate are subject to the requirements of compulsory registration, even though they would not otherwise be so.[2] This will be the case where a secure tenant had a right to buy his home under Part 5 of the HA 1985, but where the tenancy ceases to be a secure tenancy because the reversion is sold to a private sector landlord. That transfer of the reversion must be registered as part of the means by which the tenant's right to buy is preserved.

Leases granted for more than 7 years

2.15 The most striking change in the requirement of compulsory registration concerns the grant of leases. Under the LRA 2002, the grant of a lease for a term of more than 7 years from the date of the grant must be registered if that grant is made for valuable or other consideration, is by way of gift or is in pursuance of an order of the court.[3] This is a significant extension from the former requirement that only leases granted for more than 21 years were compulsorily registrable. The change is carried through into other provisions of the Act. Thus:

- a lessee holding under an unregistered lease which has more than 7 years to run may, if he chooses, voluntarily register the title to that lease;[4]
- the transfer of an unregistered lease with more than 7 years to run is subject to the requirement of compulsory registration;[5]
- where a proprietor of a registered estate grants a lease for more than 7 years that is a registrable disposition;[6] and
- an unregistered lease will only override first registration or a registered disposition if it is not otherwise registrable and is for a term not exceeding 7 years.[7]

These changes were amongst the most contentious aspects of the Act during its passage through Parliament and they prompted divisions in

---

[1]   Schedule 9A, para 2(1).
[2]   LRA 2002, s 4(1)(b).
[3]   Ibid, s 4(1)(c). For the meaning of 'valuable or other consideration' and 'gift', see para **2.12** and LRA 2002, s 4(6), (7).
[4]   LRA 2002, s 3(3); para **2.5**.
[5]   Ibid, s 4(1)(a); para **2.12**.
[6]   Ibid, s 27(2)(b)(i). See para **3.15**.
[7]   Ibid, Sch 1, para 1 (first registration); Sch 3, para 1 (registered dispositions); paras **2.48**, **3.92**.

both Houses.[1] The reasons for them appear both from the Law Commission Report[2] and from the debates in Parliament.

2.16 One of the goals of the LRA 2002 is to pave the way for a system of conveyancing that is wholly electronic and therefore entirely registered. It is intended that, in time, all dispositions of land that are required to be made by deed should be effected electronically and registered.[3] If that is to happen all leases granted for more than 3 years will, in due course, have to be brought within the compulsory registration provisions of the Act.[4] The LRA 2002 contains powers that will enable that reduction to be made by statutory instrument.[5] Furthermore, under the Act, there is a power to enter a notice in the register in respect of a lease granted for a term of more than 3 years (and not merely in respect of a lease granted for more than 7 years).[6]

2.17 The reduction in the length of registrable lease from those in excess of 21 years to those granted for more than 7 years is not only the first step towards the Act's ultimate goal. It also means that the great majority of business leases will become registrable.[7] Although at one time such leases were normally granted for terms of more than 21 years, most are now granted for 10- or 15-year terms. It was a major shortcoming in the registered system that the principal form of commercial dealing with land, namely the business lease, could not be registered. It followed that such leases had to be dealt with in accordance with the principles of unregistered conveyancing. An important factor that persuaded the Government to make the reduction in the length of registrable leases is the transparency of the property market.[8] This reduction needs to be viewed against two other factors.

---

1 See *Hansard* (HL), 8 November 2001, vol 628, cols 309, 310; *Hansard* (HC), 11 December 2001, Report of Standing Committee D (proposed Conservative amendment to Cl 4).

2 See (2001) Law Com No 271, paras 2.6, 3.14–3.17. There had been prior consultation on the length of registrable leases: see (1998) Law Com No 254, paras 3.7–3.10. The outcome was, however, inconclusive.

3 See (2001) Law Com No 271, para 3.17.

4 The only leases that can be created orally without a deed are those granted for 3 years or less at the best rent which can be reasonably obtained without taking a fine: LPA 1925, s 54(2).

5 LRA 2002, s 118(1). The Lord Chancellor must consult before he exercises the power: s 118(3).

6 This follows from LRA 2002, s 33(b); para **3.49**.

7 It was stated by Mr Michael Wills MP (the Parliamentary Secretary in the Lord Chancellor's Department) in Parliament that 'The Land Registry can ... expect the Bill's proposals to result in between 20,000 and 30,000 new leases, plus assignments of extant unregistered leases where the un-expired residue exceeds the relevant minimum': *Hansard* (HC), 11 December 2001, Report of Standing Committee D, discussion of a proposed Conservative amendment to Cl 4.

8 See, eg, the comments of Mr Michael Wills MP, *Hansard* (HC), 11 December 2001, Report of Standing Committee D, discussion of a proposed Conservative amendment to Cl 4.

The first is the open register, which has become the principal source of accurate information about property dealings that have to be registered. Secondly, under the LRA 1925, it was not possible to inspect leases or charges referred to in the register.[1] The LRA 2002 removes that restriction,[2] although it is anticipated that rules will be made[3] that are likely to reflect the provisions of Part II of the Freedom of Information Act 2000 (FIA 2000) which exempt certain information from disclosure under that Act. In particular, it is anticipated that information contained in leases and charges will be exempted from disclosure, if such disclosure would be likely to prejudice the commercial interests of any person.[4] There is little doubt that the information that will become accessible will provide a much fuller and more accurate picture of the leasehold market than is presently available and will be widely used by surveyors and valuers. There will also be conveyancing advantages.[5] Registration will facilitate dealings not only with business leases themselves but also with the reversions on such leases. For example, where there is a large commercial building occupied by many tenants and sub-tenants, it will in time become possible to see from the register exactly what those interests are. This is not presently possible because many of the leases will not be registered and extensive enquiries may, therefore, have to be made.

Reversionary leases

2.18 Another important change that the LRA 2002 has introduced is the requirement that all leases of whatever length that are granted out of unregistered land must be registered if they are to take effect in possession more than 3 months from the date of the grant.[6] The reason for this requirement is that such reversionary leases are otherwise very hard to discover. This change, which reflected the outcome of consultation,[7] is consistent with the stated goal of the Act to make the register as conclusive as possible and thereby to eliminate additional enquiries.[8] It needs to be kept in mind, as such reversionary leases are not uncommon.

---

[1]   See LRA 1925, s 112(1)(b).
[2]   LRA 2002, s 66(1)(b). See para **5.18**.
[3]   Under LRA 2002, s 66(2)(a).
[4]   See FIA 2000, s 43(2).
[5]   Although these will not necessarily be enjoyed by all leaseholders who have to register their leases under the LRA 2002.
[6]   LRA 2002, s 4(1)(d).
[7]   See (1998) Law Com No 254, paras 5.91, 5.94; (2001) Law Com No 271, para 3.32.
[8]   See para **1.7**.

Grant of a right to buy lease

2.19 The grant of a right to buy lease under Part 5 of the HA 1985 remains subject to the requirement of compulsory registration, regardless of the length of that lease.[1]

Grant of a lease to which s 171A of the HA 1985 applies

2.20 It has been explained in para **2.14** that where land is subject to a secure tenancy and the tenant has a right to buy under Part 5 of the HA 1985, a transfer by the landlord of its interest to a private sector landlord must be completed by registration of the transferee's title (if that interest is not already registered). This is so even though the provisions on compulsory registration would not otherwise apply. The same is true where, instead of transferring its interest, the landlord grants a lease of the reversion to a private sector landlord: that lease must be registered whatever its length.[2] Once again, the LRA 2002 replicates the previous law.

Protected first legal mortgages

2.21 Certain legal mortgages of unregistered land trigger the requirement of compulsory registration of the estate that is charged. This will be the case where the owner of an unregistered legal estate, that is either a freehold or a lease with more than 7 years unexpired, creates a protected first legal mortgage.[3] To fall within these provisions, the mortgage must take effect on its creation as one that is to be protected by the deposit of documents of title relating to the mortgaged estate.[4] It must also rank in priority ahead of any other mortgages which then affect the mortgaged estate.[5] Although these provisions of the Act largely replicate the effect of their equivalent in the LRA 1925,[6] they go further in one respect. To reflect the reduction in the length of lease that is required to be registered,[7] they apply to a mortgage of a lease with more than 7 years to run.[8]

---

[1]   LRA 2002, s 4(1)(e), replacing in part HA 1985, s 154.
[2]   LRA 1925, s 4(1)(f), replacing HA 1985, Sch 9A, para 2(1).
[3]   LRA 2002, s 4(1)(g).
[4]   Ibid, s 4(8)(a).
[5]   Ibid, s 4(8)(b).
[6]   See LRA 1925, s 123(2) (as substituted by LRA 1997).
[7]   See para **2.15**.
[8]   Under LRA 1925, s 123(2), the requirement of registration applied only to protected mortgages of leases granted for more than 21 years.

Power to add further triggers to compulsory registration

2.22 Under s 5 of the LRA 2002, the Lord Chancellor may by order amend s 4 of the Act so as to add to the events[1] that trigger the requirement of registration.[2] The power is exercisable by statutory instrument.[3] Before exercising the power the Lord Chancellor is under an obligation to consult on the proposed order.[4] The 'events' to which the section refers is an event relating to any of the following interests in unregistered land:

(a)   an estate in land;
(b)   a rentcharge;
(c)   a franchise; and
(d)   a *profit à prendre* in gross.[5]

This power is wider in a number of respects than its equivalent in the LRA 1925.[6] In particular, under the LRA 1925, the power could only be employed to add to the *dispositions* of, or otherwise affecting a legal estate in unregistered land that were required to be registered. Because that power was confined to 'dispositions', it was narrower than the power contained in the LRA 2002, which applies to 'events'.[7]

The requirement of registration and its enforcement

2.23 The LRA 2002 does not change the nature of the requirement of registration or the sanctions for failing to comply with that

---

[1]   This word echoes the language of LRA 2002, s 4(1), which specifies the events to which the requirement of registration applies.
[2]   LRA 2002, s 5(1)(a). He may also make such consequential amendments of any provision of any Act, or having effect under any Act (such as delegated legislation) as he thinks appropriate: s 5(1)(b).
[3]   Subject to annulment in pursuance of a resolution of either House of Parliament: see LRA 2002, s 128(4).
[4]   LRA 2002, s 5(4). There was no equivalent obligation in relation to the similar power contained in LRA 1925, s 2(4), although in practice it would not have been exercised without prior consultation.
[5]   LRA 2002, s 5(2). The power cannot, however, be exercised to require the title to an estate granted to a person as mortgagee to be registered: s 5(3). There is no point in requiring a mortgagee to register its interest if the estate charged is not registered.
[6]   See s 123(4), (5) (as substituted by LRA 1997).
[7]   It is a moot point whether (for example) it would have been possible under LRA 1925, s 123(4), to provide that where there was a disposition of unregistered land of a particular description (such as the grant of a lease) the grantor could be required to register the estate out of which he had made the grant. It would plainly be possible under LRA 2002, s 5. In the passage of the Act through Parliament, there was an attempt by Lord Goodhart to extend the triggers in s 4 to include the case given in the example: see *Hansard* (HL), 17 July 2001, vol 626, col 1389. Although the Government was sympathetic, it was concerned that it would be cumbersome in practice, particularly where landowners granted short leases of small parcels of land: see the response of Baroness Scotland of Asthal (the Parliamentary Secretary): *Hansard* (HL), 17 July 2001,vol 626, col 1390.

requirement.[1] First, the Act sets out who must apply for registration and when.[2] Where the requirement to register arises because of the creation of a first legal mortgage,[3] the estate that has to be registered is that which is mortgaged and it is incumbent on the owner of that estate to apply for registration within 2 months of the creation of the mortgage.[4] In all other cases, the grantee or transferee must apply for the registration of the estate transferred or granted within 2 months of the grant or transfer.[5] It is open to any interested person to apply to the registrar for an extension of the 2-month period for registration. He may by order extend the period to a specified later date if he is satisfied that there is a good reason to do so.[6]

2.24 Secondly, the LRA 2002 specifies the effect of non-compliance with the requirement of registration.[7] If registration does not take place within 2 months (or such longer period as the registrar may previously have specified by order), the transfer, grant or creation becomes void in so far as it transferred, granted or created a legal estate.[8] In the case of a transfer, the title to the legal estate then reverts to the transferor who holds it on a bare trust for the transferee.[9] In all other cases, the grant or creation has effect as a contract made for valuable consideration to grant or create the legal estate concerned.[10] If the period of 2 months has elapsed since the relevant event occurred but subsequently, following an application to him, the registrar then extends the period by order,[11] the transfer, grant or creation is treated as if it had never become void.[12]

---

[1]   For the previous law, see LRA 1925, s 123A (as inserted by LRA 1997).

[2]   LRA 2002, s 6.

[3]   See para **2.21**.

[4]   LRA 2002, s 6(1), (2), (4). Rules may make provision whereby the mortgagee can apply for the registration of the estate charged by the mortgage whether or not the mortgagor consents: s 6(6). This replicates LRA 1925, s 123A(10)(b). For the rule made under that power, see LRR 1925, r 19(2).

[5]   LRA 2002, s 6(1), (3), (4). Registration need not be in the name of the grantee or transferee. It could (for example) be vested in a nominee or a person to whom the grantee or transferee had assigned his interest.

[6]   Ibid, s 6(4), (5).

[7]   Ibid, s 7.

[8]   Ibid, s 7(1).

[9]   Ibid, s 7(2)(a). The fact that the legal estate may revert in this way does not mean that the transferee of a fee simple initially had a determinable (and therefore an equitable) fee simple: see s 7(4).

[10]   Ibid, s 7(2)(b). As such it is vulnerable should the grantor or the person creating the mortgage execute a subsequent disposition of the legal estate. The estate contract may not bind that subsequent disponee unless it has been registered as a Class C(iv) land charge under LCA 1972, s 2(4): see LCA 1972, s 4(6).

[11]   Under LRA 2002, s 6(5); see also para **2.23**.

[12]   Ibid, s 7(3).

2.25 Thirdly, the Act makes provision as to what should happen if a disposition of a legal estate becomes void for non-registration so that it has to be repeated.[1] The transferee, grantee or mortgagor is liable to the other party for all the proper costs of, or incidental to, executing afresh the transfer, grant or mortgage.[2] He is also liable to indemnify the other party in respect of any liability reasonably incurred by him because of the failure to comply with the requirement of registration.[3] In relation to these matters, the Act does no more than set out the default position. It is open to the parties to agree otherwise.[4] In the case of a protected first legal mortgage, the parties to the charge may well agree to change the default position because the mortgagee will necessarily have custody of the documents of title that are needed to secure registration of the underlying legal estate.

Dispositions pending registration

2.26 The LRA 2002 contains a rule-making power which will apply the provisions of the Act to a dealing with unregistered land that occurs *after* a disposition has been made that triggers the requirement of compulsory registration but before the disposition is registered.[5] This replicates a power previously found in the LRA 1925.[6]

CLASSES OF TITLE

The class of title given on first registration

2.27 On an application for first registration, whether that application is voluntary or one which has to be made, the applicant will be registered with a particular class of title on satisfying the requirements of the registrar. The LRA 2002 does not change the classes of title with which an applicant for first registration may be registered.[7] Nor does it alter the nature of those classes of title. An applicant who seeks to be

---

[1]   LRA 2002, s 8.
[2]   Ibid, s 8(a).
[3]   Ibid, s 8(b).
[4]   LRA 1925, s 123A(8) stated explicitly that this was the case. However, 'Although not expressly stated as in the earlier provision, there is nothing in the Bill which prevents that liability being placed elsewhere on agreement between the parties. Indeed, there will usually be discussions between a buyer's advisers and those acting for the lender during the conveyancing process about the post-completion submission of a single application to the Land Registry covering all aspects of the transaction': Baroness Scotland of Asthal, *Hansard* (HL), 30 October 2001, vol 627, col 1321.
[5]   LRA 2002, Sch 10, para 1.
[6]   See s 123A(10). See LRR 1925, r 73.
[7]   LRA 2002, ss 9 (freehold title), 10 (leasehold title).

registered as proprietor of a freehold estate may be registered with any
of the following titles:

(1) *Absolute title* will be appropriate if the registrar is of the opinion that
the title is such that a willing buyer could properly be advised to
accept by a competent professional adviser.[1] The registrar may
register a title with absolute title even if it is open to objection,
provided that he considers that the defect is not such as will cause
the holding under the title to be disturbed.[2] The vast majority of
freehold titles are registered with absolute title.

(2) *Qualified title* will be appropriate if the title has only been established
for a limited period or subject to certain limitations that cannot be
disregarded because there is a risk that they may cause the holding
under the title to be disturbed.[3] Qualified title is very rare.[4]

(3) *Possessory title* is a residual category. It will be appropriate where the
applicant for registration is either in actual possession of the land or
in receipt of the rents and profits by virtue of his estate, and there is
no other class of title with which it may be registered.[5] In practice,
possessory title is given where the applicant's title deeds have been
lost or destroyed or where he claims title by adverse possession. In
either case the registrar will have no evidence as to the title.

2.28 Where the applicant seeks to be registered as proprietor of a
leasehold estate he may be registered with one of the following titles:

(1) *Absolute title* will be appropriate if (i) the title satisfies the
requirements mentioned in para **2.27**; *and* (ii) the registrar approves
the lessor's title to grant the lease.[6] The latter requirement will only
be satisfied if the lessor's title has itself already been registered with
absolute title or if the registrar has examined that title and is
satisfied with it. It should be noted that the Act changes the rules as
to the title which a lessor is required to deduce under a contract to
grant a lease that is subject to the requirement of compulsory
registration.[7] A lessor is now required to deduce his title to the

---

[1]   LRA 2002, s 9(2).
[2]   Ibid, s 9(3).
[3]   Ibid, s 9(4).
[4]   The example given in (2001) Law Com No 271, para 3.43(2) is where it was apparent to the registrar
      that the transfer to the applicant for first registration had been in breach of trust.
[5]   LRA 2002, s 9(5).
[6]   Ibid, s 10(2), (4).
[7]   Ibid, Sch 11, para 2(2), introducing a new LPA 1925, s 44(4A).

intending lessee unless the parties agree otherwise (a reversal of the principle that had applied previously).[1]

(2) *Good leasehold title* will be the appropriate title if the applicant can satisfy only the first of the two conditions for an absolute leasehold title set out in (1) but not the second.

(3) *Qualified title* will be appropriate if the title to either the lease or the reversion has been established only for a limited period or subject to certain limitations that cannot be disregarded because there is a risk that they may cause the holding under the title to be disturbed.[2]

(4) *Possessory title* will be the appropriate title in the same circumstances as it is where the title is freehold.[3]

Upgrading titles

The registrar's power to upgrade titles that are not absolute

2.29 Part 6 of the LRA 2002 contains provisions which empower the registrar to upgrade a title that is not absolute in certain circumstances.[4] First, if at any time the registrar is satisfied as to the title to a relevant estate that is not registered with absolute title he may upgrade the title. In deciding whether or not he is satisfied, he must apply the same standards as he would on first registration.[5] The registrar may upgrade as follows:

(a) from possessory or qualified freehold to absolute;[6]

(b) from good leasehold title to an absolute if he is satisfied as to the superior title;[7]

(c) from possessory or qualified leasehold title to good leasehold if he is satisfied as to the title to the leasehold estate;[8] and

---

[1]   The intention is obviously to encourage the first registration of leaseholds with absolute title wherever possible. However, it is often the case that no contract will precede the grant of a lease, so that this change will not apply. In any event, the lease may come in for registration either on an assignment or on an application for voluntary registration where there has been no triggering event.

[2]   LRA 2002, s 10(5).

[3]   Ibid, s 10(6). See para **2.27**(3).

[4]   Ibid, s 62. The provisions are similar but not identical to those that were found in LRA 1925, s 77 (as substituted by LRA 1986).

[5]   LRA 2002, s 62(8).

[6]   Ibid, s 62(1). For example, if an estate had been registered with a possessory title because the documents of title had been lost (see para **2.27**(3)), it could be upgraded to absolute if the title deeds subsequently came to light and the title was sufficiently proved. Before a qualified title could be upgraded, the registrar would have to be satisfied that the particular problem that prompted the initial registration had ceased to cast doubt on the title.

[7]   Ibid, s 62(2). This might happen where, eg, the title to the freehold reversion was registered.

[8]   Ibid, s 62(3)(a).

(d) from possessory or qualified leasehold title to absolute if he is satisfied both as to the title to the lease and as to the superior title.[1]

2.30 Secondly, the registrar may upgrade a possessory freehold title to absolute and a possessory leasehold to good leasehold provided that:

(a) the title has been entered in the register for at least 12 years;[2] and
(b) the proprietor is in possession of the land.[3]

The proprietor will be in possession of the land for these purposes if it is physically either in his possession or in the possession of a person who is entitled to be registered as proprietor.[4] A proprietor will also be regarded as being in possession where:

(a) he is a landlord and the estate is in the physical possession of his tenant (or any sub-tenant to whom he had underlet);
(b) he is a mortgagor and the estate is in the physical possession of the mortgagee (or any tenant to whom the mortgagee had leased the land under his power of leasing);
(c) he is a licensor and the estate is in the physical possession of a licensee; and
(d) he is a trustee and the estate is in the physical possession of a beneficiary under the trust.[5]

It is explained in Chapter 5 that this definition of proprietor in possession is also relevant in the context of rectification of the register.[6]

2.31 The powers to upgrade explained in paras **2.29** and **2.30** cannot be exercised if:

---

[1] LRA 2002, s 62(3)(b).
[2] There is a power to change this period by order: LRA 2002, s 62(9). Such an order has to be made by statutory instrument and is subject to annulment in pursuance of a resolution of either House of Parliament: LRA 2002, s 128(4)(d). The period of 12 years is indirectly linked to the limitation period under LA 1980, s 15 (12-year limitation period in actions to recover possession of land). After 12 years, any adverse rights are likely to have been barred even if they were not at the time of first registration. Although LA 1980 does not apply to registered estates under the Act (as explained in Chapter 8), it does continue to apply to matters excluded from the effect of first registration, as where registration is with a possessory title.
[3] LRA 2002, s 62(4), (5).
[4] Ibid, s 131(1). Examples of persons who are entitled to be registered as proprietor include the registered proprietor's trustee in bankruptcy, his personal representatives, or a beneficiary under a bare trust for whom he holds as nominee. It will not include a squatter who is entitled to be registered under the provisions of Sch 6 to the Act: s 131(3).
[5] Ibid, s 131(2).
[6] See para **5.56**.

(a)   there is outstanding any claim that is adverse to the title of the registered proprietor; and

(b)   that claim is made by virtue of an estate, right or interest whose enforceability is preserved by the existing entry about the class of title.[1]

This provision is not new[2] and its purpose is to ensure that where there is such an outstanding claim it is resolved before title can be upgraded.

2.32 The LRA 2002 makes one material change in relation to upgrading title. Under the LRA 1925, upgrading could only happen if either the registrar decided to act on his own initiative or the registered proprietor applied to have the title upgraded.[3] It was not open to anyone else to apply for such upgrading, even though other persons might have had a very good reason for wishing to do so. Obvious cases were a mortgagee or an executor who, in either case, wished to exercise his power of sale. The most that he could do was to request the registrar to exercise his powers. The category of persons who can apply is significantly widened by the Act and comprises:

(a)   the registered proprietor of the estate in question;

(b)   a person who is entitled to be registered as proprietor of that estate;

(c)   the proprietor of a registered charge affecting that estate; and

(d)   a person interested in a registered estate which derives from the estate in question (such as a tenant).[4]

The effect of upgrading title

2.33 The LRA 1925 did not set out the effect of upgrading a title, but left the matter implicit. By contrast, s 63 of the LRA 2002 does specify the effect of upgrading title. Where a title is upgraded to absolute, the proprietor ceases to hold the estate subject to any estate, right or interest whose enforceability was preserved by virtue of the previous entry as to the class of title.[5] The same is true where a possessor or qualified leasehold title is upgraded to good leasehold, except that the upgrading does not affect or prejudice the enforcement of any estate,

---

1   LRA 2002, s 62(6).
2   See LRA 1925, s 77(4).
3   Ibid, s 77(1)–(3).
4   LRA 2002, s 62(7).
5   Ibid, s 63(1).

right or interest which affects or is in derogation of the lessor's title to grant the lease.[1]

Indemnity

2.34 It follows from what is said in para **2.33** that upgrading a title involves an element of risk. An estate, right or interest may be defeated in the process. The LRA 2002, therefore, like the LRA 1925 before it,[2] provides for the payment of indemnity by the registrar for any person who suffers loss by reason of the change of title.[3]

THE EFFECT OF FIRST REGISTRATION

Introduction

2.35 The effect of first registration depends upon the class of title with which the estate is registered. As a general principle and, as a result of the LRA 2002, subject to an important exception,[4] first registration does not affect priorities but merely reflects priorities that have already been determined. First registration may be voluntary so that there may have been no disposition to trigger registration. In any event, even where there is some disposition, that disposition precedes registration and any issue of competing priorities will be resolved at the time of that disposition. That resolution will depend upon the principles of unregistered conveyancing that necessarily apply to that disposition.

Freehold title

Absolute title

2.36 Where a first registered proprietor of a freehold estate is registered with absolute title, the estate is vested in him together with all interests subsisting for the benefit of that estate.[5] The estate is held subject to four matters which affect the estate on the date of first registration. These require explanation.

2.37 First, it is held subject to interests which are the subject of an

---

1   LRA 2002, s 63(2).
2   LRA 1925, s 77(6).
3   LRA 2002, Sch 8, para 1(2)(a). For indemnity, see para **5.67**.
4   See para **2.39**.
5   LRA 2002, s 11(2), (3).

entry in relation to the estate.[1] The entries in question will be notices, restrictions and registered charges.[2] On an application for first registration, the registrar will, in accordance with rules,[3] make entries in the register in respect of those interests that appear from the title to affect the estate. For example, if the property is subject to an easement, he will enter a notice in respect of that encumbrance on the charges register of the title. If the registered proprietor has limited powers of disposition, he will enter a restriction to reflect this fact.

2.38 Secondly, the registered estate is held subject to certain unregistered interests.[4] These interests – known under the LRA 1925 (but not under the LRA 2002) as 'overriding interests' – are explained at paras **2.46** et seq.

2.39 Thirdly, the estate is held subject to interests acquired under the LA 1980 of which the proprietor has notice.[5] This principle is new to the LRA 2002 and it marks a striking change in the law. To understand the reasons for it, it is necessary to explain the problem that it seeks to address. Under the LRA 1925, the first registered proprietor took the estate subject to rights previously acquired by any squatter under the LA 1980.[6] This was so whether or not the squatter was in actual occupation at the time when the proprietor was first registered. Furthermore, it was immaterial that the squatter's rights were undiscoverable. The following example will demonstrate how this might happen and the injustice that it could bring.

> A squatter was in adverse possession of unregistered land for more than 12 years. His own title[7] had therefore become indefeasible because the former owner's title had been extinguished.[8] The squatter subsequently left the land and the former owner resumed possession. Two years later, that former owner sold and conveyed the land as the apparent paper owner to a buyer, who became the first registered proprietor. If the squatter re-appeared less than 12 years after the former owner had resumed possession,[9] he would be able to recover the land from the

---

[1] LRA 2002, s 11(4)(a).

[2] For notices and restrictions, see Chapter 3. For registered charges, see Chapter 4.

[3] Made under LRA 2002, s 14; para **2.54**.

[4] Ibid, s 11(4)(b).

[5] Ibid, s 11(4)(c).

[6] LRA 1925, ss 5(b), 70(1)(f).

[7] A squatter has an independent and distinct fee simple absolute in possession from the moment that he takes adverse possession: see *Rosenberg v Cook* (1881) 8 QBD 162, at p 165.

[8] See LA 1980, ss 15, 17.

[9] Obviously, if more than 12 years had elapsed since the former owner had resumed possession of the land, the squatter's rights would themselves have been barred and extinguished under LA 1980.

buyer.[1] As his interest was an overriding interest that was binding on the buyer, that buyer would be unable to recover indemnity.[2] This was so even though the buyer had purchased from the apparent paper owner and could not reasonably have discovered that the land did in fact belong to an absent squatter.

2.40 The outcome in that example is self-evidently unsatisfactory. It seriously undermines the conclusive nature of the register of title and the guarantee of title that registration brings with it. The LRA 2002 therefore addresses the problem. Under the Act, where a person is registered as first registered proprietor in circumstances where a squatter is in fact entitled to the land by reason of his prior adverse possession, the squatter's right will only bind the first registered proprietor in two circumstances. The first (which is more fully explained at paras **2.48**(2) and **2.49**(2)) is where the squatter is in actual occupation of the land at the time of first registration. Although by virtue of that actual occupation the squatter's right to the land will override first registration,[3] that right should be readily discoverable from the fact of the squatter's presence. The second case, which is relevant here, is where the first registered proprietor has notice of the squatter's interest even though he is not in actual occupation.[4] As a result, if the facts given in the example in para **2.39** were to happen, the buyer of the land would take it free of the squatter's rights on first registration. This is so even though the squatter's rights bound him in the period between the conveyance of the land to him and the moment of first registration. This is the new principle which the LRA 2002 introduces and it constitutes an exception to the general rule, explained above,[5] that first registration does not affect priorities but merely reflects the state of the title as it was on the date of first registration. A squatter who acquires title to unregistered land by adverse possession and who ceases to occupy it should therefore take steps to protect his

---

[1] Even though the buyer was a proprietor who was in possession, the register could and probably would be rectified against him: see LRA 1925, s 82(3).

[2] See *Re Chowood's Registered Land* [1933] Ch 574. The buyer would not suffer loss by reason of the rectification (as required by LRA 1925, s 83(1)), but because he had acquired the land subject to an overriding interest.

[3] LRA 2002, Sch 1, para 2.

[4] Ibid, s 11(4)(c). The Act says 'notice' and not 'knowledge' (as it does elsewhere in the Act). It follows that the first registered proprietor will be bound by squatter's rights of which he ought to have known as well as those of which he actually knows. First registration may not have been prompted by any disposition and may be voluntary, or it may have been triggered by a gift (whether *inter vivos* or testamentary). It follows that the usual enquiries and inspections that would have been made on a purchase will not have been made. What constitutes notice must, therefore, be judged according to the circumstances and not according to one yardstick.

[5] See para **2.35**.

interest by applying for first registration of title.[1] The LRA 2002 contains a transitional provision whereby any squatter who, under the LA 1980, had become entitled to the land by virtue of his adverse possession, will be protected for a period of 3 years.[2] His rights will override any first registration in that period even though he is not in actual occupation. This will give such persons a reasonable opportunity to apply for registration during that transitional period, although it does of course mean that the evil which the LRA 2002 addresses remains for that period.[3]

2.41 Fourthly, where the registered proprietor is either not entitled to the estate for his own benefit at all or is not solely entitled, he holds the estate subject to such of the interests of those beneficially entitled as he has notice of.[4] This provision ensures that, for example, where the first registered proprietor holds the estate on trust, he does not take free of those trusts.[5] However, the provision is not limited to interests under a trust, but could include, for example, the rights of a person with an equity arising by proprietary estoppel.

Qualified and possessory titles

2.42 Registration of a freehold with a qualified title has the same effect as does registration with an absolute title, with one exception. It does not affect the enforcement of any estate, right or interest which appears from the register to be excepted from the effect of registration.[6] Similarly, registration with possessory title has the same effect as registration with absolute title but, again, with an exception. It does not affect the enforcement of any estate, right or interest that is adverse to, or in derogation of, the proprietor's title, which is either subsisting at the time of first registration or is capable of arising.[7] For example, if the first registered proprietor was registered with possessory freehold title but it subsequently transpired that her title was only leasehold and not

---

[1]   They will not be able to lodge a caution against first registration: see LRA 2002, s 15(3); also para **2.58**.
[2]   Ibid, Sch 12, para 7.
[3]   The 3-year transitional period was criticised during the passage of the Act through Parliament by Lord Lester of Herne Hill: see *Hansard* (HL), 30 October 2001, vol 627, cols 1329–1332. His concern was whether the provision was compatible with the Human Rights Act 1998. However, it appears that he did not appreciate that a squatter would be protected if he were in actual occupation of the land affected: see col 1336. A 3-year transitional period would appear to be proportionate when balancing the claims of innocent purchasers in possession against absent squatters who have done nothing to protect their rights.
[4]   LRA 2002, s 11(5).
[5]   Cf LRA 1925, s 5(c) (the equivalent provision under the previous law).
[6]   LRA 2002, s 11(6).
[7]   Ibid, s 11(7).

freehold, registration with a possessory title would not prevent the freeholder from enforcing his rights on the termination of the lease.

Leasehold title

Absolute title

2.43 Where a first registered proprietor is registered with an absolute title to a leasehold estate, the effect is the same as where a person is registered as first registered proprietor of a freehold with an absolute title, with one exception.[1] The proprietor of the lease holds it subject not only to the four matters explained in paras **2.37–2.41**, but also to the implied and express covenants, obligations and liabilities incident to the leasehold estate.[2] Those burdens found in the lease that create proprietary rights, such as the landlord's right of re-entry or any restrictive covenants, are not noted on the register, but by virtue of this provision they still bind the lessee. The register will refer to the lease and it therefore constitutes part of the register. Any person who was intending to deal with the land (whether the lease, the reversion or perhaps some derivative interest) would inspect the lease and would therefore be aware of its contents.

Good leasehold title

2.44 First registration with a good leasehold title has the same effect as the first registration of a leaseholder with absolute title, except that it does not prejudice the enforcement of any estate, right or interest affecting, or in derogation of, the title of the lessor to grant the lease.[3]

Qualified and possessory titles

2.45 The first registration of a person as the proprietor of a leasehold estate with qualified or possessory title has the same effect as registration with absolute title, but subject to the same exceptions that have been explained in para **2.42** in relation to qualified and possessory freehold title.[4]

---

[1]   LRA 2002, s 12(2)–(4).
[2]   Ibid, s 12(4)(a).
[3]   Ibid, s 12(6).
[4]   Ibid, s 12(7), (8).

Unregistered interests which override first registration

Introduction

2.46 It has been explained above that, on first registration, the proprietor takes the estate subject to, amongst other matters, certain unregistered interests.[1] Overriding interests, as they were known under the LRA 1925, are a well-known and unsatisfactory feature of registered conveyancing. The existence of rights that affect a registered estate but do not appear on the register run counter to the objectives of a system of registered title. Such interests are necessarily incompatible with the fundamental objective of the LRA 2002, explained in Chapter 1, which is to make the register as complete and accurate a record of the title at any given time as is possible. The Act contains many provisions by which the impact of such unregistered interests can be minimised. These are explained at various places in the course of this book.[2]

2.47 In s 70(1) of the LRA 1925,[3] no explicit distinction was drawn between those unregistered interests that overrode first registration and those that overrode registered dispositions. However, such a distinction necessarily exists and the LRA 2002 makes this clear. It lists the unregistered interests that override first registration in Sch 1 and those that override registered dispositions in Sch 3. The lists are not the same.[4] As has been indicated above,[5] subject to one exception that is introduced by the LRA 2002,[6] first registration reflects the state of the title at the time of first registration and does not change the priority of interests that affect it. This is because first registration does not bring about any disposition of the land, whereas the registration of a registered disposition necessarily does. Thus in Sch 3, whether or not the person to whom a registered disposition has been made is bound by an unregistered interests depends, in some cases, on whether he made any enquiries about such rights or whether they met certain requirements as to their discoverability. However, such issues have no meaning in relation to first registration and there are no equivalent provisions in Sch 1. Whether or not the rights that fall within that

---

[1] See para **2.38**.
[2] See paras **2.49–2.52**, **3.92**, **3.93**, **3.109**.
[3] The subsection of LRA 1925 that listed overriding interests.
[4] The distinction puzzled Lord Kingsland when the Bill received its Second Reading in the Lords: see *Hansard* (HL), 3 July 2001, vol 626, col 794.
[5] See para **2.35**.
[6] See para **2.39**.

Schedule bind the first registered proprietor will have been determined before he applies for first registration.[1]

The interests that will override first registration

2.48 Schedule 1 to the LRA 2002 lists 14 interests that will bind the first registered proprietor even though they are not protected on the register. There is a fifteenth by virtue of s 90 of the Act. The interests are as follows.

(1)   Any lease granted for a term of 7 years or less unless it is required to be registered under the provisions explained at paras **2.18–2.20**.[2] This is the logical concomitant of the provisions on the compulsory registration of leases explained earlier in this chapter.[3] Those leases that are not subject to the requirement of registration necessarily override first registration even though they are not registered.[4]

(2)   An interest belonging to a person in actual occupation, so far as relating to land of which he is in actual occupation.[5] This provision partially replicates s 70(1)(g) of the LRA 1925 and, as was the case under that Act,[6] it is not possible to protect by actual occupation an interest under a settlement under the Settled Land Act 1925 (SLA 1925). The provision is narrower in two respects than s 70(1)(g) of the LRA 1925. First, the protection conferred on an interest is limited to the land actually occupied.[7] To the extent that the interest extends beyond that land, it is unprotected. This point is explained more fully in the context of unregistered interests which override registered dispositions, because it is only in that context that it is really material.[8] Secondly, protection is no longer given to those who are in receipt of the rents and profits of the land as well as those who are in actual occupation. This is of more significance in relation to unregistered interests that override a registered disposition and it is, once again, explained in more detail there.[9] For the reasons

---

[1]   See (2001) Law Com No 271, paras 8.3–8.5.

[2]   LRA 2002, Sch 1, para 1.

[3]   See para **2.15**.

[4]   The same protection applies to leases that were granted for more than 21 years before the Act came into force: LRA 2002, Sch 12, para 12.

[5]   LRA 2002, Sch 1, para 2.

[6]   See LRA 1925, s 86(2).

[7]   Cf *Ferrishurst Ltd v Wallcite Ltd* [1999] Ch 355, which the Act reverses.

[8]   See para **3.96**.

[9]   Ibid.

explained para **2.47**, Sch 1 does not include the words 'save where enquiry is made of such person[1] and the rights are not disclosed' that were found in s 70(1)(g) of the LRA 1925.

(3)   A legal easement or profit.[2] The only easements and profits that will be capable of overriding first registration are those that are legal. Equitable easements will never do so.[3] Furthermore, the provisions on disclosure explained below[4] should ensure that many such easements are in fact protected by notice on the register at first registration.

(4)   A customary right.[5] Customary rights are those that are enjoyed by all or some of the inhabitants of a particular locality, such as the ancient right of the freeman of the borough of Huntingdon to graze animals over certain land.[6]

(5)   A public right.[7] Such rights are exercisable by any person under the general law and include, for example, public rights of way.

(6)   A local land charge.[8] Local land charges operate under the quite separate regime created by the Local Land Charges Act 1975, which makes provision for their registration in local registers. Those registers are themselves being computerised by local authorities and it will become possible to access them through the National Land Information Service (NLIS).

(7)   Certain mineral rights. Three classes of mineral right override first registration. First, any interest in any coal or coal mines, the rights attached to such interests and certain other rights under the Coal Industry Act 1994 are all incapable of any form of registration under the Act[9] and override first registration as unregistered interests.[10] The extent and complexity of coal rights made it difficult to register them. However, the Coal Authority provides a system of coal mining searches so it is possible to discover what mining either has been or may in future be conducted on any particular land. Again, it is likely that it will become possible to conduct such searches on-line via NLIS. Secondly, for reasons connected with the practice of registration prior to the LRA 1925

---

[1]   That is, the person in actual occupation.
[2]   LRA 2002, Sch 1, para 3.
[3]   They could under LRA 1925, s 70(1)(a): see *Celsteel Ltd v Alton House Holdings Ltd* [1985] 1 WLR 204, at pp 219–221.
[4]   See para **2.51**.
[5]   LRA 2002, Sch 1, para 4.
[6]   See *Peggs v Lamb* [1994] Ch 172.
[7]   LRA 2002, Sch 1, para 5.
[8]   Ibid, para 6.
[9]   See LRA 2002, s 33(e); see also para **3.52**.
[10] LRA 2002, Sch 1, para 7.

in relation to mineral rights over registered land, mineral rights over land that were registered before 1898 will override first registration.[1] Thirdly, for the same reason, as regards land that was registered between 1898 and 1925, mineral rights created prior to such registration will, again, override first registration.[2]

(8)   A franchise.[3] Franchises arise out of an actual or presumed royal grant and can be valuable.[4] As explained above, it is possible for the first time under the Act to register such rights with their own titles.[5]

(9)   A manorial right.[6] It ceased to be possible to create manorial rights after 1925. However, such rights are quite common and include the lord's sporting rights or his rights to minerals.

(10)   What is commonly called a Crown rent.[7] This is a very obscure right but may have arisen, for example, on the grant of a freehold estate by the Crown with the reservation of a rent.

(11)   A non-statutory right in respect of an embankment or river or sea wall.[8] Once again, this is an obscure form of liability. It may affect a person who owns property that fronts on to the sea or a river. It may have arisen by prescription, grant, a covenant supported by a rentcharge, custom or tenure.

(12)   What is commonly called a corn rent.[9] This is perhaps the most arcane of the interests that can override first registration.[10] Technically, it is a liability on the owner of the land to make payments by any Act of Parliament other than one of the Tithe Acts, out of or charged upon land in commutation of tithes.

(13)   PPP leases.[11] The nature of these leases and the reasons why they are outside the registered system have been explained in para **2.5**.

Limiting the scope of unregistered interests that override first registration

2.49 It has been explained above that the existence of unregistered interests that can override first registration runs counter to the

---

[1]   LRA 2002, Sch 1, para 8.
[2]   Ibid, para 9.
[3]   Ibid, para 10.
[4]   Amongst the commonest are the franchise to hold a market.
[5]   LRA 2002, s 3; see also para **2.8**.
[6]   Ibid, Sch 1, para 11.
[7]   Ibid, para 12.
[8]   Ibid, Sch 1, para 13.
[9]   Ibid, para 14.
[10] Liability to pay corn rent still exists. The principal (but not only) beneficiaries are the Church Commissioners, who no longer collect it because it is uneconomic to do so.
[11] LRA 2002, s 90(5).

fundamental objective of the Act, which is to create a register that is as far as possible conclusive as to the state of the title at any time.[1] The LRA 2002 therefore adopts a number of strategies for eliminating such interests as far as possible. The first is to restrict the interests that can override first registration. This strategy has two aspects. The first is to remove overriding status from interests which previously had it under s 70(1) of the LRA 1925. There are three such interests:

(1) Liability for the repair of a church chancel.[2] This has lost its overriding status because the Court of Appeal has held that this form of liability contravenes the European Convention on Human Rights.[3]
(2) Squatter's rights.[4] If a squatter has barred the rights of the first registered proprietor before first registration, subject to the transitional provisions that have been explained above,[5] his rights will only override first registration if at the date of first registration he was in actual occupation or the first registered proprietor had notice of his rights.[6]
(3) Estates, rights and interests excluded from the effect of first registration in the case of possessory, qualified or good leasehold titles.[7] These are dealt with in a different way under the Act by way of the provisions on priorities.[8]

The second aspect of the strategy is to narrow the scope of the interests that can override first registration. The Act does this in relation to a number of the interests that fall within Sch 1 and, in particular, in relation to the three most important categories of interest, namely, leases, the interests of persons in actual occupation and easements and profits.

2.50 Secondly, the LRA 2002 makes provision for the phasing out of five of the interests 10 years after the Act is brought into force.[9] The

---

[1] See para **2.46**.
[2] See LRA 1925, s 70(1)(c).
[3] *Aston Cantlow and Wilmcote with Billesley PCC v Wallbank* [2001] EWCA Civ 713, [2001] 3 WLR 1323. The House of Lords has granted leave to appeal: [2002] 1 WLR 713.
[4] See LRA 1925, s 70(1)(f).
[5] See para **2.40**.
[6] Ibid.
[7] See LRA 1925, s 70(1)(h).
[8] See LRA 2002, ss 29(2)(a)(iii), 30(2)(a)(iii); see also para **3.33**.
[9] Ibid, s 117.

interests are those listed in para **2.48**(8)–(12).[1] If a person enjoys the benefit of one or more of those five interests over unregistered land, he will be entitled to lodge a caution against the first registration of the land affected without charge during that 10-year period.[2] In this way he can ensure that, on the first registration of that land, his interest will be noted on the register. If he fails to lodge a caution against first registration during that 10-year period, he will not lose his right. However, there is obviously a significant risk that if the land is then registered, the interest will not be noted on the title. Solicitors and licensed conveyancers may wish to consider whether any of their clients are likely to be affected by this provision and, if they are, to draw it to their attention.

2.51 Thirdly, s 71(a) of the LRA 2002 makes provision for rules to be made requiring an applicant for first registration to provide information about an interest affecting the estate which falls within Sch 1 and is of a description prescribed by the rules. The intention is to ensure that such interests are then protected by notice on the register at first registration. It follows that the registrar will only wish to know about those interests that are clearly established and are not disputed. It is anticipated that the rules will provide guidance as to when such information must be disclosed. Although there will initially be no sanction for failing to make the necessary disclosure, once electronic conveyancing has been introduced, an obligation to comply with s 71 is likely to be a term of any network access agreement.[3]

2.52 Fourthly, under s 37(1) of the LRA 2002, the registrar is given power to enter a notice on the register in respect of any interest that falls within Sch 1, unless it is an interest of a kind that cannot be protected by notice.[4] The registrar will be under an obligation to give notice of any such entry to such persons who may be specified by rules.[5] These are likely to include the registered proprietor, any registered chargee and the person having the benefit of the interest that has been protected.

---

[1]   Namely, franchises, manorial rights, Crown rents, liability to repair embankments, sea and river walls, and corn rents. For the reasons why these five were selected, see (2001) Law Com No 271, paras 8.87–8.88.

[2]   LRA 2002, s 117(2)(a). For cautions against first registration, see paras **2.55–2.60**.

[3]   For network access agreements, see para **7.38**.

[4]   For those interests, see LRA 2002, s 33; see also paras **3.47–3.53**.

[5]   LRA 2002, s 37(2).

RULES ABOUT FIRST REGISTRATION

2.53 The LRA 2002 contains certain rule-making powers that relate to first registration. First, there is a power to make rules about what the Act calls 'dependent estates'. These are intended to make provision for three situations. The first is where a person is registered as first registered proprietor of land and that land has the benefit of a legal estate (such as an easement or a profit[1]) over other land, the title to which is not registered. The rules will make provision as to how the benefit of that legal estate is to be recorded on the register.[2] The second situation is where, on first registration, the legal estate that is to be registered is subject to a pre-existing legal mortgage. Rules will provide how the mortgagee is to be registered as proprietor of the registered charge.[3] The third situation (which is covered by the same provision as the second) is where a legal charge is created subsequent to first registration that does not have to be registered to have effect as a legal estate. This is the case in relation to certain charges of a public character that take effect as local land charges.[4] However, such charges cannot be realised until they are registered as such.[5] Once again, rules will make provision for the registration of the mortgagee as proprietor of the registered charge.[6]

2.54 It is also necessary to have rules which explain how applications for first registration are to be made, what evidence of title is required and the making of entries on the register in pursuance of the application. Section 14 of the Act contains the necessary power. The rules made under the section will deal with the making of applications, the functions of the registrar following that application and the effect of any entry made pursuant to such an application.

---

[1] Under the LRA 2002, 'legal estate' has the same meaning as under LPA 1925: LRA 2002, s 132(1). Under the LPA 1925, s 1(4), 'legal estate' includes both legal estates in land within s 1(1), and legal interests or charges in or over land within s 1(2).

[2] LRA 2002, s 13(a).

[3] Ibid, s 13(b).

[4] For example, a charge by a street works authority for the cost of executing street works under the Highways Act 1980, s 212.

[5] LRA 2002, s 55.

[6] Ibid, s 13(b).

CAUTIONS AGAINST FIRST REGISTRATION

Introduction

2.55 Cautions against first registration provide a mechanism by which a person, who has some interest in unregistered land, can ensure that he is informed of any application for the first registration of that land. He may have grounds for wishing to oppose any such application[1] or, more commonly, he wishes to ensure that, on first registration, his interest will be protected on the register. Although the LRA 2002 prospectively abolishes cautions *against dealings*,[2] it retains cautions against first registration. However, it rationalises the way in which they are recorded, it extends the circumstances in which their entry may be challenged and it places a significant limitation on what may be protected by them.

Recording cautions against first registration

2.56 Under the LRA 1925, cautions against first registration were recorded on an index map (thereby indicating that there was a caution lodged against a particular parcel of land). The details of any such caution[3] were kept on what was called a 'caution title'. Under the LRA 2002, cautions against first registration are recorded on what the Act calls 'the index'.[4] The details of any given caution are kept on a new cautions register which the Act creates.[5] Both the court and registrar are given powers to alter the register of cautions that are analogous to those that apply to the register of title[6] for the purpose of correcting a mistake or bringing the register up to date.[7] Indemnity is also payable in respect of loss suffered as a result of a mistake in the cautions register.[8]

---

[1]   Perhaps because he has some claim to the land himself.

[2]   See para **3.44**.

[3]   Namely, the cautioner's name and address, the name and address of the solicitor or licensed conveyancer who lodged the caution, the estate against which the caution had been registered and an extract from the statutory declaration in support of the application to show the nature of the cautioner's interest.

[4]   LRA 2002, s 68(1)(c). It is envisaged that the index will no longer be tied to a map but might be kept in some other (dematerialised) form. See para **5.28**.

[5]   LRA 2002, s 19.

[6]   For alteration of the register of title, see para **5.48**.

[7]   LRA 2002, ss 20, 21.

[8]   Ibid, Sch 8, para 1(1)(g). For indemnity, see para **5.67**.

Lodging cautions against first registration

2.57 Under the LRA 2002, subject to one very significant exception,[1] a person may apply to the registrar[2] to lodge a caution against first registration if he claims to be either the owner of a qualifying estate or entitled to an interest affecting such a qualifying estate.[3] For these purposes, 'a qualifying estate' means:

(a)   an estate in land;
(b)   a rentcharge;
(c)   a franchise; and
(d)   a *profit à prendre* in gross,

that relates to the land to which the caution relates.[4] Thus, for example:

(i)   a tenant holding under a lease may lodge a caution against the first registration of his landlord's reversionary freehold estate;
(ii)   a person who claims the benefit of an easement or profit over a freehold estate may lodge 'a caution against the first registration of that estate; or
(iii) a beneficiary under a trust of land may lodge a caution against the first registration of the freehold estate held by the trustees.

The cautioner[5] has a right to withdraw the caution on application to the registrar.[6]

2.58 The LRA 2002 introduces a significant limitation on the power to lodge a caution against first registration. A person may not lodge a caution against the first registration of his own estate where that estate is either a freehold estate in land or a lease of which more than 7 years remains unexpired at the time when the caution is lodged.[7] The policy of this provision is that a caution against first registration should not be

---

1   See para **2.58**.
2   See LRA 2002, s 15(4).
3   Ibid, s 15(1).
4   Ibid, s 15(2).
5   Who, for these purposes, includes not only the person who lodged the caution but also such other persons as rules may provide: see LRA 2002, s 22. The persons likely to be included in rules are the personal representatives and trustee in bankruptcy of the person who lodged the caution. The cautioner (as defined) is the only person who can object to an application to cancel a caution against first registration: s 73(2). This is an exception to the general rule that anyone may object to an application made to the registrar: s 73(1).
6   LRA 2002, s 17.
7   Ibid, s 15(3).

used as a substitute for the first registration of a title.[1] This provision
will not take effect until 2 years after the Act is brought into force.[2]
However, any caution lodged within that 2-year period will cease to
have effect at the end of it except in relation to applications for first
registration made within the period.[3]

The effect of lodging a caution against first registration

2.59 The protection that a caution against first registration confers is
limited. When there is an application for the first registration of the
unregistered legal estate to which the caution relates, the registrar must
give the cautioner notice of the application and of his right to object to
it.[4] Rules will specify the period within which the cautioner will be
entitled to object. The registrar will only be able to determine an
application for first registration once that period has elapsed unless the
cautioner indicates before that date that he does not intend to object to
the application.[5] A caution against first registration has no effect on the
validity or priority of any interest that the cautioner may have in the
legal estate to which the caution relates.[6] In essence, therefore, the
lodging of a caution has no substantive effect. It is merely a procedural
device by which a person, who has an interest in unregistered land, is
alerted to an application for first registration. He may then oppose that
application if he so wishes. This will often be done to ensure that his

---

[1] See (2001) Law Com No 271, para 3.58. In practice, it is not common for landowners to lodge cautions
against the first registration of their own estates. Nonetheless, this provision provoked criticism (and
indeed a division) in the House of Lords. This was because it was said that it would force charities to
register their lands when presently they could protect their unregistered estates by lodging a caution
against first registration: see *Hansard* (HL), 17 July 2001, vol 626, cols 1412–1417. It seems to have
been thought that lodging a caution against first registration would protect such charities from
applications by squatters: see the comments of Baroness Buscombe at col 1413. However, lodging a
caution against first registration would only be useful in this regard if the squatter had not barred and
extinguished the landowner's title. By contrast, under the provisions explained in Chapter 8,
registration of a title *will* protect a registered proprietor against an application for registration by a
squatter in most cases. In any event, the appeal to the burden placed upon charities is questionable.
Given the substantial benefits conferred on charities, there is at least a case for saying that all charities
should be required to register their land so that the information about those properties is publicly
available.

[2] LRA 2002, Sch 12, para 14(1).

[3] Ibid, Sch 12, para 14(2).

[4] Ibid, s 16(1). The Act makes provision for an agent of the applicant for first registration to give notice
to the cautioner and, if he does, this is to be treated as given by the registrar: s 16(4). The persons who
can serve such a notice will be prescribed by rules, but are likely to include solicitors and licensed
conveyancers. Similarly, the circumstances in which a notice may be served will be a matter for rules.
The intention of this provision is to enable a solicitor or licensed conveyancer, who is acting for an
applicant for first registration, to serve a notice on the cautioner at the same time as the application for
first registration. This will speed up the conveyancing process.

[5] LRA 2002, s 16(2).

[6] Ibid, s 16(3).

interest is duly protected on the register of the legal estate to which it relates.

Removing or challenging a caution against first registration

2.60 The LRA 2002 contains a number of provisions that are intended to deter the improper lodgement of cautions against first registration.

(1) Should the owner of the land become aware that there has been an application to the registrar to lodge a caution against first registration, he may object to the application under the general power conferred by the Act for any person to object to an application.[1] If that objection cannot be disposed of by agreement, it will be referred to the Adjudicator for resolution.[2]

(2) The Act gives both the owner of the legal estate affected by the caution and such other persons as may be provided in rules[3] the right to apply at any time to the registrar for the cancellation of the caution.[4] When such an application is made, the registrar must inform the cautioner[5] of the application and of the fact that, if he does not exercise his right to object within the period specified by rules, the caution must be cancelled.[6] There is one limitation on the cautioner's right to apply for the cancellation of the caution. Normally, if he consented to the entry of the caution he will be unable to do so.[7] However, even in this situation, rules may provide that, in certain circumstances, he may apply for cancellation.[8] For example, it is likely that rules will permit such an application where the cautioner's interest has determined.[9]

(3) A person may not exercise his right to lodge a caution without reasonable cause.[10] This is a statutory duty that is owed to any person who suffers damage in consequence of its breach.[11] Any

---

[1] LRA 2002, s 73; see also para **5.38**.
[2] Ibid, s 73(7). For the Adjudicator to HM Land Registry, see Chapter 9.
[3] Who are likely to include mortgagees and receivers.
[4] LRA 2002, s 18(1). Under LRA 1925, s 53(3), a landowner could only challenge the caution once he had made an application for first registration. This meant that a landowner, who wished to sell his land and was aware that there was a caution against first registration, could do nothing to remove it before the sale.
[5] As to who is the cautioner for these purposes, see LRA 2002, s 22; see also para **2.57**.
[6] LRA 2002, s 18(3), (4).
[7] Ibid, s 18(2)(a). Consent would, for these purposes, have to be in a manner prescribed by rules, in order to avoid any arguments.
[8] Ibid, s 18(2)(b).
[9] The obvious case would be where the cautioner was a lessee and his lease had determined.
[10] LRA 2002, s 77(1)(a).
[11] Ibid, s 77(2).

such breach of statutory duty will therefore be actionable in tort in the usual way.

THE SPECIAL POSITION OF THE CROWN

Voluntary first registration

2.61 The legislation governing land registration in England and Wales has always made provision for the registration of *estates* in land. However, the Crown holds substantial amounts of land not for any estate but in demesne – in other words, in its capacity as sovereign or paramount feudal lord. This land includes most of the foreshore around the coast of England and Wales, land that has escheated,[1] and land that the Crown has always held and has never granted away. Because the Crown has no estate in such land it could not, prior to the LRA 2002, register the title to it.[2] The Act changes this. It empowers Her Majesty to grant herself an estate in fee simple absolute in possession in demesne land.[3] However, such a grant will not be regarded as having been made unless an application is made to register it under s 3 of the Act within 2 months of the date of the grant or such longer period as the registrar may by order provide.[4]

Compulsory first registration

2.62 The provisions of s 4(1) of the LRA 2002 on the compulsory registration of title[5] are extended (with necessary modifications) to the grant by Her Majesty of a fee simple or a lease of more than 7 years out of demesne land.[6] These provisions do not in fact change the law as the compulsory registration requirements of the LRA 1925 applied to conveyances and grants made by Her Majesty out of demesne land.[7]

---

[1] Escheat occurs where a freehold estate determines. A common example of escheat is where a trustee in bankruptcy or a liquidator disclaims the freehold because it is onerous property. Disclaimer determines the fee simple. The property thereupon necessarily escheats.

[2] See *Scmlla Properties Ltd v Gesso Properties (BVI) Ltd* [1995] BCC 793, at p 798.

[3] LRA 2002, s 79(1). It is thought that statutory authority is required for this power as Her Majesty cannot be feudal lord and at the same time hold of herself as tenant-in-chief: see (2001) Law Com No 271, para 11.9.

[4] LRA 2002, s 79(2)–(4). The registrar can extend the 2-month period on the application of Her Majesty provided that he is satisfied that there is a good reason for doing so: s 79(4). If the registrar makes an order under s 79(4) more than 2 months after the grant, that grant will be treated as having been made notwithstanding s 79(2): s 79(5).

[5] See paras **2.11** et seq.

[6] LRA 2002, s 80(1)–(4). There is also a necessary modification to s 7(2) (effect of non-compliance with requirement of registration): s 80(5).

[7] See LRA 1925, s 123.

Cautions against first registration

2.63 The provisions of the LRA 2002 on cautions against first registration cannot apply to demesne land because such a caution can only be lodged against an unregistered legal *estate*. However, those provisions are extended to demesne land as if it were held by Her Majesty for an unregistered estate in fee simple absolute in possession.[1] It has been explained above, that 2 years after the Act comes into force, it will no longer be possible for an owner of either an unregistered fee simple or of a lease with more than 7 years unexpired to lodge a caution against the first registration of that estate. He is expected to register the title to it.[2] As the Crown has not hitherto been able to register land which Her Majesty holds in demesne, it was considered appropriate that the Crown should be permitted to lodge cautions against first registration in respect of such land until such time as it could register it. It was accepted that this would take some time.[3] The Act therefore permits the Crown to lodge cautions against the first registration of demesne land for a period of 10 years in the first instance and makes provision by which that period may be extended further by rules.[4]

---

[1] LRA 2002, s 81(1). There is power to make modifications by rules in the application of the provisions to demesne land: s 81(2).
[2] See para **2.58**.
[3] See (2001) Law Com No 271, para 11.18.
[4] LRA 2002, Sch 12, para 15(1).

CHAPTER 3

DEALINGS WITH REGISTERED LAND

THE MAIN CHANGES AT A GLANCE

3.1   This chapter is about dealings with registered land. The relevant provisions are found in three Parts of the LRA 2002. First, Part 3 of the Act is concerned with dispositions of registered land. It makes provision for the following matters:

- owner's powers;
- the protection of disponees;
- registrable dispositions;
- the effect of dispositions on priority.

Secondly, Part 4 of the LRA 2002 is concerned with notices and restrictions. Finally, Part 7 of the Act sets out provisions relating to certain special cases: the Crown, pending actions and miscellaneous matters.

3.2   The main changes made by the LRA 2002 are as follows.

- Leases granted for more than 7 years become registrable dispositions.
- The registration requirements for registrable dispositions are prescribed by the LRA 2002.
- The principles of priority that apply to registered land are modified and are set out in their entirety in statutory form.
- The status of rights of pre-emption, equities arising by estoppel and mere equities is clarified: all are treated as proprietary interests from the time of their creation.
- The methods of protecting third party interests in the register are simplified and the protection given to such interests is enhanced.

- Cautions against dealings and inhibitions are prospectively abolished. Notices and restrictions become the only two forms of protection under the LRA 2002.
- A person who applies for the entry of a notice or restriction is under a duty to act reasonably in exercising that right.
- The range of overriding interests is restricted and reduced.
- The LRA 2002 enables the Crown to grant itself a fee simple of land held by it in demesne to enable it to register such land.
- The Crown is given the power to lodge cautions against the first registration of land held in demesne;
- Entries in the register in relation to land which has escheated to the Crown remain until the land is disposed of by the Crown or pursuant to a court order.

POWERS OF DISPOSITION

The principles adopted

3.3   It was explained in Chapter 1 that the fundamental objective of the LRA 2002 is, in time, to create a conclusive register.[1] A necessary feature of a conclusive register is that it should reveal whether there is any possible defect in a registered proprietor's title. One possible risk to an intending buyer of land is that the transaction might be outside the powers of the registered proprietor. Those powers might be limited by statute, by the terms of a trust deed where the owners were trustees, or, in the case of a company, by its memorandum and articles. The LRA 1925 does not spell out explicitly what powers (if any) a registered proprietor is presumed to have. In particular, it is unclear whether a buyer can assume that a seller has unrestricted powers of disposition in the absence of any entry to the contrary in the register, such as a restriction or caution.[2] If there is to be a conclusive register, those dealing with the registered proprietor ought to be able to rely upon the register to tell them whether there are any limitations on the powers of a registered proprietor. If any limitation exists it should be reflected by an entry in the register. In the absence of any such entry in the register, a registered proprietor should be taken to have unlimited dispositive powers, and a person dealing with him should be able to rely upon the register and his title should be inviolable. However, where there are limitations on a registered proprietor's powers of disposition, but these

---

1   See para **1.7**.
2   Cf (2001) Law Com No 271, para 4.3.

are not recorded in the register, the proprietor should not escape the consequences of a disposition in contravention of those limitations.

Owner's powers

3.4 The LRA 2002 adopts this approach. It creates the concept of 'owner's powers'. A person is entitled to exercise owner's powers in relation to a registered estate or charge if he is:

— the registered proprietor, or
— entitled to be registered as the proprietor.[1]

3.5 In relation to a registered estate, owner's powers consist of:

— the power to make a disposition of any kind permitted by the general law in relation to an interest of that description, except a mortgage by demise or sub-demise;[2] and
— the power to charge the estate at law with the payment of money.[3]

Three points in this provision require explanation. First, the dispositions permitted by the general law are subject to any limitations imposed by that general law, such as the requirement that, to overreach an interest under a trust of land, payment of any capital monies must be made to two trustees.[4] For example, if X holds registered land on trust for Y, and charges the land to Z, that disposition will undoubtedly create a valid charge: X can convey a legal estate to Z. However, it will not overreach Y's beneficial interest under the trust, because Z pays the mortgage monies to just one trustee, X, and not to two.[5] If Y is in actual occupation, her unregistered interest will override Z's charge.[6] Secondly, the reason why mortgages by demise or sub-demise cannot be created in relation to registered land is because they have long been obsolete.[7] Thirdly, the power to charge the estate at law with the payment of money is the way in which registered land has always been

---

[1]   LRA 2002, s 24(1).
[2]   Ibid, s 23(1)(a).
[3]   Ibid, s 23(1)(b).
[4]   LPA 1925, s 27(2). The LRA 2002 makes provision for the entry of restrictions in the register to ensure that there will be at least two trustees on the making of a disposition: see LRA 2002, ss 42, 44.
[5]   For the sake of the example, it is assumed that Y has not entered a restriction to protect her interest. Cf para **3.8**.
[6]   See LRA 2002, Sch 3, para 2; see also para **3.96**.
[7]   See para **4.3**.

mortgaged since the Land Transfer Act 1875, and it has no equivalent in unregistered land.[1] It continues to be available under the LRA 2002.

3.6   In relation to a registered charge, owner's powers consist of:

–   the power to make a disposition of any kind permitted by the general law in relation to an interest of that description, other than a legal sub-mortgage;[2] and
–   the power to charge at law with the payment of money indebtedness secured by the registered charge.[3]

For these purposes, a 'legal sub-mortgage' is defined as a transfer by way of mortgage, a sub-mortgage by sub-demise, or a charge by way of legal mortgage.[4] The effect of the LRA 2002 therefore is to place just one restriction on the dispositive powers of a registered chargee. He can only create a sub-charge by one method, namely that of charging the indebtedness that is secured by the registered charge. In fact, that apparent restriction is simply a restatement of the present law.[5]

3.7   The LRA 2002 provides that a registrable disposition of a registered estate or charge only has effect if it complies with such requirements as to form and content as rules may provide.[6] This involves a small change in the law. At present, although it is possible to prescribe the form and content of most registered dispositions,[7] there is an exception in relation to registered charges.[8] Furthermore, in practice, the form and content of registered leases has never been prescribed, even though they could have been.

Protection of disponees

3.8   As a general rule, a person's right to exercise owner's powers in relation to a registered estate or charge is to be taken to be free from any limitation affecting the validity of a disposition.[9] In accordance with the principle set out in para **3.3**, this rule will only be displaced if a

---

1   For the present law, see LRA 1925, s 25(1)(a), which gives the proprietor of registered land the power to charge the registered land with the payment at an appointed time of any principal sum.
2   LRA 2002, s 23(2)(a).
3   Ibid, s 23(2)(b).
4   Ibid, s 23(3).
5   See LRR 1925, r 163(1); (2001) Law Com No 271, para 7.11.
6   LRA 2002, s 25(1).
7   See LRA 1925, ss 18(1), 21(1).
8   Ibid, s 25(2).
9   LRA 2002, s 26(1).

limitation is reflected by an entry in the register, or if a limitation is imposed by, or under, the LRA 2002.[1] That entry in the register might be a restriction or a caution against dealings although, for the future, the appropriate form of entry will be by way of a restriction only: cautions are prospectively abolished.[2] However, this presumption only operates to protect the disponee's title. It does not make the disposition lawful if the registered proprietor's powers were in fact limited, but there was no entry in the register to reflect this.[3]

An example

3.9   The workings of the new principles set out in paras **3.3–3.8** can be illustrated by an example. This example demonstrates that the protection given by the LRA 2002 does not apply to the transferor who has acted in breach of his obligations. It also shows that although the transferee's title is inviolable, he may be under other forms of liability if he was knowingly implicated in the breach of duty by the transferor.[4]

3.10   A and B hold registered land on trust for C for life, thereafter for D absolutely. Under the terms of the trust, A and B may not sell the land without the prior written consent of D. There is no restriction in the register to ensure that no sale can take place without D's consent. A and B sell the land to E without obtaining D's consent. E's title cannot be challenged by D. A and B are in breach of trust and D can take proceedings against them accordingly. If D could show that E knew that A and B were acting in breach of trust by transferring the land:

– she could not challenge E's title; but
– she could take proceedings against him on the basis that he was liable in equity for the knowing receipt of property transferred in breach of trust.

Liability for knowing receipt is merely a personal liability to account for the loss suffered by D. It does not give rise to a proprietary claim by D against the land which E acquired.

---

[1]   LRA 2002, s 26(2).
[2]   See para **3.44**.
[3]   LRA 2002, s 26(3).
[4]   Cf (2001) Law Com No 271, paras 4.10, 4.11.

REGISTRABLE DISPOSITIONS

Introduction

3.11 Section 27 is one of the most important sections in the LRA 2002. It defines the categories of disposition of registered land that must be completed by registration. Such registrable dispositions are particularly significant as, on registration, they take effect as legal estates at law, and are given a special priority. The provisions governing registrable dispositions are similar to, but not identical with, the equivalent provisions of the LRA 1925.[1]

3.12 As indicated above, the uniting characteristic of the dispositions in question is that they are required to be registered and do not operate at law (but only in equity) until what the LRA 2002 calls 'the registration requirements' are met.[2] Those registration requirements are set out in Sch 2 to the Act.[3] The LRA 2002 deals separately with dispositions of:

– a registered estate; and
– a registered charge.

A registered estate means a legal estate the title to which is entered in the register, other than a registered charge.[4] Not all such legal estates can be registered with their own titles under the Act. However, the following estates can:[5]

– a fee simple absolute in possession;
– certain leasehold estates;[6]
– a rentcharge;
– a franchise;
– a *profit à prendre* in gross; and
– a manor.[7]

---

[1] See LRA 1925, ss 18 and 21.
[2] LRA 2002, s 27(1). This provision will cease to apply to any given disposition as and when compulsory electronic conveyancing is introduced in relation to it: see LRA 2002, s 93(4); see also para **7.54**.
[3] See LRA 2002, s 27(4).
[4] LRA 2002, s 132(1).
[5] Cf para **2.3**. Legal estates that cannot be registered with their own titles include legal easements and those *profits à prendre* that do not exist in gross.
[6] See paras **2.15–2.20**.
[7] Any manor that has not been registered with its own title before the LRA 2002 comes into force will not be capable of registration thereafter: see para **2.9**.

It is necessary to explain both the dispositions that are registrable dispositions and the registration requirements for each.

Registrable dispositions of a registered estate

Transfers

3.13 Subject to the three exceptions mentioned in para **3.14**, a transfer of a registered estate is required to be registered.[1] For practical purposes, the only legal estates that can be transferred are those which are registered with their own titles.[2] The registration requirements for such transfers are that the transferee or his successor in title must be registered as proprietor of the registered estate.[3] Where there is a transfer of part of the registered estate, such details of the transfer as rules may provide must be entered in the register in relation to the registered estate out of which the transfer is made.[4]

3.14 The three exceptional cases where a transfer is not required to be registered are all transfers by operation of law.[5] They are as follows.

- A transfer on the death of a sole individual proprietor. The legal title vests by operation of law in the deceased's executors or, if there are none, in the Public Trustee. Once there has been a grant of administration, the personal representatives may apply to the registrar to be registered as proprietors,[6] although they are not bound to do so.[7]
- A transfer on the bankruptcy of a sole individual proprietor. An insolvent's entire estate vests automatically in his trustee in bankruptcy on his appointment or, if there is no such appointment, in the Official Receiver.[8] As with personal representatives, the

---

[1] LRA 2002, s 27(2)(a).
[2] On rare occasions, it may be possible to sever a *profit à prendre* of common that is appurtenant so that it becomes a *profit à prendre* of common in gross: see *Bettison v Langton* [2002] 1 AC 27, and the authorities considered there. Rights of common must be registered under the Commons Registration Act 1965 (CRA 1965), s 1, and cannot be registered under LRA 2002: see LRA 2002, s 33(d); see also para **3.51**.
[3] LRA 2002, Sch 2, para 2(1).
[4] Ibid, Sch 2, para 2(2). This accords with the present practice of the Registry.
[5] See ibid, s 27(5).
[6] See ibid, Sch 4, paras 7(d) (application to the registrar), 5(b) (altering the register to bring it up to date). For alteration of the register, see paras **5.48** et seq.
[7] Often personal representatives do not register themselves as proprietors, but sell the land in their representative capacity or assent to its vesting in the person entitled to it under the deceased's will or intestacy.
[8] Insolvency Act 1986 (IA 1986), s 306.

trustee in bankruptcy may apply to the registrar to be registered as proprietor.

— A transfer on the dissolution of a sole corporate proprietor. On the dissolution of a company its property passes as bona vacantia to the Crown or to the Duchy of Cornwall or Lancaster.[1] Once again, it is open to the Crown or Royal Duchy to apply to the registrar to be registered as proprietor.

The grant of certain leases

3.15 The grant of a lease of registered land will be a registrable disposition and must be registered if it is one of the following:[2]

— the grant of a lease for a term of more than 7 years from the date of the grant;
— the grant of a reversionary lease to take effect in possession after the end of the period of 3 months beginning with the date of the grant;
— the grant of a lease under which the right to possession is discontinuous;[3]
— the grant of a lease in pursuance of the right to buy conferred by Part 5 of the HA 1985 (as now); or
— the grant of a lease in circumstances where s 171A of the HA 1985 applies (as now).[4]

With one exception, the extension of leases that are registrable dispositions mirrors the changes that have been made to the rules on compulsory first registration that have been explained in Chapter 2.[5] The one exception is that *all* discontinuous leases of whatever length granted out of registered land are registrable dispositions. Although discontinuous leases of any length granted out of unregistered land are voluntarily registrable,[6] only those granted for a term of more than 7 years after the LRA 2002 comes into force will be subject to compulsory first registration. The reason why discontinuous leases granted out of registered land are always registrable dispositions is because of the difficulty of discovering them if they are not registered.

---

[1] Companies Act 1985, s 654.
[2] LRA 2002, s 27(2)(b).
[3] For discontinuous leases, see para **2.5**.
[4] For an explanation of HA 1985, s 171A, see para **2.20**.
[5] See paras **2.15–2.20**, where the reasons for the changes are explained.
[6] See para **2.5**.

There are two classes of lease of registered land that are not registrable dispositions:

- leases granted for 7 years or less[1] except where they are required to be registered for some other reason; and
- PPP leases of underground railways and ancillary property granted pursuant to the GLAA 1999 (if such leases are ever in fact granted).[2]

Such leases are unregistered interests that will override a registrable disposition.[3]

3.16 Where a lease is a registrable disposition, the grantee of the lease or his successor in title must be entered in the register as the proprietor of the lease, and a notice in respect of the lease must also be entered against the superior title.[4]

Leases of franchises and manors

3.17 The LRA 2002 makes no provision for the registration of a *grant* of a manor or a franchise because none is required. Even if the Crown can still grant a manor today (which seems unlikely), it would not be possible to register that grant under the Act.[5] If the Crown were to grant any new franchise, it could be registered, if the grantee so wished, under the new provisions for voluntary first registration.[6] The LRA 2002 does make provision for the registration of leases granted of a manor or franchise, where the title to that manor or franchise is registered. Any lease of whatever length of such a franchise or manor is a registrable disposition,[7] although such cases are likely to be very rare indeed. *All* leases are registrable because of the difficulty of discovering them if they were not. Where the lease is granted for a term of more than 7 years, the grantee or his successor in title will be registered with his own title and a notice in respect of that lease entered in the register of the manor or franchise.[8] Where the lease is granted for a term of

---

[1] This period may and almost certainly will be reduced in due course by statutory instrument to include leases granted for 3 years or less: LRA 2002, s 118(1)(d); see also paras **2.6**, **2.16**.
[2] LRA 2002, s 90(3)(a). See also para **2.5**.
[3] See paras **3.93**, **3.95**.
[4] LRA 2002, Sch 2, para 3.
[5] See para **2.9**.
[6] See paras **2.7–2.8**.
[7] LRA 2002, s 27(2)(c).
[8] Ibid, Sch 2, para 4(2).

7 years or less, a notice must be entered in the register of the manor or franchise.[1]

Express grant or reservation of a legal easement, right of privilege

3.18 Subject to two qualifications, the express grant or reservation of a legal easement, right or privilege[2] over registered land is a registrable disposition.[3] In practice this will apply to easements and to *profits à prendre*, whether those profits are in gross or appurtenant to an estate. The two qualifications to the requirement of registration are as follows.

— First, the grant of a right of common, which must be registered under the CRA 1965,[4] is not registrable under the LRA 2002.[5] This restates the present law.
— Secondly, the grant of an easement or a *profit à prendre* as a result of the operation of s 62 of the LPA 1925 is not a registrable disposition.[6] Although technically s 62 operates as an express grant (because it writes words into a conveyance),[7] in reality it is a form of implied grant. Frequently, the parties will not have appreciated at the time of the conveyance that the section has operated, and it would be unreasonable to expect them to register a grant of which they were unaware.

3.19 The registration requirements are as follows.

— First, where the disposition involves the grant or reservation of a *profit à prendre* in gross[8] for an interest equivalent to a fee simple or a term of more than 7 years, the grantee or his successor in title must be entered in the register as the proprietor of the profit. In other words, the profit will be registered with its own title. A notice of the right must also be entered in the register of the title affected by it.[9]
— Secondly, in any other case, a notice of the interest must be entered in the register of the title affected by it. If the easement or profit is for the benefit of another registered estate, the proprietor of that

1   LRA 2002, Sch 2, para 5(2).
2   Cf LPA 1925, s 1(2)(a).
3   LRA 2002, s 27(2)(d).
4   See CRA 1965, s 1.
5   LRA 2002, s 27(2)(d). See also s 33(d).
6   Ibid, s 27(7). For LPA 1925, s 62, see Harpum, *Megarry & Wade's Law of Real Property* (Sweet & Maxwell, 6th edn, 2000), para 18-108.
7   See Harpum, *Megarry & Wade's Law of Real Property*, op cit, n 6, para 18-113.
8   Such as shooting or fishing rights.
9   LRA 2002, Sch 2, para 6.

registered estate must be registered as proprietor of that easement or profit.[1]

There is a very important point that must be stressed. *The express grant or reservation of an easement or profit is a registrable disposition however long or short the duration of the grant or reservation may be.* For example, if an easement is granted for the benefit of a lease of 5 years' duration, the lease cannot be registered with its own title,[2] but the easement must be noted in the register nonetheless.[3] Under the LRA 2002 – unlike the present law – an easement or profit that has been expressly granted or reserved but has not been registered can never override a registered disposition.[4]

Express grant or reservation of a rentcharge or a legal right of entry

3.20 The express grant or reservation of either:

- a rentcharge in possession issuing out of or charged on land being either perpetual or for a term of years absolute;[5] or
- a right of entry exercisable over or in respect of a legal term of years absolute, or annexed for any purpose, to a legal rentcharge;[6]

is a registrable disposition.[7]

3.21 Where the disposition involves the grant or reservation of a legal rentcharge with its own title for an interest that is either:

- equivalent to an estate in fee simple; or
- for a term of years exceeding 7 years,

the grantee or his successors in title must be entered in the register as the proprietor of the interest created, and a notice in respect of the rentcharge must also be entered in the register.[8] In every other case, a notice in respect of the interest must be entered in the register and, where the interest is for the benefit of a registered estate, the registered

---

1   LRA 2002, Sch 2, para 7. Obviously this cannot be done where the easement or profit is for the benefit of an estate in unregistered land. Nor can it be done in respect of an easement that is granted for the benefit of a lease that was not capable of registration when it was granted.
2   Although it may be noted in the register: see LRA 2002, s 33(b); see also para **3.49**.
3   Rules will no doubt provide for the form of notice.
4   See para **3.95**.
5   Cf LPA 1925, s 1(2)(b).
6   Ibid, s 1(2)(e).
7   LRA 2002, s 27(2)(e).
8   Ibid, Sch 2, para 6.

proprietor must also be entered in the register of the land benefited as the proprietor of the interest.[1]

The grant of a legal charge

3.22 The grant of a legal charge is a registrable disposition.[2] To register the charge, the chargee or his successor in title must be entered in the register as the proprietor of the charge.[3] By way of exception to this general rule, where a charge arises under statutory powers and is registrable as a local land charge, it does not have to be registered under the LRA 2002.[4] It takes effect as an unregistered interest that overrides a registered disposition.[5] However, it cannot be realised unless it is registered as a registered charge.[6] The Act does not change the law in this regard[7] and the point is explained more fully in Chapter 4.[8]

3.23 It will be apparent that, except in the cases of a transfer and the creation of a legal charge, the registrar must always enter a notice of a registrable disposition in relation to the registered estate out of which it is made and which it therefore affects. The LRA 2002 does in fact contain a general provision to that effect.[9]

Dispositions of a registered charge

3.24 In the case of a registered charge:

–   a transfer of that charge; and
–   the grant of a sub-charge;

are both registrable dispositions.[10] The registration requirement for a transfer is that the transferee or his successor in title must be entered in the register as proprietor.[11] The registration requirement for a

---

1   LRA 2002, Sch 2, para 7(2).
2   Ibid, s 27(2)(f).
3   Ibid, Sch 2, para 8.
4   Ibid, s 27(5)(c).
5   Ibid, Sch 3, para 6; see also para **3.93**.
6   Ibid, s 55.
7   Cf LRA 1925, s 70(1)(i).
8   See para **4.17**.
9   LRA 2002, s 38. The entry of a notice must always be made in relation to the registered estate affected by the interest concerned: s 32(2).
10   Ibid, s 27(3).
11   Ibid, Sch 2, para 10.

sub-charge is that the sub-chargee or his successor in title must be registered as the proprietor of the sub-charge.[1]

Applications for registration

3.25 The way in which applications for registration will be made is a matter for rules.[2] At present, unless the proprietor's land certificate has been retained by the Registry, it has to be produced in order to register a registrable disposition.[3] As is explained in Chapter 5, given the much diminished role of land certificates under the LRA 2002, it is most unlikely that this requirement will be replicated under the new rules.[4]

PRIORITIES

Introduction

3.26 The present law governing the priority of competing interests in registered land is a patchwork of statute and common law. Where the LRA 1925 was silent – principally in relation to the priority of competing minor interests[5] – the judges have filled the gaps as best they can by reference to the general principles of priority that apply between competing equitable interests.[6] The LRA 2002 has a completely statutory scheme of priorities. The rules that it lays down are simpler than are those that presently apply.[7]

The basic rule

3.27 Under s 28(1) of the LRA 2002, the basic rule of priority, which is subject to two important exceptions,[8] is that the priority of an interest affecting the title to a registered estate or charge is not affected by a disposition of the estate or charge. It makes no difference for the purposes of this rule whether the interest or disposition is registered.[9] In cases falling within the general rule, the priority of any interest in registered land is simply determined by the date of its creation. The first interest in time of creation prevails. Unlike the present law on

---

1 LRA 2002, Sch 2, para 11.
2 Ibid, s 27(6).
3 LRA 1925, s 64(1)(a).
4 See paras **5.42–5.44**.
5 The term 'minor interest' is not used by the LRA 2002.
6 See (1998) Law Com No 254, paras 7.15–7.19.
7 See, generally, (2001) Law Com No 271, Part V.
8 See below.
9 LRA 2002, s 28(2).

competing minor interests, that first in time rule is unqualified. At present, the priority of competing minor interests is determined by the general rule applicable to equitable interests, namely, *where the equities are equal*, the first in time prevails. The law on when the equities are or are not equal has been the source of some difficulty and uncertainty and it has no place in the new scheme. The two exceptions to the general first in time of creation rule are:

– the special rules of priority that apply to registrable dispositions for valuable consideration that have been registered;[1] and
– the rules of priority applicable to Inland Revenue charges.[2]

3.28 It should be noted that, under the provisions of the LRA 2002 that deal with e-conveyancing, it will in due course become impossible to create or dispose of many estates, rights and interests in registered land except by simultaneously registering them.[3] In this way the priority of such interests will always be apparent from the register. It also means that the principal exception to the basic rule, that applies to registrable dispositions for valuable consideration that have been registered, will cease to have much importance. The basic first in time of creation rule contained in s 28(1) of the LRA 2002 will indeed be the principal rule as to the priority of competing interests.

Registrable dispositions for valuable consideration that have been registered

The special rule of priority

3.29 The first exception to the basic rule of priority in s 28(1) stated above is as follows. If a registrable disposition of a registered estate or charge is made for valuable consideration, completion of the disposition by registration has the effect of postponing to the interest under the disposition any interest affecting the estate or charge immediately before the disposition whose priority is not protected at the time of registration.[4] In having a special rule of priority for registrable dispositions made for valuable consideration, the LRA 2002

---

[1]   See para **3.29**.
[2]   See para **3.37**.
[3]   LRA 2002, s 93; see also paras **7.53** et seq.
[4]   Ibid, ss 29(1) (dispositions of registered estates), 30(1) (dispositions of registered charges).

follows the LRA 1925.[1] The elements of this exception are important and require explanation.

3.30 First, there must be a registrable disposition of a registered estate or charge. It has been explained above:

- which transactions are registrable dispositions under the LRA 2002; and
- that such transactions are required to be registered.[2]

3.31 Secondly, the registrable disposition must be made for valuable consideration. For the purposes of the LRA 2002, valuable consideration does not include either marriage consideration,[3] or a nominal consideration in money.[4] If the registrable disposition is made other than for valuable consideration (as defined), the basic rule of priority in s 28(1) applies.

3.32 Thirdly, the registrable disposition is given priority over any interest:

- which affects the estate or charge *immediately prior to the disposition*; and
- whose priority is not protected *at the time of registration*.

There are obvious reasons why these different times have been chosen. When the LRA 2002 first comes into force, there will continue to be a period of time between the making of a disposition and its subsequent registration – the so-called registration gap.[5] A result of the gap is that if the disponee created an interest in favour of a third party during the registration gap, he would not be able to rely on the special rule of priority to take free of it. That is obviously right in principle. There is one potential trap – as there is under the present law[6] – to which practitioners need to be alert. In those cases where the seller is to retain an unpaid vendor's lien over the land after its transfer, it is imperative that he should register that lien against his own title immediately after

---

1   See LRA 1925, ss 20(1), 23(1).
2   See paras **3.11** et seq; and see LRA 2002, ss 27 and 132(1).
3   This is a change in the law: cf LRA 1925, s 3(xxxi).
4   LRA 2002, s 132(1).
5   The position will change when e-conveyancing is introduced. Under the system of e-conveyancing which the LRA 2002 creates, the making of a disposition and its registration occur simultaneously. The registration gap will, therefore, disappear. See para **3.28**.
6   See *Orakpo v Manson Investments Ltd* [1977] 1 WLR 347, at pp 360, 369.

making the contract of sale. The lien arises on the making of the contract[1] and if it is not protected in the register at the time of registration, the buyer will take free of it under the special rule of priority for registrable dispositions.[2]

3.33 Fourthly, a disponee *will* take subject to interests that are protected at the time of registration. The LRA 2002 explains[3] that an interest will be protected for these purposes if it is:

- a registered charge;[4]
- the subject of a notice in the register;[5]
- one which overrides a registered disposition under any of the paragraphs of Sch 3, unless that interest has been the subject of a notice in the register at any time since the coming into force of the sections conferring special priority;[6] or
- one which appears from the register to be excepted from the effect of registration (as where the disposition is of an estate which has some title other than absolute).[7]

In the case of a disposition of a leasehold estate, or of a charge relating to such an estate, the burden of any interest incident to the estate will also be protected.[8] This would include, for example, the burden of any restrictive covenants affecting that estate.[9]

3.34 Fifthly, the interrelationship of the basic rule and the special rule of priority needs to be understood. If an interest has priority over a subsequent interest under the basic rule, the person having that priority never needs to rely upon the special rule of priority applicable to registrable dispositions. The special rule enables a registered disponee to reverse priorities where there is in existence an unprotected interest that has priority to his own interest under the basic rule. This can be illustrated by an example. W, the registered proprietor of freehold land charges the property to X Bank Plc, which registers its registered

---

1   See *Barclays Bank plc v Estates & Commercial Ltd (in liquidation)* [1997] 1 WLR 415, at pp 419–420.
2   Cf (2001) Law Com No 271, para 5.10. This point arises in practice quite often.
3   See LRA 2002, ss 29(2), 30(2).
4   For registered charges, see Chapter 4.
5   For protection by way of a notice, see para **3.46**.
6   LRA 2002, ss 29(3), 30(3). The effect of this exception is that if an unregistered interest is noted in the register and, by mistake, that notice is deleted from the register, the interest is no longer protected. Its former overriding status does not revive.
7   See ibid, ss 11, 12; see also paras **2.42** et seq.
8   Ibid, ss 29(2)(b), 30(2)(b).
9   Such restrictive covenants are not capable of registration: see LRA 2002, s 33(c); see also para **3.47**.

charge. W then contracts to sell the land to Y, who protects her estate contract by entering a notice in the register of title of the land. Before the contract to sell can be completed, W defaults on the mortgage payments and X Bank plc exercises its power of sale and contracts to sell the land to Z. Z takes the land free of Y's estate contract, even though it has been noted in the register. Z's priority derives from X Bank plc's charge which was created before Y's estate contract and therefore had priority over it.[1] It should be noted, in this example, that only the basic rule of priority is in play. It is unnecessary to have recourse to the special rule of priority that is given to registrable dispositions.

The grant of leases that are not registrable dispositions

3.35 The LRA 2002 – like the LRA 1925[2] – makes provision for the priority of those leases granted out of a registered estate that are not registrable dispositions.[3] Under the LRA 2002, where the grant of a leasehold estate in land out of a registered estate does not involve a registrable disposition, the special rule of priority applicable to a registered disposition nonetheless applies as if:

– the grant involved such a disposition; and
– the disposition were registered at the time of the grant.[4]

The priority of competing registered charges

3.36 The LRA 2002 makes specific provision for the priority of competing registered charges.[5] This is explained in Chapter 4.[6]

Inland Revenue charges

3.37 Like the LRA 1925,[7] the LRA 2002 preserves the special rules applicable to the priority of Inland Revenue charges under the Inheritance Tax Act 1984. The effect of a disposition of a registered estate or charge on a charge for unpaid tax under s 237 of the Inheritance Tax Act 1984 is to be determined in accordance with

---

[1]   Having created the charge in favour of X Bank plc, W could only contract to sell his equity of redemption. That equity of redemption is overreached by X Bank plc's sale of W's land to Z: see *Duke v Robson* [1973] 1 WLR 267.

[2]   See LRA 1925, ss 19(2), 22(2).

[3]   For leases that are registrable dispositions, see para **3.15**.

[4]   LRA 2002, s 29(4).

[5]   Ibid, s 48.

[6]   See para **4.10**.

[7]   See LRA 1925, s 73.

ss 237(6) and 238 of the Inheritance Tax Act 1984, under which a purchaser in good faith for money or money's worth takes free from the charge in the absence of registration.[1]

The effect of notice and knowledge on priority under the LRA 2002

3.38 It will be apparent from the rules of priority set out above that questions of knowledge or notice are not directly relevant in determining whether or not a disponee of an interest in registered land is bound by a prior interest.[2] However, such concepts do have a minor role under the LRA 2002 in certain clearly defined circumstances. In some cases this is because there is a pre-existing statutory regime where notice determines whether a disponee is bound by some pre-existing interest. Thus, whether or not a disponee takes subject to an Inland Revenue charge depends upon notice. The LRA 2002 applies the principles laid down in the Inheritance Tax Act 1984, as has been explained.[3] Similarly, the effect of a disposition by a registered proprietor after bankruptcy depends upon the principles of good faith and notice laid down in the IA 1986.[4] In other cases the LRA 2002 employs concepts of knowledge or notice to protect a registered proprietor from unregistered interests that he could not readily discover. This is one device that the Act uses as part of its strategy to reduce the impact of unregistered interests that override first registration or a registered disposition.[5] Thus, as has been explained, a first registered proprietor will be bound by interests acquired under the Limitation Act 1980 only if he has notice of those interests.[6] Furthermore, as is explained below,[7] certain unregistered interests will override registered dispositions only if they are known or easily discoverable.

Special cases

3.39 In relation to three types of interest, the LRA 2002 clarifies or changes its status in such a way that it may or will affect its priority. The

---

1   LRA 2002, s 31.
2   The LRA 2002, s 78, preserves the rule, presently found in LRA 1925, s 74, that the registrar is not affected with notice of any trust.
3   See para **3.37**.
4   See para **3.116**.
5   Cf para **2.46**.
6   LRA 2002, ss 11(4)(c), 12(4)(d); see also para **2.39**.
7   See paras **3.92** et seq.

three types of interest are rights of pre-emption, an equity arising by estoppel and a mere equity.

Rights of pre-emption

3.40   The precise status of rights of pre-emption in terms of when they take their priority as proprietary rights is uncertain. In dicta in *Pritchard v Briggs*,[1] a majority of the Court of Appeal suggested that a right of pre-emption was not a proprietary right unless and until the grantor chose to sell, at which point it became an option. However, this is not an easy rule to apply and it has given rise to some difficulty in practice.[2] For the future, in relation to registered land, the LRA 2002 reverses the effect of the dicta in *Pritchard v Briggs* if indeed they represent the law. Subject to the rules regarding the effect of dispositions on priority that have been explained above,[3] the LRA 2002 provides that a right of pre-emption in relation to registered land created on or after the Act comes into force has effect from the time of creation as an interest binding successors in title.[4]

An equity arising by estoppel

3.41   Where a party, X, acts to his detriment in reliance upon an expectation created (whether by encouragement or acquiescence) by a landowner, Y, that X will acquire some right over Y's land, an equity arises in X's favour. This 'equity' arising by estoppel is a right to go to a court to seek relief. It lies in the court's discretion how best to give effect to that equity and it will give X the minimum necessary to do justice.[5] This may or may not mean that X acquires a proprietary right over Y's land, although commonly it will.[6] If the court does grant X a proprietary right, that interest can be protected in the register in the appropriate way. However, there is some doubt as to the status of the 'equity' which arises in X's favour before such time as the court gives effect to it. Although the point has never been finally determined, the weight of authority undoubtedly favours the view that such an equity is a proprietary right, and this is reflected in the practice of HM Land

---

[1]   [1980] Ch 338.
[2]   See (2001) Law Com No 271, para 5.26.
[3]   See paras **3.27** et seq.
[4]   LRA 2002, s 115.
[5]   For these principles, see *Crabb v Arun District Council* [1976] Ch 179.
[6]   See, generally, Harpum, *Megarry & Wade's Law of Real Property* (Sweet & Maxwell, 6th edn, 2000), chapter 13.

Registry.[1] Subject to the rules about the effect of dispositions on priority,[2] the Act places the Registry's practice on a statutory footing by declaring that in relation to registered land, an equity by estoppel has effect from the time when the equity arises as an interest capable of binding successors in title.[3] A party can, therefore, protect his equity in the period after it has arisen but before a court has made an order giving effect to it, by entering a notice in the register. Alternatively, if the claimant is in actual occupation of the land in relation to which he has claimed an equity, he will be able to protect it as an unregistered interest which will override a registered disposition.[4]

A mere equity

3.42 The law recognises that there are equitable rights, usually referred to as 'mere equities', which fall short of being equitable interests.[5] It is not easy to define such interests,[6] but they include a right to have a deed set aside on grounds of fraud or undue influence, and the right to have a document (typically a conveyance) rectified for mutual mistake.[7] As regards unregistered land, it has been held that a purchaser in good faith of an *equitable* interest (as much as a purchaser of a legal estate) takes free of a mere equity.[8] What the position might be in registered land, where concepts of notice are normally irrelevant, has never been settled, but it might well be the same as where title is unregistered. The LRA 2002 clarifies the priority of a mere equity in relation to registered land as against a later equitable interest. Subject to the rules about the effect of dispositions on priority,[9] the Act declares that in relation to registered land, a mere equity has effect from the time when the equity arises as an interest capable of binding successors in title.[10] In consequence, as a mere equity is an interest for the purposes of the LRA 2002, it is brought within the general principles of priority contained in the Act. This means that a mere equity will not be defeated by a later equitable interest in registered land that is created for valuable consideration where the grantee was a buyer in good faith and without notice of the mere equity. Given the uncertainty as to what rights are

---

[1]   It will allow the entry of a caution or notice in relation to such an equity.
[2]   See paras **3.27** et seq.
[3]   LRA 2002, s 116(a).
[4]   See para **3.96**.
[5]   See Harpum, *Megarry & Wade's Law of Real Property* (Sweet & Maxwell, 6th edn, 2000), para 5-012.
[6]   See (2001) Law Com No 271, para 5.33.
[7]   See Harpum, *Megarry & Wade's Law of Real Property*, op cit, n 5, para 5-012.
[8]   *Phillips v Phillips* (1862) 4 De GF & J 208, at p 218.
[9]   See paras **3.27** et seq.
[10]   LRA 2002, s 116(b).

mere equities as opposed to equitable interests, this change should avoid difficult questions for the future. It is also consistent with the approach of the LRA 2002 under which concepts of notice are generally irrelevant in determining the priority of competing interests.

NOTICES AND RESTRICTIONS

Introduction

3.43 The LRA 1925 contains an elaborate structure for the protection of what that Act calls 'minor interests'.[1] That structure comprises notices, cautions, restrictions and inhibitions. These provisions have not worked well, particularly those on cautions against dealings.[2] Part 4 of the LRA 2002 replaces that structure.[3] Cautions against dealings and inhibitions are prospectively abolished. Notices are the appropriate method of protecting interests (other than registered charges) that are intended to endure through changes of ownership of the land affected by them, such as the burden of options, restrictive covenants and easements. Restrictions operate to prevent the registration of a disposition that does not comply with the terms of the restriction. They can be used to protect interests in land, particularly interests under trusts which are intended to be overreached on any disposition. But they are wider than that and provide a means of ensuring that bodies with limited powers keep within them. This is a matter of some importance in the light of the concept of 'owner's powers' that has been explained above.[4]

Prospective abolition of cautions against dealings

3.44 The proposals by the Law Commission and the Land Registry to abolish cautions were strongly supported on consultation, with virtually no opposition.[5] Under the LRA 2002 there is no power to lodge cautions against dealings for the future.[6] Notices and restrictions will do the work of cautions, but they will do it better. Notices will confer

---

[1]   See LRA 1925, s 3(xv).
[2]   For a critique, see (1998) Law Com No 254, Part VI. The problem with cautions is that they confer no priority, but are merely a form of machinery by which the cautioner is notified of a proposed dealing with the land. He must then defend his interest in the hope of securing a more permanent form of protection.
[3]   For detailed comment see (2001) Law Com No 271, Part VI.
[4]   See para **3.4**.
[5]   See (2001) Law Com No 271, para 6.2.
[6]   Cautions against first registration, which do not suffer from the same vice as cautions against dealings, are retained: see para **2.55**.

priority and restrictions will operate flexibly to restrict or prevent an entry in the register with regard to a registered estate or charge. In relation to existing cautions against dealings and any applications for cautions that are pending at the time that the LRA 2002 is brought into force, the relevant sections of the LRA 1925[1] continue to have effect under the transitional provisions in the LRA 2002.[2] There is also a power for rules to be made in relation to existing cautions.[3]

Abolition of inhibitions as a separate form of entry

3.45 The LRA 2002 does not contain any separate category of entries corresponding to an inhibition: an order made by the court or registrar that inhibits the registration or entry of any dealing in relation to any registered land or charge.[4] Inhibitions are just the most extreme form of restriction on the power of the registered proprietor to make a disposition of registered land,[5] and, as such, are subsumed within restrictions. The provisions of the LRA 2002 on restrictions apply to inhibitions or restrictions entered under the LRA 1925,[6] thereby obviating the need for any further transitional provisions.

Notices

The nature and effect of a notice

3.46 The LRA 2002 explains the nature and effect of a notice. A notice is an entry in the register in respect of the burden of an interest affecting a registered estate or charge.[7] However, as is explained in the next paragraph, it is not the burden of every interest that can be protected by a notice. The entry of a notice is to be made in relation to the registered estate or charge affected by the interest concerned.[8] If the interest in question is a registered estate and a registrable lease is granted out of the registered freehold, a notice will, therefore, be entered in respect of it on the title to the freehold estate.[9] As under the LRA 1925, the fact that an interest is the subject of a notice does not

---

[1]   Namely, LRA 1925, ss 55, 56.
[2]   LRA 2002, Sch 12, paras 2(3) and 5.
[3]   Ibid, Sch 12, para 2(4). This power will enable the existing provisions in LRR 1925 in relation to cautions – which are necessary to their operation – to be replicated.
[4]   LRA 1925, s 57.
[5]   The entry of an inhibition prevents the entry of *any* dealing in the register: LRA 1925, s 57(1).
[6]   LRA 2002, Sch 12, para 2(2).
[7]   Ibid, s 32(1).
[8]   Ibid, s 32(2).
[9]   Ibid, Sch 2, para 3(2).

necessarily mean that the interest is valid. It does mean that the priority of the interest, if it is valid, is protected for the purposes of the special provisions on priority contained in ss 29 and 30 of the LRA 2002.[1] If, for example, parties had entered into an agreement that was not a binding contract because it failed to comply with the formal requirements of s 2 of the Law of Property (Miscellaneous Provisions) Act 1989 (LP(MP)A 1989), the entry of a notice in respect of the contract would not validate it. The form and content of notices in the register will be a matter for rules.[2]

3.47 Section 33 of the LRA 2002 lists six interests that are *not* capable of being protected by a notice. With one important exception, the Act replicates the previous law. The list of excepted interests is informative because it sheds further light on the nature and function of a notice under the Act.

3.48 First, it is not possible to enter a notice in respect of an interest under a trust of land, or a settlement under the SLA 1925.[3] Where there is a disposition of land held in trust, the disponee does not expect to take subject to the beneficial interests. The interests should instead be overreached. Any capital monies should therefore be paid to the trustees, of whom there should be at least two (unless the trustee is a trust corporation).[4] A restriction is both the appropriate and, under the LRA 2002, the *only* form of entry that can be made to ensure that this occurs.[5] An interest under a trust includes a charging order over an interest under a trust, which can also only be protected by the entry of a restriction.[6]

3.49 Secondly, a notice cannot be entered in respect of a lease granted for a term of 3 years or less and which is not otherwise required to be registered.[7] This provision is a notable change from the present law under which leases granted for a term of 21 years or less cannot be the subject of a notice unless they are otherwise required to be registered. It might have been expected that, following the reduction of the length of registrable leases from those granted for more than 21 years to those granted for a term of more than 7 years, it would not be possible to

---

[1]   LRA 2002, s 32(3); LRA 1925, s 52(1).
[2]   LRA 2002, s 39.
[3]   Ibid, s 33(a).
[4]   SLA 1925, s 94(1); LPA 1925, s 27(2).
[5]   LRA 2002, s 42(1)(b).
[6]   Ibid, s 42(1)(c), (4); see also para **3.72**.
[7]   Ibid, s 33(b).

enter a notice in respect of a lease granted for 7 years or less (except in those cases where it was otherwise required to be registered). There are two reasons why a period of more than 3 (rather than 7) years was chosen.[1] First, as has been explained, it is intended that the length of registrable leases should in due course be reduced from a period of more than 7 years to a period of more than 3 years.[2] The provision on the entry of notices is an earnest of that intention. Secondly, it has been explained that, under the LRA 2002, *any* easement or profit that is expressly granted or reserved must be registered.[3] In those circumstances, where a short lease is granted and is subject to or has the benefit of an easement, the lessee may choose to enter a notice in relation to the lease as well as the easement.

3.50 Thirdly, a restrictive covenant made between a lessor and lessee, so far as relating to the demised premises, cannot be the subject of a notice in the register.[4] These covenants are not noted, as they are normally apparent from the lease. This is a more limited exception than that contained in the LRA 1925[5] under which any restrictive covenant made between lessor and lessee could not be protected by the entry of a notice in the register, even if it related to land not comprised in the lease. The exception under the LRA 1925 was too wide because it meant that restrictive covenants between lessor and lessee that related to property other than that demised could not be noted in the register.[6]

3.51 Fourthly, as under the present law, an interest which is capable of being registered under the CRA 1965 cannot be noted in the register.[7] Rights of common which are registrable under the CRA 1965 cannot presently be registered under the LRA 1925[8] nor will they be registrable under the LRA 2002.[9]

3.52 Fifthly, no notice may be entered in respect of an interest in any coal or coal mine, the rights attached to any such interest and the rights of any person under ss 38, 49 or 51 of the Coal Industry Act 1994.[10]

---

[1]   See (2001) Law Com No 271, para 6.11.
[2]   See paras **2.6**, **2.16** and **3.15**.
[3]   See para **3.19**.
[4]   LRA 2002, s 33(c).
[5]   See LRA 1925, s 50(1).
[6]   See *Oceanic Village Ltd v United Attractions Ltd* [2000] Ch 234, at pp 252–254.
[7]   LRA 2002, s 33(d).
[8]   CRA 1965, s 1.
[9]   See LRA 2002, Sch 11, para 7(2) (amending CRA 1965).
[10] LRA 2002, s 33(e).

Once again, this replicates the present law. It is in practice impossible to locate and therefore to map all rights to coal.

3.53 Finally, no notice may be entered in relation to a PPP lease created under the provisions of the GLAA 1999.[1] The curious status of PPP leases and their nature has already been explained.[2]

The circumstances in which a notice may be entered in the register

3.54 The circumstances in which a notice may be entered in the register include the following.

- On the first registration of a freehold or leasehold estate the registrar will note against the title the burden of any interest which affects the land of which he is aware, unless the interest is one that cannot be protected by notice.[3]
- Where it appears to the registrar that a registered estate is subject to an unregistered interest that falls within any of the paragraphs of Sch 1 to the LRA 2002[4] and is not excluded by s 33,[5] he may enter a notice in respect of that interest.[6] In other words, if the registrar discovers an unregistered interest of a kind that overrides first registration, he has the power to note it on the register. This has already been explained.[7]
- Where a person is registered as proprietor of an interest under one of the registrable dispositions listed below, the registrar *must* enter a notice in the register in respect of that interest.[8] The registrable dispositions in question are:
  - the grant of any lease that is required to be registered;[9]
  - where the registered estate is a franchise or manor, the grant of any lease of that franchise or manor;[10]
  - the express grant or reservation of an easement, right or privilege for an interest equivalent to an estate in fee simple absolute in possession or a term of years absolute, other than a

---

1   LRA 2002, s 90(4).
2   See para **2.5**.
3   LRA 2002, ss 11(4)(a), 12(4)(b).
4   See paras **2.48** et seq.
5   See paras **3.47** et seq.
6   LRA 2002, s 37.
7   See para **2.52**.
8   LRA 2002, s 38.
9   Ibid, Sch 2, para 3(2); s 27(2)(b).
10   Ibid, Sch 2, paras 4(2), 5(2); s 27(2)(c).

right of common which is capable of being registered under the CRA 1965;[1]

- the express grant or reservation of a rentcharge in possession which is either perpetual or for a term of years absolute;[2] and
- the express grant or reservation of a right of entry exercisable over or in respect of a legal lease, or annexed, for any purpose, to a legal rentcharge.[3]

– Where such an entry is necessary to update the register.[4] The sort of circumstances in which that might arise might be where, for example, the registrar discovers that due to a mistake, the burden of a registered disposition was not protected (as it should have been) by the entry of a notice.

– On application to the registrar: this category will, in practice, be the most important. The circumstances in which a person may make such an application are explained in detail below.

Applications for the entry of a notice

Introduction

3.55 A person who claims to be entitled to the benefit of an interest affecting a registered estate or charge may, if the interest is not excluded by s 33, apply to the registrar for the entry in the register of a notice in respect of the interest.[5] Subject to rules, an application under this section may be for either an agreed notice,[6] or a unilateral notice,[7] although in some cases it may have to be for an agreed notice.[8] In both cases the notice will protect the priority of the interest, if valid, as against a subsequent registered disposition.

Agreed notices

3.56 The registrar may only approve an application for an agreed notice in three circumstances.[9] These are as follows.

---

[1]　LRA 2002, Sch 2, para 6(2); s 27(2)(d).
[2]　Ibid, Sch 2, para 7(2); s 27(2)(e).
[3]　Ibid, Sch 2, para 7(2); s 27(2)(e).
[4]　Ibid, Sch 4, para 5(b). Cf paras **5.51**, **5.58**.
[5]　Ibid, s 34(1).
[6]　Ibid, s 34(2)(a).
[7]　Ibid, s 34(2)(b).
[8]　See para **3.57**.
[9]　LRA 2002, s 34(3), (4).

– The first situation is where the applicant is either the registered proprietor, or a person entitled to be registered as proprietor of the registered estate or charge that is to be affected by the notice.

– The second situation is where either the registered proprietor or the person entitled to be registered as proprietor of the registered estate or charge that is to be affected by the notice consents to the entry of the notice.

– The third situation is where the registrar is satisfied as to the validity of the applicant's claim.[1]

3.57 Agreed notices do not differ in substance from notices under the LRA 1925 except that it will not be necessary (as it is now) for the registered proprietor's land certificate to be produced to secure their entry.[2] In the first two situations, the entry of an agreed notice is consensual. In the third situation it is not. Such a non-consensual application may be made where an applicant can demonstrate to the satisfaction of the registrar that the registered proprietor has in fact granted him an interest even if the proprietor will not agree to the entry. This already happens under the present law. Rules are likely to provide that, in relation to certain types of application, probably those that can at present be protected by a notice without production of the proprietor's land certificate,[3] an agreed notice will be the only form of entry. An example would be a spouse's charge in respect of his or her matrimonial home rights under s 31(10) of the Family Law Act 1986.

3.58 Unlike the position in relation to unilateral notices that is explained below,[4] there is no procedure for the cancellation of an agreed notice (whether consensual or non-consensual) on application by the registered proprietor or some person entitled to be registered as proprietor. Should the interest in respect of which the notice is entered come to an end, the notice can and should be removed by the registrar under his powers to keep the register up to date.[5]

Unilateral notices

3.59 A unilateral notice may be entered on application without the consent of the registered proprietor of the estate or charge affected by it. The registrar does not have to be satisfied (as he would if the

---

[1]   Cf LRA 1925, s 48(2).
[2]   For the much-diminished role of land certificates under LRA 2002, see paras **5.42–5.44**.
[3]   Cf LRA 1925, s 64(5)–(7).
[4]   See para **3.62**.
[5]   LRA 2002, Sch 4, para 5(b); see also para **5.58**.

application were for an agreed notice) that the applicant's claim is valid.
A unilateral notice must indicate that it is such a notice, and identify
who is the beneficiary of the notice.[1] The purpose of a unilateral notice
is to allow a person claiming an interest to protect its priority on the
register (to the extent that it is valid), even though he cannot obtain the
concurrence of the registered proprietor.[2] At present a person in that
position can only enter a caution, which does not protect the priority of
the interest that the applicant claims. The person shown in the register
as the beneficiary of a unilateral notice or such other persons as rules
may provide,[3] may apply to the registrar for the removal of the notice
from the register.[4]

3.60 There are obvious dangers in permitting such unilateral entries.
The procedure could be abused and (for example) serious damage
could be inflicted on a registered proprietor who was trying to sell his
property by a disgruntled person who had unsuccessfully tried to
purchase the land. The LRA 2002 therefore contains safeguards against
abuse.

3.61 First, the LRA 2002 creates a procedure for notifying the
registered proprietor. If the registrar enters a unilateral notice in the
register in pursuance of an application, he must give notice of the entry
to:

– the proprietor of the registered estate or charge to which it relates,
  and
– such other persons as rules may provide.[5]

3.62 Secondly, the LRA 2002 confers on both the registered
proprietor of a registered estate or charge and any person who is
entitled to be registered as proprietor, the right to apply to the registrar

---

[1] LRA 2002, s 35(2). According to the Law Commission and the Land Registry, it is unlikely that
     anything else will appear on the register: see (2001) Law Com No 271, para 6.26. In particular, the entry
     will not identify the interest which the entry seeks to protect. At present, it is not uncommon for
     cautions to be entered in respect of interests that are not disputed between the parties but where they
     wish to protect the confidentiality of the particular transaction. A caution does not indicate the nature
     of the interest claimed. The Law Commission and Land Registry accepted that it was legitimate for
     parties to wish to preserve the confidential nature of transactions. The practice in relation to cautions is
     therefore to be carried through to unilateral notices.
[2] Or a person entitled to be registered.
[3] Who are likely to include the beneficiary's personal representatives (if he is dead) or his trustee in
     bankruptcy (if he is insolvent).
[4] LRA 2002, s 35(3).
[5] Ibid, s 35(1). Rules are likely to provide for the notification of persons such as the liquidator, where the
     registered proprietor is a company and is in liquidation at the relevant time.

for the cancellation of a unilateral notice.[1] If an application is made for the cancellation of a unilateral notice the registrar must notify the beneficiary of the notice[2] of:

— the application; and
— the fact that the registrar must cancel the notice if the beneficiary of the notice does not exercise his right to object to the application before the end of such period as rules may provide.[3]

3.63 On such an application to the registrar for cancellation, the following may occur. First, the notice may be cancelled by the registrar because the beneficiary of the notice does not oppose the application. Secondly, the beneficiary of the notice may object to the application. If he does, unless the matter can be disposed of by agreement between the parties, the registrar is bound to refer the matter to the Adjudicator for determination,[4] except where the registrar is satisfied that the objection is groundless.[5] When the matter goes to the Adjudicator, there are various conclusions which he may reach. He may (for example) determine that:

— the person who had entered a unilateral notice was entitled to do so, and that the unilateral notice should, therefore, be replaced by a more permanent form of protection, such as an agreed notice or a registered charge;
— although the beneficiary of the notice does have an interest that is entitled to be protected in the register, a unilateral notice is not the appropriate entry, but that a restriction should be entered instead; or
— the beneficiary of the unilateral notice had no right to enter the notice and he may therefore direct that it should be cancelled.

3.64 The third form of protection against the improper entry of a unilateral notice takes the form of a financial deterrent. A person who applies for the entry of such a notice without reasonable cause will be in

---

[1] LRA 2002, s 36(1).
[2] This means not only the person shown as the beneficiary of the notice in the register, but such other persons as rules may provide: see LRA 2002, s 36(4). Such persons are likely to include the personal representatives of the beneficiary (if he has died) and his trustee in bankruptcy (if he is insolvent).
[3] LRA 2002, s 36(2), (3).
[4] Ibid, s 73(7); see also paras **5.38** et seq.
[5] Ibid, s 73(6). This might be the case if it was apparent that the beneficiary of the notice had no interest that was capable of being protected by a notice.

breach of statutory duty. As such, he will be liable in damages in tort to any person who suffers damage in consequence of that breach.[1]

Restrictions

Nature and effect

3.65 A restriction is an entry in the register regulating the circumstances in which a disposition of a registered estate or charge may be the subject of an entry in the register.[2] A restriction can be entered, therefore, only in respect of a disposition of a registered estate or charge in relation to which some entry in the register may be made. No restriction can be entered in relation to dealings with unregistered interests as there is no title in the register against which to enter it, and no restriction can be entered to prevent any disposition of registered land in relation to which no entry in the register is needed. The entry of a restriction is to be made in relation to the registered estate or charge to which it relates.[3]

3.66 A restriction may in particular prohibit the making of:

- an entry in respect of any disposition (thereby freezing the register);[4] or
- a disposition of a kind specified in the restriction (as where a registered proprietor had only limited powers of disposition).[5]

The restriction may prohibit the making of a particular entry indefinitely,[6] for the period specified in the restriction,[7] or until the occurrence of an event specified in the restriction,[8] such as the giving of notice, the obtaining of a consent, or the making of an order by the court or registrar.[9]

3.67 As a general rule, where a restriction is entered in the register, no entry in respect of a disposition to which the restriction applies may be

---

1   LRA 2002, ss 77(1)(b), 77(2).
2   Ibid, s 40(1).
3   Ibid, s 40(4).
4   Such an entry would be appropriate where a person obtained a freezing injunction in relation to any dealings with the property.
5   LRA 2002, s 40(2)(a).
6   As where the registered proprietor's powers were limited.
7   As where the proprietor had contracted not to make a disposition of the property for that period.
8   LRA 2002, s 40(2)(b).
9   Ibid, s 40(3).

made in the register except in accordance with the terms of the restriction.[1] This rule is subject to one qualification. On the application of a person who appears to the registrar to have a sufficient interest in the restriction,[2] the registrar has power to make an order to:

− disapply a restriction in relation to a disposition specified in the order or dispositions of a kind specified in the order; or
− provide that a restriction has effect subject to certain specified modifications, in relation to a disposition specified in the order or dispositions of a kind specified in the order.[3]

The sort of case where the registrar might exercise his power would be where a disposition could only be made with the consent of a named individual and he could not be traced. The registrar could dispense with the requirement of consent, thereby obviating the need for an application to the court.[4] This power to modify a restriction is not new. At present a restriction is always made subject to any order of the registrar.

The entry of restrictions

Introduction
3.68 Under the LRA 2002, in the circumstances specified:

− the registrar *may* enter a restriction;
− the registrar *must* enter a restriction;
− an application *may* be made to the registrar for the entry of a restriction;
− an application *must* be made to the registrar for the entry of a restriction; and
− the court *may* order the registrar to enter a restriction.

When the registrar may enter a restriction
3.69 The registrar has power to enter a restriction in the register if it appears to him that it is necessary or desirable to do so for any one of three purposes.[5]

---

[1]   LRA 2002, s 41(1).
[2]   Ibid, s 41(3).
[3]   Ibid, s 41(2).
[4]   It seems unlikely that this power could be exercised where, as in the Trusts of Land and Appointment of Trustees Act 1996 (TLATA 1996), s 14, there is specific provision for the *court* to dispense with the requirement of consent.
[5]   LRA 2002, s 42(1).

3.70 The first purpose is for preventing invalidity or unlawfulness in relation to dispositions of a registered estate or charge.[1] The following are examples of when a restriction might be entered for that purpose.[2]

— Where the registered proprietor of an estate or charge is a body which has limited powers, as, for example, in relation to a corporation. If no restriction were entered recording the limitation, the proprietor's powers of disposition would, as regards any disponee, be taken to be free of any limitation affecting the validity of that disposition.[3]

— An entry might also be made to prevent a breach of contract, such as where the registered proprietor has contracted with a third party that he will not make any disposition either at all or without the consent of the third party. A right of pre-emption could, therefore, be the subject of a restriction. So too could the case where a chargor contracts with a chargee that he will not further charge or otherwise dispose the registered estate without the chargee's consent.

— An entry may also restrict a disposition in breach of trust. An example of this is where trustees of land are required to obtain the consent to a disposition of the beneficiaries of full age who are beneficially entitled to an interest in possession in the land.[4]

3.71 The second purpose for which the registrar may enter a restriction is for securing that interests which are capable of being overreached on a disposition of a registered estate or charge are overreached.[5] If there is a disposition by trustees of land or by a tenant for life under the SLA 1925,[6] if overreaching is to take place any capital monies that arise must be paid to:

— the trustees of land (in the case of a trust of land); or
— the trustees of the settlement (in the case of a settlement under the SLA 1925).

In either case there must be at least two trustees, unless the trustee is a trust corporation.[7] To ensure that overreaching does take place, the

---

1   LRA 2002, s 42(1)(a).
2   See (2001) Law Com No 271, para 6.40, from which these examples are drawn.
3   See LRA 2002, ss 26, 52; see also, paras **3.8** and **4.8**.
4   Such persons should be consulted by reason of TLATA 1996, s 11.
5   LRA 2002, s 42(1)(b).
6   Or by a person having the powers of a tenant for life under SLA 1925, s 20.
7   See LPA 1925, s 27(2); SLA 1925, s 94(1).

registrar may enter a restriction to ensure that the proceeds of any disposition are paid to at least two trustees or a trust corporation. As explained below, the registrar is under a *duty* to enter a restriction in certain cases to ensure that overreaching takes place.[1]

3.72 The third purpose for which the registrar may enter a restriction is to protect a right or claim in relation to a registered estate or charge.[2] An example would be where a person claimed to be entitled under a resulting or constructive trust because he had contributed to the cost of the acquisition of the property in question. The restriction might record that no disposition of the land should be registered without the consent of the person claiming the interest. The LRA 2002 expressly provides that a person entitled to the benefit of a charging order relating to an interest under a trust shall be treated as having a right or claim in relation to the trust property.[3] A restriction can, therefore, be entered in relation to the order, and is likely to be in the form that no disposition should be made of the registered estate held in trust without the prior notification of the person having the benefit of the charging order.[4] The reason for this provision is as follows. Under the LRA 1925, charging orders over beneficial interests under a trust of land were protected by the entry of a caution against dealings. This will no longer be possible under the LRA 2002 as cautions are prospectively abolished. Furthermore, it will not be possible to protect such charging orders by the entry of a notice because the order relates to an interest under a trust of land.[5]

3.73 Although a restriction may be entered by the registrar to protect a right or claim in relation to a registered estate or charge,[6] he may not exercise that power for the purpose of protecting the priority of an interest which is, or could be, the subject of a notice.[7] The reason for this limitation is to reinforce the principle that a notice is the correct form of entry to protect the priority of an interest. By its very nature a restriction does not confer priority on a right or interest (although it may have that effect indirectly because it may prevent the registration of some disposition that would affect the priority of the right or interest in question). It should be stressed that the LRA 2002 does not prohibit

---

[1] See para **3.75**.
[2] LRA 2002, s 42(1)(c).
[3] Ibid, s 42(4).
[4] (2001) Law Com No 271, para 6.43.
[5] LRA 2002, s 33(a).
[6] See para **3.72**.
[7] LRA 2002, s 42(2).

the entry of both a restriction and a notice in relation to the same right or interest if there is a good reason to have both.[1] However, the situations in which it will be appropriate are unlikely to be ones where the purpose of the restriction is to protect a right or claim in relation to a registered estate or charge.

3.74 Where the registrar enters a restriction under the powers referred to above he must normally give notice of the entry to the proprietor of the registered estate or charge concerned.[2] If the registered proprietor wishes to challenge the exercise of the registrar's power, he must do so by an application for judicial review. The Adjudicator does not have jurisdiction in this case because the entry of a restriction does not arise out of any application to which the registered proprietor may object.[3] In one situation the registrar does not have to notify the registered proprietor where he exercises his power to enter a restriction, namely where the entry is made in pursuance of an application by a person under s 43 of the LRA 2002. Applications under s 43 are explained at para **3.76**.

When the registrar must enter a restriction
3.75 The registrar must enter a restriction in the following cases.

– Where he enters two or more persons as the joint proprietors of a registered estate in land. In such circumstances he must enter such restrictions as rules may provide, for the purpose of securing that interests which are capable of being overreached on a disposition of the estate are overreached.[4]
– In other cases where the LRA 2002 requires him to enter a restriction. An example is a bankruptcy restriction,[5] which is explained at para **3.115**.
– Where any enactment requires the entry of a restriction. The form of restriction is to be such as rules may provide.[6] There are in fact many statutes that require the entry of a restriction.[7]

---

[1]   For example, in relation to a right of pre-emption, a notice could be entered to protect the priority of the interest and a restriction could be entered to prevent any specified disposition without the consent of the grantee of the right of pre-emption.
[2]   LRA 2002, s 42(3).
[3]   See ibid, ss 73, 108; see also paras **5.38** et seq.
[4]   Ibid, s 44(1). This replicates the present position.
[5]   Ibid, s 86(2).
[6]   Ibid, s 44(2).
[7]   For example, by statute certain public corporations, charities, public sector landlords and other bodies require the consent of the Charity Commission or (as the case may be) the Secretary of State to a disposal of land. A restriction must be entered in such cases.

Where a person may apply for the entry of a restriction

3.76 A person may apply to the registrar to exercise his power to enter a restriction explained in paras **3.69** et seq[1] in three circumstances.

- The first is where he is the proprietor of the registered estate or charge to which the application relates, or a person entitled to be registered as proprietor of that estate or charge.[2]
- The second is where the proprietor of the registered estate or charge to which the application relates, or a person entitled to be registered as proprietor, consents to the application.[3]
- The third is where the applicant otherwise has a sufficient interest in the making of the entry.[4]

As with the entry in the register of notices under the LRA 2002, the production of the registered proprietor's land certificate will not be required in order to enter a restriction on application.

3.77 There is a power for rules to make provision about:

- the form of consent for the purposes of an application when the relevant registered proprietor or a person entitled to be registered as such proprietor consents to the application;[5] and
- classes of persons who are to be regarded as otherwise having a sufficient interest in the making of the entry.[6] It is thought that these classes of persons may include a beneficiary under a trust of land, the Charity Commission in relation to registered land held upon charitable trusts and a receiver, administrative receiver or sequestrator appointed in respect of registered land or a registered charge.[7]

3.78 The rules may specify standard forms of restriction.[8] The LRA 2002 contains provisions – as the LRA 1925 does at present[9] – to protect the registrar from having to give effect to and police unreasonable and inconvenient restrictions. If an application is made

---

[1]   That is, under LRA 2002, s 42(1).
[2]   Ibid, s 43(1)(a).
[3]   Ibid, s 43(1)(b).
[4]   Ibid, s 43(1)(c).
[5]   Ibid, s 43(2)(b).
[6]   Ibid, s 43(2)(c).
[7]   See (2001) Law Com No 271, para 6.49.
[8]   LRA 2002, s 43(2)(d).
[9]   LRA 1925, s 58(2).

for the entry of a restriction which is not in a form specified under the rules, the registrar may only approve the application if it appears to him that:

- the terms of the proposed application are reasonable;[1] and
- applying the proposed restriction would be straightforward and would not place an unreasonable burden on him.[2]

Where a person must apply for the entry of a restriction
3.79 There is a power to make rules that will *require* an application for a restriction to be made in such circumstances and by such persons as the rules may specify.[3] There are situations under the present law where there is such a duty, as where the powers of trustees of land have been limited under s 8 of the TLATA 1996.[4] These will no doubt be replicated in rules made under the LRA 2002.

Where the court may order the entry of a restriction
3.80 The court may make an order requiring the registrar to enter a restriction in the register where it appears to the court that it is necessary or desirable to do so for the purpose of protecting a right or clause in relation to a registered estate or charge.[5] A court is likely to exercise this power in similar circumstances to those where, under the present law, it would order the entry of an inhibition. However, the position under the LRA 2002 is more flexible. An inhibition prevents the entry in the register of *any* dealing with a particular registered estate or charge: in effect it freezes the register.[6] As has been explained above, a restriction need not be so sweeping in its effect, and might, for example, preclude a particular kind of entry.[7] The court, like the registrar,[8] may not enter a restriction to protect the priority of an interest which is, or could be, the subject of a notice.[9]

3.81 Given that in most cases where the court orders the entry of a restriction, it is likely to freeze the register, a potential issue of priority might arise. In Chapter 5 it is explained that, under the LRA 2002,

---

1   LRA 2002, s 43(3)(a).
2   Ibid, s 43(3)(b).
3   Ibid, s 43(2)(a).
4   See LRR 1925, rr 59A, 106A(1).
5   LRA 2002, s 46(1).
6   See LRA 1925, s 57.
7   See paras **3.65**, **3.66**.
8   See LRA 2002, s 42(2); see also para **3.73**.
9   LRA 2002, s 46(2).

priority protection can be obtained by an intending purchaser either by making a priority search or by applying for the entry of a notice in the register in relation to his estate contract to buy the land.[1] What this means is that, during the priority period,[2] any entry made in the register will be postponed to the purchaser's protected application to register the disposition in his favour.[3] There is the possibility of a conflict between the court's power to order the entry of a restriction and this priority protection. If a purchaser has, say, made a priority search, and during the period of priority the court orders the entry of a restriction under the powers explained in para **3.80**, the issue arises as to whether the purchaser's protected application to register the sale or other disposition in his favour has priority over the restriction, or vice versa.[4]

3.82 The general principle in the LRA 2002 is that the priority protection obtained by the purchaser prevails.[5] However, the court may include in an order requiring the registrar to enter a restriction, a direction that an entry made in pursuance of the order is to have overriding priority.[6] If it does, the restriction will prevail over the purchaser's priority protection. If that does happen, the purchaser's position could be seriously prejudiced. The Act therefore provides that the court may make the exercise of the power to order overriding priority subject to such terms and conditions as it thinks fit.[7] In practice the court is likely to require an undertaking from the applicant that he should indemnify any person acting in good faith who has suffered loss as a result of the court's direction.[8] The situation is analogous to the grant of an interim injunction, where a similar undertaking in damages is required.

Safeguards against improper applications for a restriction

3.83 It has been explained above that it will not be necessary to produce the registered proprietor's land certificate on application for the entry of a restriction.[9] The LRA 2002 does, however, contain two

---

1   LRA 2002, s 72; see also para **5.33**.
2   The commencement and duration of the priority period are a matter for rules: LRA 2002, s 72(6), (7).
3   LRA 2002, s 72(2).
4   This problem could arise under the present law when the court orders the entry of an inhibition. There is no reported case in which the point has arisen.
5   This is a necessary inference from LRA 2002, ss 46(3), 72(2), (4).
6   LRA 2002, s 46(3).
7   Ibid, s 46(5).
8   (2001) Law Com No 271, para 6.53. It seems probable that Rules of Court will be made to ensure that such an undertaking is normally required.
9   See para **3.76**.

safeguards to protect a registered proprietor from the improper entry of restrictions.

3.84 The first safeguard is that a person must not exercise his right to apply for a restriction without reasonable cause.[1] Any person who enters a restriction without reasonable cause commits a breach of statutory duty and is liable to any person who suffers damage as a consequence.[2]

3.85 The second safeguard is to provide a procedure by which, when an application is made for a restriction that affects a registered estate or charge, the proprietor is notified of the application and may object to it.[3] Under the LRA 2002, a registered proprietor will be notified of *any* application for the entry of a restriction that relates to his estate or charge, except for the following:

– an application which is made by or with the consent of the registered proprietor or a person entitled to be registered as proprietor;
– an application which, by rules, is *required* to be made, as explained in para **3.79**; and
– an application which reflects a limitation under either an order of the court or registrar, or an undertaking given in place of such order.[4]

3.86 Where an application is notifiable, the registrar must give notice of the application not only to the proprietor of the registered estate or charge to which it relates,[5] but also to such other persons as rules may provide.[6] The latter are likely to include registered chargees and others who have a direct interest in any disposition of the property.[7]

3.87 The registrar may not determine an application for a restriction which is notifiable until the end of such period for making objections as rules provide, unless every person notified has either exercised his right to object to the application or has given the registrar notice that he does

---

[1]   LRA 2002, s 77(1)(b). See also (in relation to notices), para **3.64**.
[2]   Ibid, s 77(2).
[3]   Ibid, s 45.
[4]   Ibid, s 45(3).
[5]   Ibid, s 45(1)(a).
[6]   Ibid, s 45(1)(b).
[7]   See (2001) Law Com No 271, para 6.56.

not intend to do so.[1] If the registered proprietor[2] objects to the application, the usual procedures for dealing with contested applications apply.[3] If, therefore, the objection cannot be resolved by agreement, it will be referred to the Adjudicator for determination.[4]

3.88 It will be noted that the procedure applicable to notifiable restrictions is different from that which applies to unilateral notices. As has been explained, a unilateral notice will be entered in the register and the registered proprietor may then seek its cancellation.[5] The priority of the interest noted on the register is therefore protected pending any such application for its cancellation. By contrast, a notifiable restriction is not entered in the register until the registered proprietor[6] has had the opportunity to object to it. A restriction, unlike a notice, does not protect priority and there is, therefore, no reason why any objection to it should not be dealt with prior to its entry in the register rather than afterwards.

Withdrawal of a restriction

3.89 The LRA 2002 provides that a person may apply to the registrar for the withdrawal of a restriction if the restriction was entered in such circumstances as rules may provide, and the applicant is of such a description as rules may provide.[7] Where a restriction has been entered on the application of a particular person, he or his estate may wish to apply for it to be withdrawn once it is spent. However, there is nothing in the Act to limit the power to cases of restrictions entered on application. Even if the registrar has entered a restriction in circumstances where he is required to,[8] as where he enters two or more persons as the joint proprietors of a registered estate in land to ensure that overreaching takes place on any disposition,[9] the entry may still be spent in time. For example, a surviving co-owner may become absolutely entitled to the land and may wish to have the restriction removed.

---

[1] LRA 2002, s 45(2).
[2] Or other person specified by rules under LRA 2002, s 45(1)(b); see also para **3.86**.
[3] Cf paras **5.38** et seq.
[4] LRA 2002, s 73.
[5] Ibid, s 36; see also para **3.62**.
[6] Or other person entitled by rules to object.
[7] LRA 2002, s 47.
[8] See para **3.75**
[9] LRA 2002, s 44(1); see also para **3.75**.

Pending land actions, writs, orders and deeds of arrangements

3.90   As a result of the prospective abolition of cautions, the LRA 2002 has to make specific provision for certain matters which, under the LRA 1925, can only be protected by the entry of a caution. The matters are:

– pending land actions;[1]
– writs or orders affecting land issued or made by any court for the purpose of enforcing a judgment or recognisance;[2]
– an order appointing a receiver or sequestrator of land;[3] and
– a deed of arrangement within the meaning of the Deeds of Arrangement Act 1914.[4]

All of these matters are to be treated as 'an interest affecting an estate or charge' for the purposes of the LRA 2002.[5] It is necessary that *some* entry be made in the register to protect them, not least because such interests cannot be protected as unregistered interests that override first registration or a registered disposition.[6]

3.91   The position adopted by the LRA 2002 is as follows.[7] As regards both pending land actions and any writs or orders affecting land for the purpose of enforcing a judgment or recognisance, a notice, restriction or both may be entered.[8] However, an order appointing a receiver or sequestrator of land and a deed of arrangement can only be protected by the entry of a restriction. The Act prohibits the entry of a notice.[9] The reasons for this are as follows.[10] First, an order appointing a receiver or sequestrator of land sometimes creates an interest in land and sometimes does not.[11] It may not be easy to tell in any given case. It is therefore appropriate to require one form of entry in every case. A restriction is the logical form of entry because it does not confer priority. Secondly, a deed of arrangement is analogous to a bankruptcy

---

1   See LCA 1972, s 5(1)(a).
2   Ibid, s 6(1)(a).
3   Ibid, s 6(1)(b).
4   Ibid, s 7(1). Deed of Arrangement has the same meaning as in the Deeds of Arrangement Act 1914: LRA 2002, s 87(5).
5   LRA 2002, s 87(1).
6   Ibid, s 87(3).
7   The LRA 2002 contains a power to modify its application in relation to these matters by the making of rules: see s 87(4). Cf (2001) Law Com No 271, para 6.61.
8   This is a necessary inference from LRA 2002, s 87(2).
9   LRA 2002, s 87(2).
10   See (2001) Law Com No 271, para 6.60.
11   *Clayhope Properties Ltd v Evans and Jennings* [1986] 1 WLR 1223, at p 1228.

order in that it protects the interests of creditors in the period between an assignment by a debtor to his trustee for the benefit of his creditors and the registration of the trustee as proprietor of the property. As a restriction is used to protect a bankruptcy order,[1] it is also appropriate that it should be employed to protect deeds of arrangement.

UNREGISTERED INTERESTS WHICH OVERRIDE A REGISTERED DISPOSITION

Introduction

3.92 It has been explained above that, on a registered disposition for valuable consideration, the disponee takes his interest subject to interests that have priority to his own interest and are protected.[2] Amongst the interests that are protected are the unregistered interests listed in Sch 3 to the LRA 2002.[3] It was explained in Chapter 2 that the Act contains two lists of unregistered interests that override respectively (1) first registration, and (2) a registered disposition, and the reasons were given as to why these lists were not the same.[4] It was also explained that to enable the LRA 2002 to achieve its objective of creating in time a conclusive register,[5] it necessarily contained provisions for limiting the impact of such unregistered interests.[6] The range of unregistered interests that will override a registered disposition is considerably narrower than the list of overriding interests that is presently found in s 70 of the LRA 1925. Unlike the position on first registration, an issue of priority arises where there is a registered disposition. In principle it is wrong that a purchaser for valuable consideration should be bound by an interest that is neither registered nor easily discoverable. The Law Commission and Land Registry concluded that 'interests should *only* have overriding status where protection against buyers was needed, but where it was neither reasonable to expect nor sensible to require any entry on the register'.[7] The list of overriding interests in Sch 3 reflects this intention. It should be noted that the introduction of electronic conveyancing will of itself eliminate many unregistered interests because, under the system of

---

[1]   LRA 2002, s 86(4); see also para **3.115**.
[2]   Ibid, ss 29, 30; see also paras **3.29**, **3.33**.
[3]   LRA 2002, ss 29(2)(a)(ii), 30(2)(a)(ii).
[4]   See para **2.47**.
[5]   See para **1.7**.
[6]   See para **2.46**.
[7]   (2001) Law Com No 271, para 8.6.

e-conveyancing that the LRA 2002 creates, it will be necessary to register a disposition at the same time as it is made.[1]

The unregistered interests that will override a registered disposition

3.93 Schedule 3 lists 14 unregistered interests that will bind a registered disponee for valuable consideration. A fifteenth overriding unregistered interest is found in s 90 of the LRA 2002.[2] Twelve of the 15 interests that override a registered disposition are the same as the interests that override first registration. These have already been explained in para **2.48** and therefore little more needs to be said about them. The 12 interests that are the same are as follows:

(a)   a customary right;[3]
(b)   a public right;[4]
(c)   a local land charge;[5]
(d)   certain mineral rights, including rights to coal and mineral rights that were granted before 1926;[6]
(e)   a franchise;[7]
(f)   a manorial right;[8]
(g)   what is usually called a 'Crown rent';[9]
(h)   a non-statutory right in respect of an embankment or river or sea wall;[10]
(i)   a right to payment in lieu of tithe;[11] and
(j)   a PPP lease.[12]

Many of these interests can no longer be created. The ones that can be are public rights, local land charges (which are, in any event, otherwise protected), franchises (at least in theory), and PPP leases (although it remains to be seen whether these will ever be granted). Furthermore, under the LRA 2002, the rights listed at (e)–(i) will lose their overriding

---

[1]   See para **7.5**.
[2]   Cf the position on first registration under LRA 2002, Sch 1; see also para **2.48**.
[3]   LRA 2002, Sch 3, para 4.
[4]   Ibid, Sch 3, para 5.
[5]   Ibid, Sch 3, para 6.
[6]   Ibid, Sch 3, paras 7–9.
[7]   Ibid, Sch 3, para 10.
[8]   Ibid, Sch 3, para 11.
[9]   Ibid, Sch 3, para 12.
[10]   Ibid, Sch 3, para 13.
[11]   Ibid, Sch 3, para 14.
[12]   Ibid, s 90(5).

status 10 years after the Act comes into force.[1] During that 10-year period, no fee will be charged for the entry of a notice in the register to protect the interest in question. Once the 10-year period has elapsed, if no notice has been entered in the register, the interest will not be lost, but it will be unprotected as against a registered disposition for valuable consideration.[2]

3.94 The LRA 2002 does make significant changes in relation to the three most important categories of unregistered interest that can override a registered disposition. It does so having regard to the principles set out in para **3.92**. The three categories of interest are short leases, the rights of persons in actual occupation and legal easements and *profits à prendre*.

Certain short leases

3.95 Any lease that was granted for a term not exceeding 7 years except for:

- a lease granted out of unregistered land that was required to be registered under the provisions on first registration explained at paras **2.18–2.20**, even though it was for a term of 7 years or less; or
- a lease granted out of registered land that was a registrable disposition even though it was for a term of 7 years or less.[3]

In short, if a lease is required to be registered, it cannot override a registered disposition if it is not in fact registered. Conversely, if a lease cannot be registered, it necessarily overrides a registered disposition.[4]

Interests of persons in actual occupation

The general rule
3.96 The general rule is that an unregistered interest belonging at the time of the disposition to a person in actual occupation, so far as relating to land of which he is in actual occupation will override a registrable disposition.[5] That general rule is itself narrower than the

---

1   LRA 2002, s 117; see also para **2.50**.
2   See ibid, ss 29, 30.
3   Ibid, Sch 3, para 1. For the leases that are registrable dispositions even though they are for a term of 7 years or less, see LRA 2002, s 27(2)(b)(ii)–(v); see also para **3.15**.
4   The same protection applies to leases that were granted for more than 21 years before the LRA 2002 came into force: LRA 2002, Sch 12, para 12.
5   Ibid, Sch 3, para 2. The 'interest' must, therefore, be an interest in land for the purposes of the Act because it must relate to land.

equivalent provision under the present law, s 70(1)(g) of the LRA 1925 as it has been interpreted, in two respects.

–   First, it confines the protection to the land actually occupied, thereby reversing the decision of the Court of Appeal in *Ferrishurst Ltd v Wallcite Ltd*.[1] In that case it was held that a person in actual occupation of part of a registered title who had rights over the whole could, by virtue of his possession of part, protect his rights over the whole. The decision runs counter to the aim of the LRA 2002 to reduce the impact of unregistered interests that can override first registration or a registrable disposition. Its effect was to place an unreasonable burden of enquiry on a purchaser of registered land.
–   Secondly, the protection given by s 70(1)(g) of LRA 1925 to persons who are not in actual occupation of registered land but are in receipt of the rents and profits is not replicated in the LRA 2002.[2] The position of those who, immediately before the Act comes into force, are protected because they are in receipt of rents and profits is, however, preserved by the transitional provisions of the Act.[3] If, however, such persons cease to be in receipt of the rents and profits of the land at any time thereafter, their interests are no longer protected.[4] If, for example, at the time when the LRA 2002 comes into force, there is a sub-lessee in possession, but the lease out of which that sub-lease was granted is not registered, the head lessee's interest will be protected until the sub-lease terminates. If the head lessee were then to grant a new sub-lease, the fact that he would be in receipt of the rents and profits from the new sub-lease would not protect him.

The general rule as to the protection of the interests of occupiers is, however, subject to four important exceptions.

The four exceptions to the general rule
3.97   The first exception is an interest under a settlement under the

---

1   [1999] Ch 355. See (2001) Law Com No 271, paras 8.56–8.58.
2   This applies not only to unregistered interests that override registered dispositions but also to unregistered interests that override first registration: LRA 2002, Sch 1, para 2. However, on first registration, the fact that there are superior unregistered interests will normally be reflected in the class of title that is given, which will typically be a good leasehold title. That of itself will protect the rights of those with a superior title: see LRA 2002, s 12(6); see also para **2.44**.
3   LRA 2002, Sch 3, para 2A(1), inserted by Sch 12, para 8.
4   Ibid, Sch 3, para 2A(2), inserted by Sch 12, para 8.

SLA 1925.[1] Such an interest must be protected by the entry of appropriate restrictions in the register. This exception involves no change in the law.[2]

3.98 The second exception is an interest of a person of whom inquiry was made before the disposition and who failed to disclose the right when he could reasonably have been expected to do so.[3] This exception replicates the position under s 70(1)(g) of the LRA 1925.

3.99 The third exception is an interest:

– which belongs to a person whose occupation would not have been obvious on a reasonably careful inspection of the land at the time of the disposition; and
– of which the person to whom the disposition is made does not have actual knowledge at that time.[4]

This exception is new and is a significant limitation on this category of unregistered interest.

3.100 First, as regards the first of the two limbs, it should be noted that it is not the occupier's *interest* that has to be apparent on a careful inspection of the land, but his *occupation*. The test is *not* whether a buyer has *constructive notice* of the occupier's occupation, but whether that person's occupation was *obvious* on a reasonably careful inspection of the land at the relevant time. This concept is borrowed from the law on sale of land.[5] A seller of land is obliged to disclose to an intending buyer interests affecting the property that are latent, in other words, interests that are *not* obvious on a reasonable inspection of the land. In this context the Court of Appeal has expressly rejected the view that, because a person has constructive notice of an interest, that interest is patent.[6] As it relates to the discoverability of the occupation rather than

---

[1] LRA 2002, Sch 3, para 2(a).
[2] Cf LRA 1925, s 86(2). Astonishingly, this provision provoked an unsuccessful division during the Bill's passage through Parliament: see *Hansard* (HL), vol 628, cols 314–317 (there were only three divisions during the passage of the Bill through the House of Lords). Given that new settlements can no longer be created and that any problems with unintended settlements are likely to have surfaced, the concern over this point is puzzling.
[3] LRA 2002, Sch 3, para 2(b).
[4] Ibid, Sch 3, para 2(c).
[5] See (2001) Law Com No 271, para 8.62.
[6] *Caballero v Henty* (1874) LR 9 Ch App 447.

the interest, the application of the principle is analogous rather than direct.

3.101 Secondly, to fall within the exception, the disponee will have to satisfy *both* limbs of the exception. If he does not, he will be bound by the interest of the person in occupation. Thus:

- if a person's occupation is *not* obvious under the first limb, a purchaser will still be bound by that interest if he had actual knowledge of the occupier's interest; and
- if a person's occupation *is* obvious under the first limb, a buyer will be bound by the occupier's interest even if he did not have actual knowledge of that interest because he failed to make inquiry of the occupier.

3.102 The purpose of this third exception is clear: the unregistered interests of occupiers should only be binding on a buyer if those interests were either readily discoverable or already known to the buyer. The objective of the LRA 2002 is to eliminate as far as possible inquiries beyond the register.[1]

3.103 The fourth exception to the general principle is a leasehold estate granted to take effect in possession after the end of the period of 3 months beginning with the date of the grant and which has not taken effect in possession at the time of the disposition.[2] This exception necessarily follows from the requirement that a reversionary lease that takes effect in possession more than 3 months after grant has to be registered.[3] This exception will not commonly arise. For it to do so:

- a lease of land would have to be granted to a person to take effect in possession more than 3 months after the grant;
- that grantee would either have to be in actual occupation when the grant was made (as where he has an existing lease) or be permitted to go into occupation before the lease takes effect;
- a registered disposition would then have to be made of the land affected by the reversionary lease before the lease takes effect in possession but after the tenant went into actual occupation.

---

[1]   See paras **1.7, 1.8**.
[2]   LRA 2002, Sch 3, para 2(d).
[3]   Ibid, ss 4(1)(d) (compulsory first registration), 27(2)(b)(ii).

Legal easements and profits

The general principle

3.104   The circumstances in which an unregistered easement or *profit à prendre* will override a registered disposition are substantially curtailed by the LRA 2002. The general principle is that an unregistered legal easement or *profit à prendre* will override a registered disposition. It is significant that only *legal* easements and profits can override a registered disposition. This means that an easement or profit that is expressly granted or reserved after the LRA 2002 comes into force but is not registered can *never* override a registrable disposition, as it can under the present law.[1] It follows that the only legal easements or profits that will override a registered disposition will be:

— those in existence when the LRA 2002 came into force but which had not been registered; and
— those that arise subsequently by prescription or by implied grant or reservation.

As is explained below, there are important transitional provisions in relation to easements and profits that are overriding interests at the time when the LRA 2002 comes into force but would not be under the Act.[2]

The exceptions to the general rule

3.105   The general provision in para **3.104** is subject to a very significant exception. An unregistered legal easement or *profit à prendre* which is *not* registered under the CRA 1965, which has *not* been exercised within one year of the date of the disposition, and which at the time of the disposition:

— is *not* within the actual knowledge of the person to whom the disposition is made; or
— would *not* have been obvious on a reasonably careful inspection of the land over which the easement or profit is exercisable,

---

[1]   The LRA 2002 therefore reverses the effect of part of the decision in *Celsteel Ltd v Alton House Holdings Ltd* [1985] 1 WLR 204, at pp 219–221.
[2]   See para **3.108**.

will *not* override first registration.[1] Stated positively, an unregistered legal easement or profit *will* override a registered disposition if:

- it is a right of common that has been registered under the CRA 1965;[2] or
- it is actually known to the disponee under the registered disposition; or
- it would have been obvious on a reasonably careful inspection of the servient tenement; or
- the person entitled to the easement on profit proves that it has been exercised within one year of the disposition.

3.106 This provision may at first sight seem puzzling, but on closer analysis, the reasons for it become clear.

- First, if the easement or profit is a right of common that has been registered under the CRA 1965, then it is readily discoverable from a search of the commons register. It is protected on a register which any buyer should inspect.
- Secondly, when a person sells land, he must disclose to the intending buyer prior to contract the existence of any latent defects in title, including any easements or profits. A defect in title is latent if it is not obvious on a reasonable inspection of the land affected by it.[3] There is, however, no duty to disclose latent defects in title of which the intending buyer actually knows.[4] The LRA 2002 applies these principles to the issue of whether an unregistered easement or profit should override a registered disposition. If a legal easement or profit is either known to a buyer or obvious, he is not prejudiced if he takes the land subject to it.
- Thirdly, many landowners have legal easements over their neighbours' lands of which their neighbours may be unaware and which are not obvious. The commonest examples are rights for the passage of utilities and drainage rights. Many such rights are not protected in the register but have been used for many years. To deal with such cases and to prevent important rights being defeated, the LRA 2002 provides that legal easements and profits will override a

---

[1]   LRA 2002, Sch 3, para 3.

[2]   Cf para **3.18**.

[3]   It has been repeatedly stated that a defect is patent and does not have to be disclosed to an intending buyer if it is obvious: see, eg, *Ashburner v Sewell* [1891] 3 Ch 405, at pp 408–409; approved by the House of Lords in *Shonleigh Nominees Ltd v Attorney-General (at the Relation of Hampshire County Council)* [1974] 1 WLR 305, at pp 311, 315, 323–324.

[4]   See, eg, *Re Gloag and Miller's Contract* (1883) 23 ChD 320, at p 327.

registered disposition if they have been exercised within one year of the disposition. This is a limited pragmatic exception by which rights that may not be readily discoverable are nonetheless protected. In practice, standard forms of enquiry before contract are likely to be instituted to try to identify such rights in any event.

3.107 One important effect of these provisions should be noted. It is comparatively easy to acquire an easement or profit from 20 years' user under the doctrine of prescription by lost modern grant. However, once an easement has been acquired, it is virtually impossible to prove that it has been released by abandonment because it has not been exercised for many years.[1] Under the LRA 2002, subject to the transitional provisions explained below, a purchaser of registered land will not be bound by a long-dormant unregistered easement or profit that has not been exercised for many years and which is not obvious on a reasonably careful inspection of the land affected by it. It is clear that this result is intended.[2]

Transitional provisions

3.108 As a result of the far-reaching nature of the changes that the LRA 2002 makes in relation to easements and profits, there are generous transitional provisions. First, any easement or profit that is an overriding interest immediately before the Act comes into force will retain that status.[3] Obviously with the passage of time it will become increasingly difficult to prove that such a right was an overriding interest at that date. There are, in any event, provisions which are intended to ensure that such rights are entered in the register.[4] Secondly, for a period of 3 years after the LRA 2002 comes into force, *any* unregistered legal easement or profit will override a registered disposition.[5] This will in practice protect those easements or profits that come into being within that 3-year period by way of prescription or implied grant or reservation.

Ensuring that unregistered interests are registered

3.109 It has been explained, in the context of unregistered interests that override first registration, that the LRA 2002 contains provisions

---

[1]   See, eg, *Benn v Hardinge* (1992) 66 P&CR 246 (175 years' non-use of a right of way did not amount to abandonment).
[2]   See (2001) Law Com No 271, paras 8.65, 8.72.
[3]   LRA 2002, Sch 12, para 9.
[4]   See para **3.109**.
[5]   LRA 2002, Sch 12, para 10.

which are intended to ensure that unregistered interests are entered on the register.[1] One of these provisions also applies in relation to unregistered interests that override a registered disposition. Section 71(b) of the LRA 2002 makes provision for rules to be made requiring a person who is applying to register a registrable disposition to provide the registrar with information about an interest affecting the estate which falls within Sch 3 and is of a description prescribed by the rules.[2]

SPECIAL CASES

Introduction

3.110   Part 7 of the LRA 2002 makes provision for a number of special cases. Some of the matters in Part 7 have already been discussed. It is, however, necessary to say something about the Crown, insolvency and settlements.

The Crown

3.111   In Chapter 2 it was explained how the LRA 2002 contains provisions that will enable the Crown to register land that it holds in demesne as paramount feudal lord, something it cannot presently do.[3] It is thought that the Crown will take advantage of this new power. The provisions of the LRA 2002 on adverse possession[4] provide an incentive for it to do so. This is particularly so in relation to Crown land that is vulnerable to adverse possession such as the foreshore[5] and, in due course, those parts of the sea bed beyond the county boundaries that will become registrable under the Act.[6]

3.112   The LRA 2002 contains other provisions concerning the Crown. These only require brief mention because they are unlikely to affect most practitioners.[7] One issue that does arise from time to time is

---

[1]   See paras **2.51**, **2.52**.
[2]   Cf para **2.51**.
[3]   See paras **2.61**, **2.62**.
[4]   Explained in Chapter 8.
[5]   See para **8.62**.
[6]   See LRA 2002, s 130(b). Like LRA 1925, LRA 2002 applies to land covered by internal waters that falls within the body of a county: see s 130(a). The applicability may be extended by order out to the base lines that define the territorial limits of the UK.
[7]   See LRA 2002, ss 83 (Crown and Duchy land: representation), 84 (disapplication of certain requirements as to formalities and enrolment) and 85 (bona vacantia).

that of escheat.[1] Where a freehold estate terminates the land escheats, usually to the Crown,[2] and it then becomes part of the Crown's demesne land.[3] The usual reason why this happens is because the Treasury Solicitor disclaims onerous property that passed to him by way of bona vacantia when a company became insolvent.[4] The problem that the escheat of a registered freehold creates is that, because the freehold has terminated, the title has to be removed from the register. This obviously runs counter to the objective of securing the registration of all land in England and Wales. The LRA 2002 therefore contains a rule-making power that will ensure that where registered freehold land escheats, the title can remain on the register. It is likely that appropriate restrictions will be entered in the register to ensure that there can be no dealing with that land except (say) by order of the court or on the application of the Crown Estate.[5]

Insolvency

Introduction

3.113 Section 86 of the LRA 2002 makes detailed provision for the situation where a registered proprietor becomes insolvent. The Act retains the essentials of the practice under the LRA 1925, with such modifications as are necessary because of the prospective abolition of inhibitions.[6]

Procedure in relation to bankruptcy petitions

3.114 Where a bankruptcy petition is made, it must be registered as a pending action under the LCA 1972.[7] Under the LRA 2002, as soon as is practicable after the registration of the petition in bankruptcy, the registrar must enter a notice in respect of the pending action in the

---

1. The matter is explained in detail in (2001) Law Com No 271, paras 11.20–11.30. See also *Scmlla Properties Ltd v Gesso Properties (BVI) Ltd* [1995] BCC 793, the leading modern authority on escheat.
2. Technically, escheat is to the lord of whom the land was held. Land is usually held directly of the Crown, although it may be held of one of the two Royal Duchies (Cornwall or Lancaster). It is extremely unlikely that any other person would succeed in proving that he was a mesne lord, although we are aware of at least one individual who makes claims of this kind.
3. It is administered by the Crown Estate.
4. See Companies Act 1985, ss 654, 656.
5. See LRA 2002, s 82.
6. Cf LRA 1925, s 61(3), which requires the registrar to enter a *bankruptcy inhibition* as soon as possible after the registration of a bankruptcy order under LCA 1972.
7. LCA 1972, s 5(1)(b). The requirement that a land charge be entered is imposed by the Insolvency Rules 1986, SI 1986/1925. Under LRA 2002, s 86(7), nothing in s 86 requires a person to whom a registrable disposition is made to make any search under LCA 1972. Registration under LCA 1972 cannot affect an estate in registered land.

register in relation to any registered estate or charge which *appears* to him to be affected.[1] Unless this notice is cancelled by the registrar in the manner provided for in rules, the notice continues in force until either a restriction is entered in the register or the trustee in bankruptcy is registered as proprietor.[2]

Bankruptcy order

3.115　A similar procedure applies when a bankruptcy order is made. Once again, the bankruptcy order should be registered under the LCA 1972.[3] As soon as practicable after that happens, the registrar must enter a restriction in relation to any registered estate or charge which appears to him to be affected by the order. The terms of that restriction must reflect the limitation under s 284 of the IA 1986 that a disposition by a bankrupt is void unless it is made with the consent of, or is subsequently ratified by, the court.[4]

Protection of purchasers

3.116　Neither a petition in bankruptcy nor a bankruptcy order is an interest affecting an estate or charge for the purposes of the LRA 2002.[5] It follows that the effect of such a petition or order is outside the provisions on priority explained above.[6] As mentioned in para **3.38**, the LRA 2002 follows instead the provisions of the IA 1986 in this regard. It provides that where the proprietor of a registered estate or charge is adjudged bankrupt, the title of his trustee in bankruptcy is void as against a person to whom a registrable disposition of the estate or charge is made if:

(a)　the disposition is made for valuable consideration;
(b)　the person to whom the disposition is made acts in good faith; and
(c)　at the time of the disposition:
　　(i)　no notice or restriction has been entered under s 86 in relation to the registered estate or charge, and
　　(ii)　the person to whom the disposition is made has no notice of the bankruptcy petition or the adjudication.[7]

---

[1]　LRA 2002, s 86(2). The use of the word 'appears' is deliberate. If the bankrupt has a common name, it can often be difficult to identify the land in question.
[2]　LRA 2002, s 86(3).
[3]　See LCA 1972, s 6(1)(c).
[4]　LRA 2002, s 86(4).
[5]　Ibid, s 86(1).
[6]　See paras **3.27** et seq.
[7]　LRA 2002, s 86(5).

This provision only applies if the relevant registration requirements set out in Sch 2 to the LRA 2002 are met in relation to the disposition.[1]

Settlements

3.117 The LRA 1925 contains detailed provisions on the treatment of settled land where the title is registered. However, it ceased to be possible to create new settlements after 1996.[2] The LRA 2002 therefore leaves the application of the principles of registered land to settlements to rules (to the extent that those are thought to be necessary).[3]

---

[1] LRA 2002, s 86(6).
[2] TLATA 1996, s 2.
[3] LRA 2002, s 89.

CHAPTER 4

CHARGES OVER REGISTERED LAND

THE MAIN CHANGES AT A GLANCE

4.1   Although a number of provisions of the LRA 2002 are concerned with charges over registered land, Part 5 is exclusively concerned with them. The Act, whether in Part 5 or elsewhere, makes provision for the following matters:

— the nature of registered charges and sub-charges;
— the powers enjoyed by chargees and sub-chargees;
— the priority of competing advances;
— tacking and further advances;
— the realisation of a chargee's security; and
— certain miscellaneous matters.

For the purposes of the Act, 'charge' is widely defined to include 'any mortgage, charge or lien for securing money or money's worth'.[1]

4.2   The main changes made by the LRA 2002 are as follows.

— It is no longer possible to create a legal mortgage of registered land by demise or sub-demise.
— The present practice by which a second chargee notifies a first chargee of its charge in order to ensure the priority of that second charge over any further advances by the first chargee is given statutory effect.
— It creates a new method protecting further advances, by permitting the parties to agree a maximum sum for which a charge shall stand as security which is then appropriately protected on the register. That charge then has priority over any subsequent charges until the maximum sum secured is reached.

---

[1]   LRA 2002, s 132(1).

- Where a chargee exercises its power of sale and there is a surplus after the charge is discharged, the chargee will in practice have to search the register to ascertain whether there are any other charges. This is because it will be fixed with notice of anything in the register.
- A duty is imposed on the registrar to notify existing chargees of any overriding statutory charge when it is registered. Indemnity is payable for any loss suffered by reason of a failure by the registrar.

THE NATURE OF REGISTERED CHARGES AND SUB-CHARGES

4.3   Under the LRA 2002, it ceases to be possible to create a mortgage of registered land by demise or sub-demise.[1] This is merely a recognition of reality and is unlikely to have any practical effect. Even under the LRA 1925, there was a presumption that a registered charge took effect as a charge by way of legal mortgage,[2] but in any event, mortgages by demise or sub-demise have been obsolete for some considerable time. Legal charges of registered land can either be created as charges expressed to be by way of legal mortgage or by charging the estate with the payment of money, the means traditionally associated with registered land.[3] In either event, the charge has effect on registration as a charge by deed by way of legal mortgage.[4]

4.4   A mortgagee has an interest which he can charge and a sub-mortgage is simply a mortgage of a mortgage. Under the LRA 2002, there is only one way that the proprietor of a registered charge can create a legal sub-charge, namely by charging with the payment of money the indebtedness secured by the registered charge.[5] All other means are precluded.[6]

4.5   In the unlikely event that the proprietor of a registered estate were to attempt to execute a mortgage by demise or sub-demise or the

---

[1]   LRA 2002, s 23(1).
[2]   See LRA 1925, s 27(1).
[3]   LRA 2002, s 23. Under the Land Transfer Act 1875, the only means of creating a legal mortgage of registered land was by means of charging the registered legal estate with the payment of money. There was no transfer or fiction of transfer of the legal estate to the mortgagee. The introduction of the charge by way of legal mortgage by LPA 1925, s 87 was intended to provide a means of harmonising the registered and unregistered systems: (2001) Law Com No 271, para 7.2.
[4]   LRA 2002, s 51.
[5]   Ibid, s 23(2)(b).
[6]   Ibid, s 23(2)(a), (3).

proprietor of a registered charge were to try to create a sub-charge in a manner prohibited by the LRA 2002, the application for registration would simply be rejected by the registrar. It may be that the charge or sub-charge will, in any event, have to be created in a prescribed form (particularly once electronic conveyancing has been introduced). There is a power under the Act to prescribe by rules the form and content of a registrable disposition of a registered estate or charge.[1] This contrasts with the previous position under the LRA 1925. Subject to certain limitations, a registered proprietor was free to create a charge in any form.[2]

EQUITABLE CHARGES

4.6   Subject to one minor change, the LRA 2002 does not alter the circumstances in which an equitable charge may be created[3] or imposed. The Act does not replicate the provision of the LRA 1925 that enabled a registered proprietor to create a lien over the registered estate by depositing his land certificate with the lender as security.[4] This is because that power had become obsolete as a result of a judicial decision.[5]

THE POWERS OF A REGISTERED CHARGEE OR SUB-CHARGEE

Power to make dispositions of the charge

4.7   Subject to the limitations on the methods of sub-charging mentioned in para **4.4**, a person who is the proprietor of a registered charge has power to make a disposition of that charge of any kind permitted by the general law.[6] The Act also confers on him the specific power to create a sub-charge.[7] It has already been explained[8] that a

---

[1]   LRA 2002, s 25(1).

[2]   LRA 1925, s 25(2).

[3]   A registered proprietor, in exercise of his owner's powers, may create such a charge to the extent that is permitted under the general law: see LRA 2002, s 23; also para **3.5**.

[4]   LRA 1925, s 66.

[5]   See *United Bank of Kuwait plc v Sahib* [1997] Ch 107. The decision was based upon LP(MP)A 1989, s 2, and its abolition of the old doctrine of part performance upon which a mortgage by deposit of title deeds (the model for the lien by deposit of the land certificate) had rested.

[6]   LRA 2002, s 23(2)(a).

[7]   Ibid, s 23(2)(b).

[8]   See para **3.8**.

proprietor of a registered estate or charge is to be taken as free from any limitation affecting the validity of the disposition unless that limitation is reflected by an entry in the register[1] or is imposed by, or under, the LRA 2002.[2] However, this presumption only operates to protect the disponee. It does not validate an unlawful disposition where, for example, there should have been a restriction on the register to indicate that there was some limitation on the registered proprietor's powers of disposition.[3] It follows that, if, say, the chargee had no power to assign its charge but had failed to ensure that there was a restriction on the register to reflect this fact, the assignee's title to the charge would be good. However, the chargee would remain subject to whatever liabilities there might be for making such an *ultra vires* disposition.

Powers in relation to the property charged

4.8 In relation to the property charged, the proprietor of a registered charge is to be taken to have all the powers of disposition conferred by law on the owner of a legal mortgage, unless there is an entry to the contrary in the register.[4] For example, if under the terms of the charge the chargee's remedies were not exercisable for the first 2 years of the mortgage,[5] or his power of leasing[6] was wholly excluded, those limitations should be the subject of a restriction in the register. Once again, the presumption created by the Act only serves to protect the disponee. It does not affect the lawfulness of the disposition.[7] Thus if a registered chargee sold the land subject to the charge when his power of sale had not arisen or had not become exercisable, the buyer's title could not be challenged. But the chargee would be liable in damages to the chargor.[8]

4.9 The registered proprietor of a sub-charge has the same powers of

---

[1]   For dispositions made after the LRA 2002 comes into force, the only relevant entry will be a restriction.
[2]   LRA 2002, s 26(1), (2). Limitations imposed by the Act include the need to comply with any rules as to form and content (s 25) and the requirements for the registration of a registered disposition (s 27(4), Sch 2).
[3]   Ibid, s 26(3).
[4]   Ibid, s 52(1).
[5]   Because the legal date for redemption was postponed: cf *Twentieth Century Banking Corporation Ltd v Wilkinson* [1977] Ch 99.
[6]   Under LPA 1925, s 99(2).
[7]   LRA 2002, s 52(2).
[8]   Cf LPA 1925, s 104(2).

disposition in relation to the property charged as does the registered chargee who has created the sub-charge.[1]

THE PRIORITY OF COMPETING CHARGES

Registered charges

4.10 Under the LRA 2002, registered charges on the same registered estate, or (in the case of sub-charges) on the same registered charge, rank in priority between themselves in the order shown in the register.[2] In other words, it is the order in which the charges are registered that determines their priority and not the date of their creation.[3] This is the same as under the LRA 1925.[4] Rules are likely to make provision as to how the priority of registered charges as between themselves is recorded on the register.[5] Because chargees may decide between themselves on some different priority from that conferred by the order of registration, rules are also likely to make provision by which such agreements can be recorded.[6]

Equitable charges

4.11 The priority of equitable charges will depend upon the general rules of priority in the Act that have already been explained.[7] In other words, the order of creation of equitable charges will be determined by the order in which the charges are created. When electronic conveyancing has become fully operative, it will in time become impossible to create equitable charges except by simultaneously registering them.[8] In those circumstances the date of registration and the date of creation will coincide, so that the register will in practice become as conclusive as to the priority of equitable charges as it is for registered charges.

---

[1] LRA 2002, s 53.

[2] Ibid, s 48(1).

[3] In time, with the introduction of electronic conveyancing, it will in any event become impossible to create or transfer most estates, rights or interests in registered land except by simultaneously registering the disposition: see para **7.54**. In those circumstances, the basic rule of priority that the first in time of creation prevails (LRA 2002, s 28) will come to coincide with the rule of priority as to competing charges contained in LRA 2002, s 48(1).

[4] See LRA 1925, s 29.

[5] LRA 2002, s 48(2)(a).

[6] Ibid, s 48(2)(b). This could be important where one chargee exercises its power of sale and there is a surplus that has to be paid to the chargee next entitled: cf s 54, para **4.18**.

[7] LRA 2002, ss 28–30; see also paras **3.27–3.35**.

[8] See para **7.54**.

TACKING AND FURTHER ADVANCES

4.12 The LRA 2002 makes very significant changes to the law on tacking and further advances. Although the rules which govern tacking and further advances in relation to charges over unregistered land are exclusively statutory,[1] those provisions did not apply to charges registered under the LRA 1925.[2] However, there was no equivalent statutory code applicable to tacking and further advances in relation to charges over registered land. The applicable law comprised the old common law rules of tacking that had been abolished in relation to unregistered land[3] with a partial statutory gloss.[4] The essential common law rule was that where a first chargee received notice of the charge of a second chargee, he could not thereafter make a further advance to the chargor that had priority over the charge of the second chargee. Because of this rule, where there is a second or subsequent charge over registered land, the new lender will notify prior lenders of his charge. This practice is widely employed by mortgage lenders in England and Wales and it works effectively. It has proved to be quicker and less cumbersome than the procedure contained in the LRA 1925 by which the registrar was obliged to give notice to any prior chargee before he registered a subsequent charge which would prejudicially affect further advances by the prior chargee.[5]

4.13 The LRA 2002 recognises that the practice of lenders is the right one and gives it statutory effect. It provides that the proprietor of a registered charge may make a further advance on the security of the charge that ranks in priority to a subsequent charge if he has not received from the subsequent chargee notice of the creation of the subsequent charge.[6]

4.14 The Act permits three other forms of tacking further advances. Two of these replicate the previous law. A proprietor of a registered

---

1   LRA 1925, s 94(1)–(3).
2   Ibid, s 94(4). Nor do they apply to charges under LRA 2002: see Sch 11, para 2(9), amending LRA 1925, s 94(4).
3   See LRA 1925, s 94(3).
4   For the statutory provisions, see LRA 1925, s 30.
5   LRA 1925, s 30(1).
6   LRA 2002, s 49(1). Notice given for the purposes of this subsection is to be treated as received when, in accordance with rules, it ought to have been received: s 49(2). It is anticipated that rules will make different provision as to the time of deemed receipt according to the means of communication employed.

charge may make a further advance that has priority over a subsequent charge if:

- that further advance was made in pursuance of an obligation and, at the time when the subsequent charge was created, that agreement was entered in the register in accordance with rules;[1] or
- the subsequent chargee agrees.[2]

4.15 The final method of tacking further advances is, however, a novelty. The proprietor of a registered charge may make a further advance having priority over a subsequent charge if the parties to the prior charge had agreed a maximum amount for which the charge was security and at the time when the subsequent charge was created, the agreement had been entered on the register in the manner specified in rules.[3] For example, X agrees that he will lend money on the security of Y's registered estate and that the maximum sum for which the charge is to stand as security is £100,000. The agreement is recorded on the register in the prescribed manner. Y borrows £50,000 from X. He then borrows a further £20,000 from Z and creates a second charge over the registered estate as security. Y then borrows a further £50,000 from X. X is secured for the full sum of £100,000 in priority to Z's second charge.

4.16 There is a power to make rules which, in relation to charges of a particular description, would either disapply this form of tacking or would require compliance with specified conditions.[4] This power has been included as a safeguard. It could be exercised if it transpired that this form of tacking was being employed oppressively in relation to particular types of charge.[5] It remains to be seen whether such rules will prove to be necessary.

REALISATION OF A CHARGEE'S SECURITY

4.17 The LRA 2002 addresses two matters concerned with the realisation of a chargee's security. The first merely replicates what was

---

[1] LRA 2002, s 49(3).

[2] Ibid, s 49(6).

[3] Ibid, s 49(4).

[4] Ibid, s 49(5).

[5] The Law Commission gave as a possible example of the sort of case where rules might be made regulated agreements secured by land mortgages under the Consumer Credit Act 1974: (2001) Law Com No 271, para 7.36.

the law under the LRA 1925. Local land charges are not normally registrable under the Act (because they are recorded instead in local land charges registers), and override both first registration and registered dispositions.[1] Some local land charges create charges over land for the payment of money, as, for example, where a street works authority incurs expenditure in executing street works.[2] The LRA 2002 provides that a charge over registered land that is a local land charge can only be realised if the title has been registered.[3] The thinking behind that provision is as follows.[4] The proprietor of a registered charge has the powers of a legal mortgagee.[5] If any person has powers of disposition over registered land, that fact should appear from the register. That is consistent with the fundamental objective of the Act to ensure that the register is as conclusive as it can be made.[6]

4.18 The second matter concerns the situation where a registered chargee exercises its power of sale and, after discharging its charge and related expenses, there is a surplus. That surplus is held upon trust and must be paid to 'the person entitled to the mortgaged property'.[7] It is not settled under the present law whether the chargee who holds the surplus should search the register to see if there are any other chargees, or whether it is entitled to pay the surplus to the chargor if it has not received notice of any subsequent charge.[8] However, in principle, there would appear to be no such obligation to search the register.[9] The LRA 2002 clarifies the position. It states that a person is to be taken to have notice of anything in the register immediately before the disposition on sale.[10] The effect of this is that a chargee exercising its power of sale must inspect the register prior to the disposition to ascertain whether there are any subsequent charges on the register. Given that the Act seeks to bring about a conclusive register, and one to which most lenders are likely to have access, this is unlikely to be an unduly onerous

---

[1]   See LRA 2002, Schs 1 and 3, para 6.
[2]   Under Highways Act 1980, s 212.
[3]   LRA 2002, s 55.
[4]   See (2001) Law Com No 271, para 7.42.
[5]   See para **4.8**.
[6]   See para **1.7**.
[7]   LPA 1925, s 105.
[8]   Where the title to land is *unregistered*, a mortgagee holding a surplus after sale *is* in practice obliged to search the Land Charges register to see if there is any subsequent charge that has been registered as a Class C(i) or C(iii) land charge. This is because registration of a land charge is actual notice to all persons for all purposes of both the charge and its registration: LPA 1925, s 198(1). There is no equivalent to s 198(1) in relation to registered land.
[9]   See Harpum, *Megarry & Wade's Law of Real Property* (Sweet & Maxwell, 6th edn, 2000), para 19-064.
[10]   LRA 2002, s 54. On sale, the interests of any subsequent chargees will be overreached: see LPA 1925, s 104(1).

requirement. It is also consistent with the principle that registration protects the right in question, in this case the interest of the subsequent chargee.[1]

OVERRIDING STATUTORY CHARGES

4.19 There are certain statutory charges that purport to take priority over any existing charges affecting the land.[2] On the assumption that such charges do indeed override prior charges – which is not settled[3] – there is no obligation on the body that has the benefit of the overriding charge to notify any prior chargees. There is an obvious danger, therefore, that a prior chargee might make a further advance, oblivious of the fact that its security has been eroded or even destroyed by the overriding statutory charge. To overcome this problem, the LRA 2002 imposes a duty on the registrar, when such an overriding charge is registered, to give notice of its creation to such persons as rules may provide.[4] Those rules will doubtless require the registrar to notify all existing chargees[5] whose interests are, in some way, protected on the register. If a person suffers loss by reason of a failure by the registrar to perform his duty, he is entitled to be indemnified.[6]

MISCELLANEOUS

Consolidation

4.20 A mortgagee has a right of consolidation.[7] This means that where a landowner has more than one charge from the same mortgagee, the mortgagee can refuse to permit the mortgagor to redeem one of the mortgages without redeeming them all. There is presently a procedure under the LRR 1925 by which the chargee's right to consolidate against the properties affected may be noted on the register.[8] Under the

---

[1] Even if a subsequent charge is *not* protected on the register, a chargee who has sold the estate subject to the charge will have to account for any surplus to the subsequent chargee if it has been given notice of its charge.

[2] They are not common. The best known (and perhaps only) example is the legal aid charge: see Legal Aid Act 1988, s 16(6); Access to Justice Act 1999 (ATJA 1999), s 10(7).

[3] See (2001) Law Com 271, para 7.41.

[4] LRA 2002, s 50.

[5] Whether their charges are legal or equitable.

[6] LRA 2002, Sch 8, para 1(1)(h).

[7] Many lending institutions include a contractual right of consolidation in their standard mortgage terms.

[8] LRR 1925, r 154.

LRA 2002, there is a rule-making power to make provision about entry in the register of a right of consolidation in relation to a registered charge.[1]

Power of joint proprietors to give receipts

4.21 The LRA 2002 contains a provision by which, where a charge is registered in the name of two or more proprietors, a valid receipt for the money secured by the charge may be given:

- by the registered proprietors;
- where one or more of those proprietors has died, by the survivor(s); and
- by the personal representative of the last survivor of the registered proprietors.[2]

This replicates the present law.[3]

---

[1]   LRA 2002, s 57.
[2]   Ibid, s 56.
[3]   See the latter part of LRA 1925, s 32.

CHAPTER 5

REGISTRATION AND THE REGISTER

THE MAIN CHANGES AT A GLANCE

5.1 Most of the provisions relating to registration and the register are contained in Part 6 of the LRA 2002.[1] The provisions of the Act governing the alteration of the register and the payment of indemnity are to be found respectively in Schs 4 and 8 to the Act.[2]

5.2 The main changes made by the LRA 2002 are as follows.

- The concept of the open register in relation both to access to the register and to reliance upon the register is extended.
- The registrar is given power to record certain defects in title on the register.
- The role of the land certificate is downgraded.
- Charge certificates are abolished.
- The concept of alteration of the register is introduced. Rectification is one specific form of alteration.
- New provisions are made for alterations to the register of cautions.
- A mortgagee in possession is classified as a proprietor in possession for the purposes of the provisions on rectification.
- The registrar is given power to pay a party's costs in relation to any alteration of the register that does not amount to rectification.

THE EFFECT OF REGISTRATION

5.3 It is a fundamental principle of registered conveyancing that it is registration that vests the legal estate in the registered proprietor.[3] In accordance with this principle, the LRA 2002 provides that if on the entry of a person in the register as the proprietor of the legal estate, the

---

1   See (2001) Law Com No 271, Part IX.
2   Ibid, Part X.
3   Cf LRA 1925, s 69(1).

legal estate would not otherwise be vested in that person, the legal estate will be deemed to be vested in him as a result of the registration.[1] What this means is that the legal estate will vest in a person even if he is registered as proprietor on the basis of a forged transfer – which is itself a nullity.[2]

5.4   There is one exception to this general principle and it gives effect to the registration requirements of Sch 2 to the LRA 2002 that were explained in Chapter 3.[3] The legal estate will not vest if, following a registrable disposition, those registration requirements are not met.[4] In the Law Commission's Report the example is given of the grant of a 99-year lease where the lease is registered with its own title, but where the registrar fails to enter a notice of the lease on the superior freehold title. The legal estate will not vest in the lessee as a result of the exception to the general principle.[5] Without this exception, the provisions of Sch 2 would not, in practice, be registration *requirements*.

THE REGISTRATION OF DEPENDENT ESTATES

5.5   The LRA 2002 makes provision as to how, what it describes as 'dependent estates', are to be entered on the register. The first case is where one legal estate – a freehold or leasehold – has the benefit of a legal estate, typically an easement or *profit à prendre* appurtenant, over some other land. The registration of a person as the proprietor of that dependent estate must be made in relation to the registered estate.[6] Thus, for example, where X is registered as proprietor of a freehold estate, 'Greenhythe', the register will also record the fact that he has the benefit of a legal easement over a neighbouring property, 'Redhills'. Secondly, the entry of a person in the register as the proprietor of a charge on a registered estate must be made in relation to the registered estate subject to the charge.[7] For example, the charges register of

---

1   LRA 2002, s 58(1). See para **3.12** for the registration requirements for registrable dispositions in Sch 2.
2   See (2001) Law Com No 271, para 9.4. In a recent decision, *Malory Enterprises Ltd v Cheshire Homes (UK) Ltd* [2002] EWCA Civ 151, [2002] 3 WLR 1, the Court of Appeal held that the registration of a proprietor under a forged disposition merely vested the bare legal estate in him. He took subject to the equitable title of the true owner. It is difficult to see how this can be correct and it appears to be based upon a misconception of the effects of registration. It is also contrary to earlier authorities, such as *Argyle Building Society v Hammond* (1984) 49 P&CR 148.
3   See paras **3.12–3.23**.
4   LRA 2002, s 58(2).
5   See (2001) Law Com No 271, para 9.5.
6   LRA 2002, s 59(1).
7   Ibid, s 59(2).

'Greenhythe' will record that Y Bank plc is the registered proprietor of a charge over 'Greenhythe'. Thirdly, if Y Bank plc, the registered chargee of 'Greenhythe', has created a sub-charge in favour of Z plc, the entry of Z plc as proprietor of the sub-charge will be made in relation to Y Bank plc's registered charge.[1]

EFFECTIVE DATE OF REGISTRATION

5.6   An entry made in the register in pursuance of an application for registration of an unregistered legal estate, or an application for registration in relation to a disposition required to be completed by registration, has effect from the time of the making of the application.[2] This reflects the present position which is found in the LRR 1925.[3]

BOUNDARIES

5.7   The LRA 2002 preserves the general boundaries rule.[4] It provides that the boundary of a registered estate shown for the purposes of the register is a general boundary, unless it is shown as having been determined under s 60 of the Act.[5] As a general boundary, the line that is shown on the registered plan does not determine the exact line of the boundary.[6] It follows, therefore, that unless fixed,[7] boundaries are not guaranteed by the Registry.

The power to determine the exact line of the boundary

5.8   The power to fix boundaries under s 60 is not new,[8] but it has seldom been used. Apparently, this has been due to the expense involved and also to the risk that it may precipitate a boundary dispute.[9] This is because it is necessary to involve the adjoining landowners in the process of fixing the boundary. It is likely that, for the future, greater use will be made of the power to fix boundaries, particularly

---

[1]   LRA 2002, s 59(3).

[2]   Ibid, s 74.

[3]   See LRR 1925, rr 24, 42 and 83 (as amended or substituted).

[4]   Despite its importance, the general boundaries rule is not found in LRA 1925 but in the rules made under it: see LRR 1925, r 278(1).

[5]   LRA 2002, s 60(1).

[6]   Ibid, s 60(2). This maintains the previous approach as set out in the LRR 1925, r 278(1).

[7]   See para **5.8**.

[8]   See LRR 1925, r 278(2).

[9]   (2001) Law Com No 271, para 9.10. See also the Land Registry's Practice Leaflet No 16: *Boundaries in Land Registration*, para 1.2.

when new estates are set out and also in those cases where the legal boundary does not coincide with the physical boundaries. Modern mapping techniques are likely to make the process easier and there is also an incentive in the LRA 2002 to do so. As is explained in Chapter 8, although it will in general be much more difficult for a squatter to acquire title to registered land under the Act than it is at present, there are situations where he will be able to do so. Perhaps the most important of these is where a person adversely possesses adjacent land and for 10 years of his adverse possession reasonably believes that he owns it.[1] However, this exception will not apply if the boundary between the two properties has been fixed and is not a general boundary.[2] There is a power under the LRA 2002 to make rules enabling or requiring the exact line of the boundary to be determined.[3] In particular rules may make provision as to the circumstances in which the exact line of a boundary may or must be determined.[4] One case where it is likely that rules will require a boundary to be fixed is where a squatter brings himself within the exception mentioned above. To ensure that he cannot acquire any further land by adverse possession under this exception, he will be required to have the new boundary fixed.[5]

Accretion and diluvion

5.9   Accretion is the addition to the bank of a river or the shore of a lake or sea of soil that raises it above the water level and, in effect, creates new land out of what was previously water. Diluvion describes the reverse process, by which banks or shores are washed away by the action of water so that they disappear under water. The operation of accretion and diluvion has particular relevance given coastal erosion and accumulation, the fact that boundaries of properties along estuaries may change all the time, and also following the floods of recent years.[6] The doctrines are also of particular importance to the Crown, which in most cases owns the foreshore. The principles governing accretion and diluvion are set out in the well-known opinion of the Privy Council in *Southern Centre of Theosophy Inc v State of South Australia.*[7]

---

[1]   LRA 2002, Sch 6, para 5(4); see also para **8.36**.
[2]   Ibid, Sch 6, para 5(4)(b).
[3]   Ibid, s 60(3).
[4]   Ibid, s 60(3)(a).
[5]   See (2001) Law Com No 271, para 9.13.
[6]   In the past few years several disputes arising from such boundary changes have been heard by the Solicitor to the Land Registry.
[7]   [1982] AC 706. See in particular, at p 716, *per* Lord Wilberforce.

5.10 In essence, those principles are that the ownership of land follows the gradual changes in boundaries caused to land that fronts on to water, whether by the action of the water, wind or tide. A landowner may gain or lose land according to these principles. The LRA 2002 reflects these principles. It provides that the fact that a registered estate in land is shown in the register as having a particular boundary (whether a general boundary or a boundary determined under s 60 of the Act) does not affect the operation of accretion or diluvion.[1]

5.11 It may be that neighbouring landowners will decide that the boundary between their respective properties should not change as a result of accretion or diluvion – the typical case would be where their properties are separated by a river.[2] Under the LRA 2002, any such agreement about the operation of accretion or diluvion in relation to a registered estate in land will have effect only if registered in accordance with rules.[3] As a result if (for example) adjoining landowners, whose properties are separated by a stream, agree that, notwithstanding any change in the course of that stream, the boundary shall remain where it is on the date of the agreement, that agreement will have to be recorded on the register.

USE OF REGISTER TO RECORD DEFECTS IN TITLE

5.12 In order to make the register as conclusive as possible, s 64 of the LRA 2002 creates a new power for the registrar to enter on the register of title the fact that a right to determine a registered estate in land has become exercisable.[4] Such a defect in title would arise out of an event which has occurred during the course of ownership of the property. The power is particularly intended to catch those cases where there are no existing mechanisms for neutralising the defect.[5] An example would be the failure by a freeholder to pay a rentcharge, where that freehold is subject to a rentcharge that is supported by a right of re-entry.[6] Another

---

[1]   LRA 2002, s 61(1).
[2]   See (2001) Law Com No 271, para 9.15.
[3]   LRA 2002, s 61(2).
[4]   Ibid, s 64(1).
[5]   See para **5.14**.
[6]   (2001) Law Com No 271, paras 9.31 and 9.33. There are undoubtedly freeholds subject to such rights of re-entry, though they are not common. In most cases, the rent owner will rely on the more limited right of entry implied in the absence of contrary intention by LPA 1925, s 121(3).

case might be where, by the operation of a statutory provision, land becomes subject to divestment on the occurrence of some event.[1]

5.13 There is a power to make rules in relation to the making of entries under s 64 and, in particular, as to the circumstances in which there will be duty to make entries, how entries may be made and as to their removal.[2]

5.14 There are circumstances where conveyancers have existing practices to identify whether an occurrence has invalidated the title,[3] and it is envisaged that such practices will continue. Section 64 of the LRA 2002 is intended to cater for those situations, such as the sale of a freehold subject to a rentcharge, for which there are no such safeguards. It is expected that the rules will confine the power to such cases. At first sight, it is not obvious how this power will be made to work in practice: conveyancers are unlikely to wish to volunteer information to the Registry that will prejudicially affect their clients' titles. However, the introduction of electronic conveyancing is likely to provide a means of ensuring that such defects are disclosed and registered. A conveyancer who enters into a network access agreement is likely to be required to provide such information under the terms of that agreement.[4]

ACCESSING INFORMATION

5.15 The LRA 2002 is intended to facilitate conveyancing and to make the property market more transparent. It is therefore not surprising that it contains provisions that extend the accessibility of the titles and cautions registers and of the information referred to in them.

---

[1]   See Harpum, *Megarry & Wade's Law of Real Property* (Sweet & Maxwell, 6th edn, 2000), para 4-042.
[2]   LRA 2002, s 64(2).
[3]   The best known example is that of an intending assignor of a lease: see (2001) Law Com No 271, para 9.32. Provided that he produces to the intending assignee the last receipt for rent prior to the assignment, there is a rebuttable statutory presumption that all the covenants and provisions of a lease have been duly performed up until the date of the assignment: see LPA 1925, s 45(2) (and in the case of an intending sub-lessee, s 45(3)). The basis for this presumption is the doctrine of waiver. A landlord who accepts rent with knowledge of a breach of covenant is taken to waive his right to forfeit for that breach.
[4]   For network access agreements, see LRA 2002, Sch 5. See also para **7.42**.

The open register

5.16 The LRA 1988 began the sequence of reforms that paved the way for the LRA 2002. It opened the register of title so that it was a public document.[1] It is no longer necessary to obtain the consent of a registered proprietor to investigate his title. Without an open register, it would not be possible to investigate title on line or conduct any form of electronic conveyancing.

5.17 Under the LRA 2002, any person may inspect and make copies of, or of any part of:

- the register of title;[2]
- any document kept by the registrar which is referred to in the register of title;[3]
- any other document kept by the registrar which relates to an application to him;[4] or
- the register of cautions against first registration.[5]

5.18 The power conferred by the LRA 2002 goes beyond that which is permitted under LRA 1925 and this is of some practical significance. In particular, it includes two important categories of document that cannot presently be inspected,[6] namely leases filed at the Land Registry[7] and charges.[8] The ability to inspect leases is of considerable practical

---

[1] LRA 1988, which substituted a new s 112 into LRA 1925. The LRA 1988 implemented the recommendations of the Law Commission in its Second Report on Land Registration, (1985) Law Com No 148.

[2] LRA 2002, s 66(1)(a).

[3] Ibid, s 66(1)(b).

[4] Ibid, s 66(1)(c). This is a new right. Previously, such documents could only be inspected at the discretion of the registrar unless the applicant fell within one of the categories specified in the Land Registration (Open Register) Rules 1991 (LRORR 1991), SI 1991/122, Sch 2 – an exception applicable to criminal investigations.

[5] LRA 2002, s 66(1)(d). The Act establishes for the first time a register of cautions against first registration. At present, cautions against first registration are recorded on the Index Map. There is presently a right to search the Index Map: LRR 1925, r 8.

[6] See LRA 1925, s 112(1)(b).

[7] Not all leases are supplied to the Land Registry. The present practice is summarised in Ruoff and Roper, *Registered Conveyancing*, at pp 21–22. When an original lessee applies for first registration he must furnish a certified copy of his lease: LRR 1925, r 21. A lease noted as an incumbrance on first registration of the title to the reversion is seldom supplied to the Registry. When an assignee of a lease applies for the first registration of his title, he is required to supply a certified copy of the assignment but may not supply a copy of the lease itself.

[8] In relation to domestic conveyancing, charges are not normally very informative. They do not disclose the amount borrowed and are often according to the standard terms and conditions of the borrower, which are lodged with HM Land Registry.

significance and the policy reasons for it have been explained in Chapter 2.[1]

5.19   The right to inspect the registers will, however, be subject to rules which may provide for exceptions to be made to the right and impose conditions on its exercise, including conditions regarding the payment of fees.[2] It is anticipated that, as a matter of principle, such rules will restrict access to documents of a commercially sensitive nature.[3] In this they will reflect the provisions of Part II of the FIA 2000 (which exempt certain information from disclosure under that Act).[4] In practice, the rights to inspect and take copies will not, therefore, be unfettered.

Official copies

5.20   As a corollary to the power to inspect and take copies, the LRA 2002 makes official copies[5] admissible in evidence to the same extent as the original. This will be the case in relation to the following:

- the register of title;[6]
- any document which is referred to in the register of title and kept by the registrar;[7]
- any other document kept by the registrar which relates to an application to him;[8] or
- the register of cautions against first registration.[9]

5.21   There is provision for rules to be made about the form of official copies, who may issue office copies,[10] applications for official

---

1   See para **2.17**.
2   LRA 2002, s 66(2)(a), (b).
3   There are said to be strong arguments relating to the property market in favour of wider publication. Such information could shed light on commercial property transactions, fostering a free and competitive market. It is thought unlikely that disclosure of amounts borrowed by individuals would be permitted: see Baroness Scotland of Asthal, *Hansard* (HL), 30 October 2001, vol 627, cols 1362–1363.
4   See para **2.17**.
5   The term 'official copy' replaces the term 'office copies' used in LRA 1925, s 113.
6   LRA 2002, s 67(1)(a).
7   Ibid, s 67(1)(b).
8   Ibid, s 67(1)(c).
9   Ibid, s 67(1)(d).
10   Under Sch 5, para 1(2)(d) of the LRA 2002, there will be power for authorised persons to issue official copies pursuant to a network access agreement. In practice, this means that solicitors and licensed conveyancers will issue such copies.

copies[1] and the conditions to be met by applicants for official copies, including conditions requiring the payment of fees.[2]

5.22 A person who relies on an official copy in which there is a mistake is not liable for loss suffered by another by reason of the mistake.[3] A person who suffers loss by reason of a mistake in an official copy is, however, entitled to be indemnified.[4]

Conclusiveness of filed copies

5.23 Under s 110(4) of the LRA 1925, the register is conclusive in relation to the abstracts and excerpts from documents referred to in it. Section 120 of the LRA 2002 contains a similar but more far-reaching provision that reflects the implications of an open register – something that did not exist in 1925. The presumption created by s 120 applies where:

– 'a disposition relates to land to which a registered estate relates', and
– an entry in the register relating to the registered estate refers to a document kept by the registrar which is not an original.[5]

In those circumstances, as between the parties to the disposition, the document kept by the registrar is to be taken to be correct,[6] and to contain all the material parts of the original document.[7] Something must be said of the two elements mentioned above.

5.24 First, the rather Delphic phrase 'a disposition relates to land to which a registered estate relates', means that the section applies in relation to the parties to the following dispositions:

(a) a registered disposition;
(b) the grant of an interest out of registered land that is not itself capable of registration, such as a lease granted for a term of 7 years or less;[8] and

---

[1] The Direct Access system has already enabled such applications to be made electronically: Directions of the Chief Land Registrar, 12 May 1997 Ruoff and Roper, *Registered Conveyancing*, F-12.
[2] LRA 2002, s 67(3)(a)–(d).
[3] Ibid, s 67(2).
[4] Ibid, Sch 8, para 1(1)(d); see also para **5.67**.
[5] Ibid, s 120(1).
[6] Ibid, s 120(2)(a).
[7] Ibid, s 120(2)(b).
[8] Which takes effect as an unregistered interest that overrides a registrable disposition: LRA 2002, Sch 3, para 1.

(c)   the disposition of an interest mentioned in (b), as where there is an
      assignment of a lease granted for a term of 7 years or less.[1]

As there is an open register, even parties to a disposition that cannot be
registered may rely upon its terms. For example, a person taking a lease
for 7 years might wish to search the superior freehold title to see if the
land was subject to restrictive covenants. The LRA 2002 – unlike
s 110(4) of the LRA 1925 – does not differentiate between registered
dispositions and other dealings with registered land.

5.25   Secondly, the second element mentioned in para **5.23** is that entry
in the register relates to a document kept by the registrar which is not
an original.[2] The presumption in s 120 of the LRA 2002 is intended to
meet the case where the register refers to an abstract, copy or extract
from a document, but where the registrar no longer keeps the original.
There is no need for any similar rule in a case where the registrar has
retained the original, as any person may inspect and copy that
document.[3]

5.26   The LRA 2002 further provides that no party to the disposition
may require production of the original document,[4] and that no party to
the disposition is to be affected by any provision of the original
document which is not contained in the document kept by the
registrar.[5] The registrar thereby precludes any further investigation in
relation to such original documents. The sense of this is obvious, given
that the registrar does not have the original document. A person who
suffers loss by reason of a mistake in a document kept by the registrar
which is not an original and is referred to in the register is, however,
entitled to be indemnified.[6]

Index

5.27   Under the LRR 1925,[7] the registrar is required to keep an Index
Map from which it is possible to ascertain whether any parcel of land is
or is not registered, and its title number if it is. The Index Map is widely
used and is of considerable practical importance. The importance of a

---

[1]   Cf (2001) Law Com No 271, para 9.50.
[2]   As is the case with many leases: see para **5.18**.
[3]   LRA 2002, s 66. See para **5.17**.
[4]   Ibid, s 120(3).
[5]   Ibid, s 120(4).
[6]   Ibid, Sch 8, para 1(1)(e); see also para **5.67**.
[7]   See r 8.

mechanism for ascertaining whether land is registered or not, is recognised in the LRA 2002. The Index (as it is now called) finds its place in the Act, and no longer merely in rules. Under the LRA 2002, the registrar must keep an Index for the purpose of enabling the following matters to be ascertained in relation to any parcel of land, whether registered or unregistered, in England and Wales:

- whether any registered estate relates to the land;
- how any such registered estate is identified for the purposes of the register;
- whether the land is affected by any caution against first registration, and if so what that caution is; and
- such other matters as rules may provide.[1]

5.28 It is provided that rules may be made as to:

- how the Index is to be kept;
- the information to be included in it;
- the form in which such information is to be kept; and
- the arrangement of that information.[2]

Rules may also make provision about official searches of the Index.[3] It will be noted from this that there is no requirement that the Index should, as now, be kept in the form of a map. Indeed, such information will increasingly be held in dematerialised form.

Historical information

5.29 The register of title is a record of the title to land as it stands at any given moment. It does not provide a history of the title. In contrast, in relation to unregistered conveyancing, a landowner is likely to know the history of his title back to a conveyance – his root of title – that was made at least 15 years prior to the conveyance under which he acquired title to the land. There are times when it is useful to know the history of a title. For example, if a parcel of land is apparently subject to an easement or restrictive covenant, it is important to know whether both the dominant and servient tenements were once in common ownership so as to extinguish the easement or covenant.[4] The registrar does in fact

---

1   LRA 2002, s 68(1). Rules may, in particular, make provision as to those matters set out in s 68(2).
2   Ibid, s 68(2)(a).
3   Ibid, s 68(2)(b).
4   For other examples, see (2001) Law Com No 271, para 9.58.

have a computerised record of the history of many titles, although it may be incomplete. At present, the registrar does sometimes provide information about the history of the title if there is a good reason to do so. Many of those who responded to the Consultative Document, *Land Registration for the Twenty-First Century*,[1] commented on the difficulties that could result from the lack of an historical record of the title.

5.30 The Law Commission and the Land Registry accepted that, where (for example) an issue or dispute had arisen which could be resolved by reference to the historical devolution of the title, it ought to be possible for a person interested to have access to such information. The LRA 2002 therefore provides that the registrar may, on application, provide information about the history of a registered title.[2] There are two important and necessary qualifications to this principle. The first is implicit. There is nothing in the LRA 2002 that requires the registrar to keep an historical record of a title. It is only to the extent that he does have such a record that the power conferred by the Act is exercisable. The second qualification is that exercise of the registrar's power will be subject to rules.[3] This is to ensure that inquiries about the historical devolution never become a routine conveyancing inquiry – it would rather defeat the point of registered title if they did.[4] Under the LRA 2002, this power to provide historical information can be contracted out.[5]

Official searches

5.31 The LRA 2002 confers an express rule-making power to make provision for official searches of the register, including searches of pending applications for first registration.[6] In particular, it is provided that rules may be made[7] providing for:

–   the form of applications for searches;

---

1   (1998) Law Com No 254.
2   LRA 2002, s 69(1).
3   Ibid, s 69(2).
4   See (2001) Law Com No 271, para 9.60. It would also add materially to the cost of conveyancing, whereas one aim of the LRA 2002 is to try to reduce conveyancing costs.
5   LRA 2002, s 69(3).
6   Ibid, s 70. For the present provision as to official searches see the Land Registration (Official Searches) Rules 1993 (LROSR 1993), SI 1993/3276. The first provision for such searches was introduced in 1930. Prior to that, searches had to be conducted in person at HM Land Registry in Lincoln's Inn Fields.
7   LRA 2002, s 70(a)–(d).

- the manner in which such applications may be made;[1]
- the form of official search certificates; and
- the manner in which such certificates may be issued.[2]

PRIORITY PROTECTION

5.32 Under the present law, when an intending purchaser makes an official search he will receive a copy of the title to land as it was on the day when the search was conducted. In order to protect the purchaser[3] from any third party rights which may supervene between the dates of search and completion, the purchaser may make an official search with priority under the LROSR 1993.[4] The official certificate of search then confers priority on the purchaser, such that any entry which is made in that register during the 30-day[5] priority period relating to that search shall be postponed to a subsequent application to register the instrument effecting the purchase.[6]

5.33 Section 72 of the LRA 2002 makes express provision for priority protection and extends the circumstances in which protection can be obtained.[7] Those circumstances are explained in para **5.34**. Provided that the application for registration is made within the priority period, it will be protected.[8] It follows that any entry made during that period will be postponed to the application for registration.[9] There are, however, two exceptions to this.

(1) The first case is where the earlier entry was made in pursuance of a protected application and the priority period relating to that application ranks first in time ahead of the one relating to the application for the other entry.[10] If, for example, A has made an application for a priority search on day 1 and B then makes

---

1   Such applications can already be made electronically by means of the Direct Access System: Notice of
     the Chief Land Registrar, 12 May 1997, Ruoff and Roper, *Registered Conveyancing*, F-14.
2   Authorised persons may be permitted to issue official search certificates pursuant to a network access
     agreement: LRA 2002, Sch 5, para 1(2)(c).
3   Defined in LROSR 1993, r 2(1) as any person including a lessee or chargee who in good faith and for
     valuable consideration acquires or intends to acquire a legal estate in land.
4   A search without priority is also possible: LROSR 1993, rr 9, 10.
5   Ibid, r 2(1).
6   Ibid, r 6.
7   See (2001) Law Com No 271, paras 9.62–9.75.
8   LRA 2002, s 72(1).
9   Ibid, s 72(2). The registrar may defer dealing with an application where a period of priority protection
     applies: s 72(5).
10   Ibid, s 72(3).

an application for a priority search on day 5, B's priority will not be protected against any application by A to be registered during the priority period consequent upon A's application.

(2) The second case is where the earlier entry is one to which a direction under s 46(3) of the LRA 2002 applies, where the court has exercised its powers to order that a restriction be entered in the register with overriding priority.[1] As has been explained,[2] when the court orders the entry of a restriction under s 46 of the Act, it may direct that the entry should have overriding priority. This means that the restriction will have priority over any priority protection already obtained by a person under s 72 of the Act. Such cases will be rare and the court will almost certainly require an undertaking in damages from the applicant for the restriction.[3]

5.34 Priority protection can be obtained in two circumstances under the LRA 2002 (and not merely one as at present).[4] The first is, as now, by making an official search with priority. This will include searches of pending applications for first registration. The second is new. Priority protection will be conferred by the noting on the register of a contract for the making of a registrable disposition of a registered estate or charge. The thinking behind this second case is that, when electronic conveyancing is introduced, it will become impossible to enter into a contract to make a disposition of a registered estate or charge, except by simultaneously noting the contract on the register.[5] This is in furtherance of the Act's stated aim of achieving a conclusive register.[6] At present, it is unusual for estate contracts to be noted on the register unless they are likely to remain in being for some time, as is the case with options and some conditional contracts. As a sort of quid pro quo for the requirement that such contracts should be noted where presently they are not, the entry of a notice will not only protect the purchaser against third parties, but will give him the additional benefit of priority protection for the priority period.

5.35 The details of priority protection are a matter for rules.[7] These rules may (and no doubt will) make provision for the keeping of records in relation to priority periods and the inspection of such

1   LRA 2002, s 72(4).
2   See para **3.82**.
3   Cf LRA 2002, s 46(5).
4   Ibid, s 72(6).
5   See para **7.54**.
6   See para **1.7**.
7   LRA 2002, s 72(6).

records.[1] This means that, as now, it will be possible to discover from a search of the register whether or not a person has the benefit of priority protection at any given time. Furthermore, rules may in particular also make provision for the following:

- the commencement and length of a priority period;
- the applications for registration to which such a period relates;[2]
- the order in which competing priority periods rank; and
- the application of the priority principle explained in para **5.32** in cases where more than one priority period relates to the same application.[3]

The last of these matters requires explanation. An intending purchaser may obtain more than one period of priority during the course of a transaction. For example, he might make a priority search before he contracts to buy the land. When the contract is made and noted on the register, another priority period will then arise. As now, it is necessary to have rules to explain the relationship between the two priority periods, especially if, after the priority search but before the making of the contract, a third person makes a priority search.[4]

APPLICATIONS TO THE REGISTRAR

General powers

5.36 The LRA 2002 contains many provisions as to when an application may be made to the registrar. The Law Commission and Land Registry listed these provisions in the final Report that accompanied the draft Bill.[5] They are as follows:

- for first registration;[6]
- to lodge or withdraw or cancel a caution against first registration;[7]
- to register a registrable disposition;[8]

---

[1]   LRA 2002, s 72(6)(b).

[2]   The protection may be for the benefit of more than one application. If an intending buyer is purchasing with the aid of a mortgage, priority protection can and should be obtained for both.

[3]   LRA 2002, s 72(7).

[4]   For the present position that will, no doubt, be replicated under the new rules, see LROSR 1993, r 8.

[5]   See (2001) Law Com No 271, para 9.76.

[6]   LRA 2002, ss 3, 4.

[7]   Ibid, ss 15, 17, 18.

[8]   Ibid, s 27.

- to enter, remove or cancel a notice;[1]
- to enter or withdraw a restriction;[2]
- to register the priority of registered charges;[3]
- to determine the exact line of a boundary;[4]
- to upgrade title;[5]
- to obtain an official copy;[6]
- to obtain an official search;[7]
- to enter into a network access agreement;[8]
- by a squatter to be registered as proprietor;[9] and
- for the Adjudicator to rectify or set aside a document.[10]

5.37 In addition to any specific rule-making powers that apply in any of the situations listed in para **5.36**, there are a number of general rule-making powers in relation to applications that are found in para 6 of Sch 10 to the LRA 2002. These permit rules to be made about the following matters.

- The first is as to the form and content of applications under the LRA 2002. As a result of this power, it will be possible to require that *all* applications should be in prescribed form. It is likely that, as electronic conveyancing is introduced, this will indeed have to be the case.[11]
- The second is as to the provision of evidence in support of certain types of application. This will necessarily vary according to the nature of the application.
- The third is as to the time at which an application is to be taken as made. This may be considered with the fourth general power, which is as to the order in which competing applications are to be taken to rank. Rules under these powers are needed so that priority can be allocated to applications made to the Registry. The Land Registry has recently moved to a system of 'real time priority' by which the priority of any application is determined by the time at which it is entered on the day list at the Registry.

---

1   LRA 2002, ss 34–36.
2   Ibid, ss 43, 47.
3   Ibid, s 48.
4   Ibid, s 60.
5   Ibid, s 62.
6   Ibid, s 67.
7   Ibid, s 70.
8   Ibid, Sch 5, para 1.
9   Ibid, Sch 6, paras 1, 6.
10   Ibid, s 106(2).
11   See (2001) Law Com No 271, para 9.78.

– Finally, rules can make provision as to the circumstances in which an alteration by the registrar, for the purpose of correcting a mistake in the application or accompanying document, will take effect as if that alteration had been made by the applicant or other interested party or parties. This power will enable the registrar to correct clerical errors in any application without having to obtain the applicant's consent.[1] The power is more fully explained at para **5.65**.

Objections to applications

5.38 Given that many of the possible applications that may be made to the registrar under the LRA 2002[2] could be disputed, the Act necessarily makes provision by which they may be challenged.[3] The general rule is that *anyone* may object to an application to the registrar.[4] That general right to object[5] is subject to two exceptions.

– First, in the case of an application for the cancellation of a caution under s 18 of the LRA 2002,[6] the person who lodged the caution and such other persons as rules may provide may object.[7]
– Secondly, on an application for the cancellation of a unilateral notice under s 36 of the Act,[8] the only persons who may object are the person shown in the register as the beneficiary of the notice to which the application relates and such other persons as rules may provide.[9]

5.39 The procedure on making an objection to an application is as follows. Unless the registrar is satisfied that the objection to the application is groundless,[10] he must give notice of the objection to the applicant.[11] In those circumstances, the registrar may not determine the application until the disposal of the objection.[12] If it is not possible

---

[1] For the present power to make such alterations, see LRR 1925, r 13.
[2] See para **5.36**.
[3] LRA 2002, s 73.
[4] Ibid, s 73(1). The right is subject to rules: see s 73(4).
[5] Cf ibid, s 132(3)(c).
[6] See para **2.60**.
[7] LRA 2002, s 73(2). The persons specified will almost certainly include the personal representatives of the person who lodged the caution if he is dead and his trustee in bankruptcy if he is insolvent.
[8] See para **3.62**.
[9] LRA 2002, s 73(3). Again, the persons who are likely to be specified in rules will no doubt include the personal representatives and the trustee in bankruptcy of the beneficiary of the unilateral notice.
[10] LRA 2002, s 73(6).
[11] Ibid, s 73(5)(a).
[12] Ibid, s 73(5)(b).

to dispose of the objection by agreement, the registrar *must* refer the objection to the Adjudicator.[1] Rules may make provision for such references.[2] The procedure before the Adjudicator is explained in Chapter 9.[3]

5.40 It should be noted that under the LRA 2002 a person must not exercise his right to object to an application without reasonable cause.[4] If he does so, he will be in breach of statutory duty and liable accordingly to any person who suffers damage in consequence.[5]

Registered charges and company charges

5.41 Where a company creates a registered charge over its property, that charge must be registered both under the LRA 2002[6] and under the Companies Act 1985.[7] In the interests of convenience, the LRA 2002 provides that rules may be made providing for the transmission of applications from the registrar to the registrar of companies.[8] When this power is exercised it should be possible to make a combined application to the Land Registry to register the charge on the register and for that application then to be forwarded to Companies House for registration in the Companies Register.

LAND AND CHARGE CERTIFICATES

5.42 At present, when a registered estate is not subject to a registered charge, the proprietor is issued with a land certificate.[9] That certificate has to be produced to the registrar:

- on an entry made in relation to a registered disposition of the estate;
- on a registered transmission of the estate on death or insolvency; and
- on the entry of a notice or restriction affecting that registered estate.

Where there is a registered charge affecting the estate, the land

---

[1]   LRA 2002, s 73(7). For the Adjudicator to HM Land Registry, see para **9.10**.
[2]   Ibid, s 73(8).
[3]   See para **9.15**.
[4]   LRA 2002, s 77(1)(c).
[5]   Ibid, s 77(2).
[6]   See ibid, s 27(2)(f); see also para **3.22**.
[7]   Companies Act 1985, Part XII.
[8]   LRA 2002, s 121.
[9]   LRA 1925, ss 63, 64. See generally (2001) Law Com No 271, paras 9.83–9.87.

certificate is 'deposited' at the Land Registry. No such deposit is made in fact: the certificate is just not issued. In such cases, in relation to the three types of transaction where the land certificate has to be produced, the Registry requires the consent of the registered proprietor or an order of the court before it will make the appropriate entry in the register. Thus, in many cases, the consent of the registered proprietor is substituted for the production of the land certificate.

5.43 In the system of electronic conveyancing that is to be created under the LRA 2002,[1] it is inevitable that the role of land certificates will be much reduced. To require the production of a paper land certificate before an entry can be made on the register would defeat one of the objectives of an electronic paperless system of conveyancing. Furthermore, the present form of the land certificate is somewhat misleading. It is a copy of the registered title as it was on the day on which the certificate was issued. However, the only true record of the title is the register as it stands at any given time.

5.44 The LRA 2002 says very little about land certificates. The only provision in the Act relating to land certificates is in Sch 10, para 4, where it is provided that rules may make provision about:

–   when a certificate of registration of title to a legal estate may be issued;
–   the form and content of such a certificate; and
–   when such a certificate must be produced or surrendered to the registrar.

It is probable that, under such rules, a land certificate will be no more than a document that certifies that the registration of a registered estate has taken place and that a named person is the registered proprietor.[2]

5.45 If the Act has little to say about land certificates, it has nothing whatever in it about charge certificates. In consequence, they are abolished.[3]

---

[1]   See Chapter 7.
[2]   See (2001) Law Com No 271, para 9.91.
[3]   See ibid, para 9.89.

ALTERATION OF THE REGISTERS

Introduction

5.46 The register may need to be altered for one of two reasons. The first is simply as part of the process of keeping the register up to date, for example by removing spent entries. The second is to correct some error or omission in the register. The first of these grounds is unremarkable. It is self-evident that the registrar should be able to up date the register, whether on his own initiative or by direction of the court after some determination. The second ground is, by contrast, of wider importance. If a mistake has been made in the register and some person has suffered loss in consequence, the registrar will pay an indemnity. This right to indemnity is the basis for 'the State guarantee of title' that the system of registered land embodies and it is explained at para **5.66**. The creation of the new register of cautions means that there is now an additional register which may require alteration.[1] This is explained at para **5.63**.[2]

5.47 The provisions of the LRA 1925 on rectification of the register are opaque and obscure the true nature of what actually happens. The LRA 2002 seeks to codify the present practice of the registrar and the courts and, at the same time, to make that process transparent on the face of the legislation.

Alteration of the register of title

5.48 The LRA 2002[3] embodies the distinction mentioned above in para **5.46** between those changes to the register that are necessary to keep the register up to date and the correction of mistakes. The basic concept employed by the Act is that of *alteration* of the register and that term covers all types of alteration that may be made in the register.[4] *Rectification* is one specific form of alteration, namely one which:

–   involves the correction of a mistake, and
–   prejudicially affects the title of a registered proprietor.[5]

---

1   See LRA 2002, ss 20, 21.
2   For the cautions register, see para **2.56**.
3   See LRA 2002, s 65 and Sch 4. Schedule 4 contains the provisions of the Act on alteration of the register.
4   See ibid, Sch 4, paras 2, 5.
5   Ibid, Sch 4, para 1.

There are two points to note about this definition of rectification. The first is that not all cases in which the register is altered to correct a mistake will be rectification – only those which prejudicially affect the title of the registered proprietor. Secondly, there will be a direct link between rectification and the right to indemnity.[1] Under the LRA 1925, there is no such link: if a person does not suffer loss as a result of rectification, he does not recover indemnity.[2] Under the LRA 2002, such a change in the register is not characterised as 'rectification', but merely as an alteration.

5.49 The LRA 2002 provides that the register may be altered to affect the priority for the future of interests affecting the registered estate or charge concerned.[3] This provision probably does no more than restate the present law. First, under the LRA 1925 it is expressly provided that there is a power to rectify the register even though it may affect derivative interests.[4] Secondly, although some doubt has been expressed on the matter, the authorities suggest that, under the LRA 1925, rectification of the register could only have prospective effect.[5]

5.50 The register may be altered either pursuant to an order of the court or by the registrar. The circumstances in which the registrar may alter the register are necessarily wider than those of the court. It is incumbent upon him to ensure that spent entries are removed. He may do this even where:

- there is no dispute between the parties; or
- no application has been made to him to alter the register.

Alteration of the register pursuant to an order of the court

The powers of the court

5.51 Under the LRA 2002, a court may make an order for alteration of the register for any one of three purposes.[6]

---

[1]   LRA 2002, Sch 8, para 1(1)(a).
[2]   See LRA 1925, s 83(1)(a). Thus, where the register is rectified to give effect to an overriding interest, the proprietor cannot recover indemnity: *Re Chowood's Registered Land* [1933] Ch 574.
[3]   LRA 2002, Sch 4, para 8.
[4]   LRA 1925, s 82(2).
[5]   See *Freer v Unwins Ltd* [1976] Ch 288, at p 296. Cf *Malory Enterprises Ltd v Cheshire Homes (UK) Ltd* [2002] EWCA Civ 151, [2002] 3 WLR 1.
[6]   LRA 2002, Sch 4, para 2(1).

- The first is for correcting a mistake. Where the alteration prejudicially affects the title of the registered proprietor, it will constitute rectification.
- The second is to bring the register up to date. If, for example, a person established in court proceedings that she had acquired a right of way by prescription over her neighbour's land, the court could (and, in practice, should) order the register to be altered to record that easement.[1]
- The third is to give effect to any estate, right or interest excepted from the effect of registration. Under the LRA 1925, where land is registered with a grade of title other than absolute, rights excepted from the effect of registration are overriding interests.[2] Under the LRA 2002 they are not. They are interests whose priority is protected, so that a purchaser of registered land takes subject to them.[3] The power to alter the register is a necessary concomitant of the way in which these rights are regulated under the Act.

Such an order has effect when served on the registrar to impose a duty on him to give effect to it.[4] Rules may make provision as to the form and service of such an order.[5]

5.52 In any proceedings in which one or more grounds for altering the register is established, a court is likely to order the registrar to make the alteration unless the case is one of rectification, where, as explained below, more restrictive rules apply.[6] It is possible in court proceedings that a court may discover that there are grounds for altering the register even though this is not an issue before the parties. Under the LRA 2002, rules may make provision about the circumstances in which there is a duty to order the alteration of the register in cases not relating to rectification.[7] It appears that such rules are likely to require the court to order alteration of the register only where that alteration arose from a determination made in the proceedings before it, and not in cases where a ground for alteration happened to come to light.[8]

---

[1]   Cf (2001) Law Com No 251, para 10.10(2).
[2]   LRA 1925, s 70(1)(h).
[3]   LRA 2002, s 29(2)(a)(iii); see also para **3.33**.
[4]   Ibid, Sch 4, para 2(2).
[5]   Ibid, Sch 4, para 4(b), (c).
[6]   See para **5.55**.
[7]   LRA 2002, Sch 4, para 4(a).
[8]   See (2001) Law Com No 271, para 10.12.

The protection given to a proprietor in possession

5.53 One of the features of the land registration system under the LRA 1925 is the protection that registration of itself confers. The LRA 1925 places restrictions on the circumstances in which the register can be rectified against a proprietor who is in possession.[1] The relevant provision is, however, obscure and badly drafted and, despite amendments to it, its meaning has been regularly litigated.[2]

5.54 The LRA 2002 not only retains the principle that protection should be given to a proprietor who is in possession, but extends and clarifies the concept of who is a proprietor in possession. Although the protection is only available in relation to those alterations that amount to rectification as defined by the Act,[3] that does not involve any erosion of the protection. This is because any form of alteration of the register that is not rectification will not, by definition, prejudicially affect the title of that registered proprietor.[4]

5.55 Under the LRA 2002, a court may not order rectification of the register so as to affect the title of a registered proprietor[5] in relation to land in his possession without his consent unless:

- he has by fraud or lack of proper care caused or substantially contributed to the mistake; or
- it would for any other reason be unjust for the alteration not to be made.[6]

5.56 A proprietor will be a proprietor in possession of land for the purposes of this provision in three circumstances.[7]

- The first is where the land is physically in his possession.[8]

---

[1]   This has been described as a principle of 'qualified indefeasibility': see (1998) Law Com No 254, para 8.47.

[2]   For an analysis of the relevant law, see (1998) Law Com No 254, paras 8.23–8.31.

[3]   See LRA 2002, Sch 4, para 3(1).

[4]   Ibid, Sch 4, para 1; see also para **5.48**.

[5]   For these purposes, the title includes the benefit of any appurtenant legal estates such as easements: see LRA 2002, Sch 4, para 3(4).

[6]   Ibid, Sch 4, para 3(2). These two exceptions replicate those in LRA 1925, s 82(3)(a) and (c). The other two exceptions found in LRA 1925, s 82(3) (giving effect to an overriding interest or to an order of the court) are no longer needed because neither involves rectification as defined by LRA 2002. Accordingly, they are not replicated: see (2001) Law Com No 271, para 10.16.

[7]   LRA 2002, s 131.

[8]   Ibid, s 131(1).

— The second is where the land is physically in the possession of a person who is entitled to be registered as proprietor, such as a proprietor's personal representative or trustee in bankruptcy, or a beneficiary under a bare trust.[1] A squatter who is entitled to be registered as proprietor under the provisions of Sch 6 to the LRA 2002,[2] is not, for these purposes, a person entitled to be registered.[3]

— The third is in certain specified relationships, where the actual or deemed[4] possession of land by another is treated as being the possession of the registered proprietor.[5]

The specified relationships that fall within the third of these circumstances are as follows:

— where a landlord is the registered proprietor and the tenant is in possession;
— where a mortgagor is the registered proprietor and the mortgagee is in possession;[6]
— where a licensor is registered proprietor and the licensee is in possession; and
— where a trustee is registered proprietor and a beneficiary is in possession.

5.57 The LRA 2002 makes provision for the converse case where a proprietor is either not in possession, or is in possession in circumstances where rectification can nonetheless be ordered.[7] It provides that, in any proceedings in which the court has power to make an order for the alteration of the register, it must do so, unless there are exceptional circumstances which justify its not doing so.[8] This is in fact a codification of the present practice of the courts.[9]

---

[1] LRA 2002, s 131(1).
[2] See para **8.43**.
[3] LRA 2002, s 131(3).
[4] In (2001) Law Com No 271, para 10.17, examples are given of situations where the other person may be treated as being in possession even when he is not actually in possession. These include where a tenant had sublet, or a mortgagee in possession had exercised its power of leasing under LPA 1925, s 99(2).
[5] LRA 2002, s 131(2).
[6] A mortgagee in possession is *not* regarded as a proprietor in possession for the purposes of LRA 1925, s 82(3): *Hayes v Nwajiaku* [1994] EGCS 106. This is, therefore, a significant extension of the law.
[7] See para **5.55**.
[8] LRA 2002, Sch 4, para 3(3).
[9] See *Epps v Esso Petroleum Co Ltd* [1973] 1 WLR 1071, at p 1078; (2001) Law Com No 271, para 10.18.

Alteration of the register other than under a court order

The powers of the registrar

5.58 Alterations to give effect to an order of the court are not common. Normally it is the registrar who makes such changes. Under the LRA 2002, the registrar has power to alter the register in the same three circumstances as the court does.[1] These have been explained at para **5.51**. In addition, the registrar may also alter the register for the purpose of removing a superfluous entry,[2] typically where an entry was spent.[3] The power to remove superfluous entries[4] and the power to bring the register up to date[5] will inevitably overlap. These powers are likely to be increasingly important with the move to electronic conveyancing. Solicitors and licensed conveyancers will be responsible for most entries that are made on the register. The registrar's functions will be increasingly to identify spent entries and to ensure that they are removed from the register.[6]

5.59 In all other respects the principles explained above[7] in relation to alteration by the court apply equally to alteration by the registrar,[8] including the protection given to a proprietor in possession.[9] Rules will make provision about applications to the registrar for the alteration of the register, including provisions requiring the making of such applications.[10] Rules will also make provision about procedure in relation to the exercise by the registrar of the power to alter the register, whether on application or otherwise.[11]

5.60 If there is an objection to an application to the registrar for the alteration of the register, the matter will be determined by the Adjudicator.[12] In making his determination, he must necessarily apply the same principles as the registrar.

---

1 LRA 2002, Sch 4, para 5(a)–(c).
2 Ibid, Sch 4, para 5(d).
3 The examples given in (2001) Law Com No 271, para 10.19, include (1) where a restriction which froze the register as a precaution ceased to be needed because the danger had passed, and (2) where a restriction on the powers of a registered proprietor had ceased to apply, as where a consent was required from a third party who had since died.
4 LRA 2002, Sch 4, para 5(d).
5 Ibid, Sch 4, para 5(b).
6 (2001) Law Com No 271, para 10.19.
7 See paras **5.52–5.57**
8 See LRA 2002, Sch 4, paras 6, 7.
9 Ibid, Sch 4, para 6(4).
10 Ibid, Sch 4, para 7(c).
11 Ibid, Sch 4, para 7(d).
12 Ibid, s 73(7). See paras **5.38–5.39**.

Alterations under network access agreements

5.61 The framework which the LRA 2002 creates for electronic conveyancing is explained in Chapter 7. One of its essential features is that solicitors and licensed conveyancers will be authorised by network access agreements to make changes to the register, usually but not exclusively on the making of a disposition of registered land. That will entail the removal of entries on the register as much as the making of new ones. On a sale of land, for example, the seller's title may be subject to a charge that will be discharged on completion. That charge will therefore have to be removed from the register. The LRA 2002 provides that a person may be authorised under a network access agreement to initiate alterations to the register of title or to the cautions register.[1] Indeed, it is visualised that authorised practitioners will have a wider role in removing spent entries that they discover when conducting conveyancing transactions.[2]

Costs in non-rectification cases

5.62 At present, the registrar has no discretion to pay costs in a case where the register is altered otherwise than by rectification. This can be a cause of hardship, as where a person incurs costs in dealing with the registrar's inquiries concerning a spent entry. The LRA 2002 remedies this shortcoming. It gives the registrar authority to pay such amount as he thinks fit in respect of any costs or expenses reasonably incurred by a person in connection with an alteration in the register that is not rectification, provided those costs were incurred with the consent of the registrar.[3] Even if the registrar's consent was not given, the registrar may still make such a payment. He may do so if:

- it appears to him that the costs or expenses had to be urgently incurred, and that it was not reasonably practicable to apply for his consent; or
- he has subsequently approved the incurring of the costs or expenses.[4]

---

[1]   LRA 2002, Sch 5, para 1(2)(b).
[2]   See (2001) Law Com No 271, para 10.23.
[3]   LRA 2002, Sch 4, para 9(1).
[4]   Ibid, Sch 4, para 9(2).

Alteration of the cautions register

5.63 The LRA 2002 makes similar provision for alterations to the new cautions register as it does in relation to the register of title.[1] First, it provides that the court may make an order for alteration of the cautions register for the purpose of:

- correcting a mistake; or
- bringing the register up to date.[2]

When such an order is served on the registrar, he is under a duty to give effect to it.[3] Rules may make provision about the circumstances in which there is a duty for the court to exercise this power,[4] the form of any order made and its service.[5]

5.64 The registrar may alter the register of cautions in the same circumstances as the court.[6] Rules may make provision about:

- the circumstances in which the registrar must exercise this power;
- how the cautions register is to be altered in exercise of that power;
- applications for the exercise of that power; and
- the procedure in relation to the exercise of that power, whether on application or otherwise.[7]

Where such an alteration is made by the registrar, the registrar may pay such amount as he thinks fit in respect of any costs reasonably incurred by a person in connection with the alteration.[8]

Alteration of documents

5.65 Not only does the registrar have power to correct mistakes in the register, but the LRA 2002 also contains a specific rule-making power to make provision that will enable the registrar to correct a mistake in an application or accompanying document.[9] In the circumstances prescribed by the rules, the correction will have the same effect as if

---

[1]   For the register of cautions, see para **2.56**.
[2]   LRA 2002, s 20(1).
[3]   Ibid, s 20(2).
[4]   Cf para **5.52**.
[5]   LRA 2002, s 20(3).
[6]   Ibid, s 21(1).
[7]   Ibid, s 21(2).
[8]   Ibid, s 21(3).
[9]   Ibid, Sch 10, para 6(e). See para **5.37**.

made by the parties. The registrar will, therefore, be able to serve notice on interested parties of his intention to correct a mistake in a particular document, and then make such a correction in the absence of any objection. Such a power was previously contained in the LRR 1925,[1] and was widely used, for example to correct a mistake in the formal parts of a lease lodged with the Registry for registration.[2]

INDEMNITY

Introduction

5.66 The law on indemnity was substantially revised by the LRA 1997.[3] The LRA 2002 therefore makes only minor changes to the law. Although the substance of the legislation is not much altered, the form of it is recast. In particular, all the grounds on which indemnity is payable are drawn together in one provision. That is not the case under the LRA 1925.

The grounds on which indemnity is payable

5.67 The LRA 2002 lists eight circumstances in which indemnity is payable.[4] A claimant who has suffered loss in such circumstances is able to recover *any* loss, direct or consequential, that flows from that particular ground.[5] Several grounds are based upon a mistake of some kind. For these purposes, 'mistake' includes an erroneous omission as well as an erroneous inclusion.[6] There is an entitlement to indemnity if a person suffers loss by reason of any of the following.

1. Rectification of the register[7]

This is perhaps the commonest ground for an award of indemnity. For the purposes of the LRA 2002, a person is to be taken to have suffered loss by reason of rectification in two specific situations. The first is where a person suffers loss where the registrar exercises his power to

---

1   LRR 1925, r 13.
2   See (2001) Law Com No 271, para 10.27.
3   LRA 1997 substituted a new LRA 1925, s 83.
4   LRA 2002, Sch 8, para 1(1).
5   See (2001) Law Com No 271, para 10.30.
6   LRA 2002, Sch 8, para 11(1).
7   Ibid, Sch 8, para 1(1)(a). An alteration of the register not amounting to rectification could not give rise to a claim for indemnity because it would not prejudicially affect the title of the registered proprietor: LRA 2002, Sch, 4, para 1; see also para **5.48**.

upgrade a title under s 62 of the LRA 2002.[1] The second is where the register is rectified against the proprietor of a registered estate or charge claiming in good faith under a forged disposition. The proprietor is to be regarded as having suffered loss by reason of such rectification as if the disposition had not been forged. But for this provision, the proprietor would be regarded as suffering no loss because a forged disposition is a nullity.[2]

2. Loss by reason of a mistake[3]

Any person who suffers loss by reason of a mistake whose correction would involve rectification of the register is entitled to an indemnity. This covers two situations. The first is where upon the exercise of the court's or registrar's discretion, rectification is not ordered. However, it is possible to suffer loss by reason of a mistake even if the register is altered.[4] The second case is where a person obtains rectification of the register in his favour but still suffers loss. To accommodate these two situations, the LRA 2002 provides that no indemnity is payable until a decision has been made about whether or not to alter the register.[5] The loss can then be assessed in the light of that decision.

3. Mistake in an official search[6]

This is self-explanatory.

4. Mistake in an official copy[7]

It has been explained above[8] that, where a person relies on an official copy in which there is a mistake, he is not liable for loss suffered by another person as a result of that mistake.[9] However, the person who suffers loss in that way is entitled to be indemnified.

5. Mistake in a document kept by the registrar which is not an original[10]

It was explained above that the register often refers to extracts from or

---

1   Ibid, Sch 8, para 1(2)(a). For the power to upgrade title under the LRA 2002, s 62, see para **2.29**.
2   See *Re Odell* [1906] 2 Ch 47, which was reversed by LRA 1925, s 83(4) (the precursor of the present provision).
3   LRA 2002, Sch 8, para 1(1)(b).
4   As in *Freer v Unwins Ltd* [1976] Ch 288.
5   LRA 2002, Sch 8, para 1(3).
6   Ibid, Sch 8, para 1(1)(c). For official searches, see para **5.31**.
7   Ibid, Sch 8, para 1(1)(d).
8   See para **5.22**.
9   LRA 2002, s 67(2).
10   Ibid, Sch 8, para 1(1)(e).

abstracts of conveyancing documents that the registrar does not retain, or of which the registrar only keeps a copy.[1] It was also explained that the Act creates a presumption by which, where there is an entry in the register to a registered estate which refers to a document kept by the registrar which is not an original, the document kept by the registrar is to be taken as correct and to contain all the material parts of the document.[2] If, however, there is in fact a mistake in such a document, any person suffering loss in consequence is entitled to an indemnity.

6. Loss or destruction of a document lodged in the registry for inspection or safe custody[3]

This provision is likely to be interpreted widely by the Land Registry so that indemnity will be payable if, for example, a document becomes unreadable because it is water damaged. For the future, documents will increasingly be held in dematerialised form, and loss and destruction will be understood accordingly.[4]

7. A mistake in the cautions register[5]

This is a new right to indemnity that arises from the creation of the cautions register.[6]

8. Failure by the registrar to perform his duty under s 50[7]

The new duty, imposed on the registrar by s 50 of the LRA 2002, to inform a chargee of the registration of an overriding charge, has already been explained.[8] If the registrar fails to perform that duty and, in consequence, the chargee suffers loss because (for example) it makes a further advance in circumstances where the property charged is not in fact good security because of the statutory charge, it will be entitled to indemnity.

The special case of mines and minerals

5.68 The LRA 2002 provides that no indemnity is payable on account of any mines or minerals, or the existence of any right to work or get

---

1   See para **5.23**.
2   LRA 2002, s 120.
3   Ibid, Sch 8, para 1(1)(f).
4   Cf (2001) Law Com No 271, para 10.36.
5   LRA 2002, Sch 8, para 1(1)(g).
6   For the cautions register, see para **2.56**.
7   LRA 2002, Sch 8, para 1(1)(h).
8   See para **4.19**.

mines or minerals, unless it is noted in the register that the title to the registered estate concerned includes the mines or minerals.[1] Registration of title to land under the Act includes mines and minerals, unless there is any entry to the contrary in the register.[2] However, the LRA 2002 follows the LRA 1925 by providing that the State guarantee of title does not extend to mines and minerals unless they are expressly included in the title and an appropriate entry is made in the register. The reasons for this limitation lie in the difficulty of discovering whether:

- the mines and minerals have been severed from the land without this being recorded on the title; or
- the land was at one time copyhold and the lord of the manor's rights to the mines and minerals were preserved when the land was enfranchised.[3]

It will only be in those rare cases where the mines and minerals are expressly included in the title that indemnity could ever be paid in relation to them.

The measure of indemnity

5.69 The purpose of indemnity is to compensate the person who has suffered loss in consequence of one or more of the eight grounds listed in para **5.67**. The losses recoverable include those that flow directly from the particular matter (such as the value of any land that the person seeking indemnity may have lost) and also any consequential losses, such as the opportunity of an advantageous sale. It is only where the losses consist entirely of costs and expenses that there are any restrictions on them. This is explained in para **5.71**.

5.70 The LRA 2002 makes provision for the case where the claim is for the loss of an estate, interest or charge.[4] Where the register is rectified, the indemnity is the value of the estate, interest or charge immediately before rectification of the register of title, but as if there were to be no rectification.[5] By contrast, where the register is not rectified, it is the value of the estate, charge or interest at the time when

---

[1] LRA 2002, Sch 8, para 2.
[2] See LRA 2002, ss 11(3), 12(3), 132(1) (definition of 'land' includes mines and minerals, whether or not held with the surface).
[3] See (2001) Law Com No 271, para 10.39.
[4] LRA 2002, Sch 8, para 6.
[5] Ibid, Sch 8, para 6(a).

the mistake which caused the loss was made.[1] The reason for the different measures is that where the register is not rectified, there is no other valuation date that can logically be taken other than the date of the mistake. In any event, it should be noted that any consequential losses are also recoverable in addition to the sum representing the value of the estate, interest or charge.[2] Furthermore, where the value of the estate, interest or charge is valued at the date of the mistake because rectification is not ordered, there is a power to award interest on the sum from that date, although the details are a matter for rules.[3] It is in fact already the present practice of the Registry to pay interest from the date of the mistake.

5.71 Costs and expenses incurred in relation to a matter giving rise to indemnity are recoverable by a person only if they were reasonably incurred by him with the consent of the registrar.[4] However, in three situations, costs and expenses can be recovered even if the registrar's prior consent has not been obtained, namely:

– where the costs or expenses incurred were incurred by the claimant urgently, and it was not reasonably practicable for him to apply for the registrar's consent in advance;[5]
– where the registrar subsequently approves the costs or expenses so that they are then treated as having been incurred with his consent;[6] and
– where a person has applied to the court to determine whether he is entitled to an indemnity at all, or to determine the amount of any indemnity.[7] The applicant does not need the prior consent of the registrar in relation to the costs of that application.

5.72 The LRA 2002 also contains a new power in relation to costs in a case where a person incurs expenses in determining whether or not he has a claim to an indemnity. This might happen, for example where the facts suggest that there might have been a mistake by the registrar but, on further investigation, this proves not to be the case. In such circumstances, the registrar is given a discretion to pay the claimant's costs or expenses provided that they were incurred reasonably and with

---

1   LRA 2002, Sch 8, para 6(b).
2   See para **5.67**.
3   LRA 2002, Sch 8, para 9.
4   Ibid, Sch 8, para 3(1).
5   Ibid, Sch 8, para 3(2).
6   Ibid, Sch 8, para 3(3).
7   Ibid, Sch 8, para 7(2).

the consent of the registrar.[1] Even if the registrar's prior consent was not obtained, he may still pay indemnity where:

- the costs or expenses incurred were incurred by the claimant urgently, and it was not reasonably practicable for him to apply for the registrar's consent in advance; or
- the registrar has subsequently approved the costs or expenses.[2]

When a claim for indemnity will fail or will be reduced

5.73 In three situations a claim for indemnity will fail. The first is where the claim is barred by lapse of time. A claim for indemnity is a simple contract debt and it arises when a person knows, or but for his own default might have known, of the existence of his claim.[3] It will, therefore, be barred 6 years after that date.[4] The second situation is where the loss suffered by the claimant is wholly or partly the result of his or her own fraud.[5] The policy reasons for this rule are self-evident. The third situation is where the loss suffered by the claimant is wholly the result of his own lack of proper care.[6] In interpreting the equivalent provision of the LRA 1925,[7] which the LRA 2002 replicates, the Court of Appeal has held that if there are in fact several causes of the claimant's loss, the claim for indemnity will not fail on this ground. This is so, even if some or all of the other causes would not have occurred but for the claimant's conduct.[8]

5.74 If the person claiming indemnity was partly but not wholly responsible for the loss which he suffered, as a result of his own lack of proper care, any indemnity payable to him will be reduced to such extent as is fair having regard to his share in the responsibility for the loss.[9] This principle of contributory negligence was first introduced by the LRA 1997.[10]

5.75 Where a claim for indemnity would be barred on grounds of fraud, or either barred or reduced because of a lack of care, it is not

---

1   LRA 2002, Sch 8, para 4(1).
2   Ibid, Sch 8, para 4(2).
3   Ibid, Sch 8, para 8.
4   See LA 1980, s 5.
5   LRA 2002, Sch 8, para 5(1)(a).
6   Ibid, Sch 8, para 5(1)(b).
7   As amended by LRA 1997.
8   *Dean v Dean* (2000) 80 P&CR 457.
9   LRA 2002, Sch 8, para 5(2).
10 See LRA 1997, s 2.

merely the person responsible whose claim is affected. Any person who derives title from him will be in the same position, unless the disposition to him was for valuable consideration and was registered or protected by an entry in the register.[1]

Claiming indemnity

5.76 Under the LRA 2002, a person is entitled to be indemnified *by the registrar*.[2] There are a number of ways in which a claim for indemnity might come to be made.

– First, it might arise out of an application to the registrar for rectification of the register.[3] If there is an objection to that application that cannot be resolved by agreement, the matter will have to be referred to the Adjudicator for determination.[4] The Adjudicator will necessarily deal with any question of indemnity that is consequent upon his decision.
– Secondly, as will be clear from the circumstances in which indemnity is payable,[5] there are many situations in which a claim for indemnity does not involve any possible issue of rectification. These will necessarily be dealt with by the registrar. Any challenge to his decision on an issue relating to indemnity would have to be by way of judicial review.[6]
– Thirdly, as now, a person is entitled to apply to the court for a determination of any question as to whether he is entitled to an indemnity, or the amount of such an indemnity.[7] He does not have to apply first to the registrar.

The registrar's rights of recourse

5.77 The LRA 2002 replicates the provisions, first introduced by the LRA 1997, that give the registrar extensive rights of recourse in cases in which he has paid indemnity.[8]

---

1   LRA 2002, Sch 8, para 5(3).
2   Ibid, Sch 8, para 1(1).
3   The procedure for such applications will be a matter for rules: see LRA 2002, Sch 4, para 7(c).
4   LRA 2002, s 73; see also para **5.38**. For the Adjudicator, see Chapter 9.
5   See para **5.67**.
6   See para **9.9**.
7   LRA 2002, Sch 8, para 7(1).
8   It is clear from the Annual Reports of HM Land Registry, that these new rights of recourse are considerably more extensive than the equivalent rights were under the LRA 1925 as originally enacted.

– First, the registrar is entitled to recover the amount paid from any person who caused or substantially contributed to the loss by fraud.[1] The registrar can make such recovery even if the recipient of the indemnity would not have been able to sue the perpetrator of the fraud had the indemnity not been paid.

– Secondly, the registrar is entitled to enforce any right of action, of whatever nature and however arising, which the claimant would have been entitled to enforce had the indemnity not been paid.[2] This would apply in cases where, for example, the error in the register resulted from negligence on the part of the professional acting for the person who suffered the loss and was subsequently indemnified, and is analogous to an insurer's right of subrogation.

– Thirdly, where the register has been rectified, the registrar may enforce any right of action, of whatever nature and however arising, which the person in whose favour the register was rectified would have been entitled to enforce if it had not been rectified.[3]

5.78 As regards the third of those cases, the Law Commission and the Land Registry in their final Report gave an example of the circumstances in which the provision might operate, and illustrates how extensive the right is. They envisaged a case where the register was rectified in favour of X because of a mistake caused by X's solicitor. As a result of the rectification, Y suffered loss for which he was indemnified by the registrar. The registrar would be entitled to recover the amount of the indemnity paid from X's solicitor. This is even though, at common law, X's solicitor might not have owed any duty of care to Y.[4]

5.79 However, although the rights of recourse are extensive, undertakings were given in Parliament both when they were first introduced under the LRA 1997 and during the passage of the Act, that they would not be invoked against solicitors and licensed conveyancers except in cases of fraud or serious cases of negligence.[5]

---

1   LRA 2002, Sch 8, para 10(1)(a).
2   Ibid, Sch 8, para 10(1)(b), 10(2)(a).
3   Ibid, Sch 8, para 10(1)(b), 10(2)(b).
4   See (2001) Law Com No 271, para 10.52.
5   See, eg, *Hansard* (HL), 8 November 2001, vol 628, col 313 (Baroness Scotland of Asthal).

CHAPTER 6

CONVEYANCING

THE MAIN CHANGES AT A GLANCE

6.1   The main changes that the LRA 2002 makes in relation to conveyancing are in its provisions on electronic conveyancing. These are considered in Chapter 7. However, the Act also makes some significant changes to other aspects of conveyancing in relation to registered land (including certain contracts to make a disposition of unregistered land that will trigger compulsory registration).

6.2   The main changes are as follows.

- The old prescriptive rules as to the proof of title which a seller of registered land has to show are replaced by a rule-making power which will enable the Lord Chancellor to make rules as to a seller's obligations in relation to his title.
- The restrictions on the title which a grantee of a lease may see are abolished where that grant is made out of a registered title and modified in relation to contracts to grant leases that trigger compulsory registration.
- Covenants for title are dealt with in a more transparent form.

PROVING TITLE

6.3   Under the LRA 1925,[1] on a sale or disposition of registered land, other than to a lessee or chargee, the registered proprietor was required to produce:

- copies of subsisting entries on the register and of filed plans;

---

[1]   LRA 1925, s 110(1), (2). For an analysis of these provisions, see (1998) Law Com No 254, paras 11.35–11.39.

– copies or abstracts of any documents noted on the register in respect of interests that would not be discharged or overridden at or prior to completion; and

– copies, abstracts and evidence in respect of estates and interests that were either appurtenant to the registered land and as to which the register was not conclusive[1] or which were excepted from the effect of registration.[2]

As regards the first two entries in the above list, the provisions were mandatory and could not be ousted by agreement to the contrary.[3]

6.4 There was also a provision in the LRA 1925 which dealt with the situation where a seller of land was not the registered proprietor of land but could require the registered proprietor to convey at his direction. This might happen where the seller had contracted to buy the land or was the beneficiary under a bare trust. He could be required by the buyer to procure either his own registration as proprietor before transferring the registered estate to the buyer, or a disposition from the proprietor to the buyer.[4] In practice this provision, which could not be ousted by contrary intention, gave rise to serious practical difficulties.[5]

6.5 The provisions of the LRA 1925 on proof of title were based upon the premise, applicable in 1925, that the register was not a public document and could only be searched with the consent of the registered proprietor.[6] That is no longer the case. The register was made public by the LRA 1988 and can be searched simply and cheaply. An increasing number of solicitors and licensed conveyancers have direct computer access to the register. The introduction of electronic conveyancing will mean that all solicitors and licensed conveyancers who are authorised to conduct such conveyancing will necessarily have on-line access to the register and will be able to call up any registered title on screen, literally at the press of a button. The provisions of the LRA 1925 now look badly out of date.

6.6 The LRA 2002 replaces these provisions with a short rule-making

---

[1]   Such as the benefit of easements.
[2]   Where the title was registered with a title that was not absolute.
[3]   LRA 1925, s 110(3).
[4]   Ibid, s 110(5).
[5]   See (1998) Law Com No 254, para 11.43.
[6]   See LRA 1925, s 110. Indeed, prior to 1930, when postal searches were introduced, the only way that the register could be searched was by attending in person at HM Land Registry in Lincoln's Inn Fields: see (2001) Law Com No 271, para 12.5.

power. This will permit the Lord Chancellor to make rules about the obligations of a seller under a contract to make a disposition for valuable consideration of a registered estate or charge with respect to proof of title or perfection of title.[1] Any rules as to the perfection of title will meet the case of the seller who is not the registered proprietor but can direct the registered proprietor to make a disposition. If the Lord Chancellor does make any rules, they may be expressed to override any contrary contractual provision that the parties may have made.[2] It is implicit in this that rules might be made that were intended to provide guidance to parties, while leaving them free to make their own arrangements. In reality, under the present registered system, the only interests in relation to which proof of title is required from a seller are those that are not protected or recorded in the register, such as unregistered interests that override first registration or registered dispositions.[3]

6.7   The fact of the open register has led to another change. Section 44 of the LRA 1925 makes provision for the statutory commencement of title. It provides, for example, that the period for the commencement of title which a purchaser may require is 15 years.[4] This has no relevance to registered title where the register stands as proof of title in place of the root and chain of title required in relation to unregistered land. Section 44 also contains provisions which preclude a person who has contracted to take the grant or assignment of a lease from calling for the freehold title.[5] Where that freehold title is registered, this provision is now meaningless because the intending grantee or assignee can inspect the register of title on the open register. The LRA 2002 therefore disapplies s 44 as regards registered land or a term of years to be derived out of registered land.[6] It also amends s 44 to create a new default position where the owner of unregistered land contracts to grant a lease that will trigger compulsory first registration of title. In that situation, those provisions of s 44 which restrict the title that the intending lessee can see,[7] will not apply.[8] The intending lessee will therefore be entitled to require the deduction of the superior title, so

---

[1]   LRA 2002, Sch 10, para 2(1). The rules would, if made, be land registration rules.
[2]   Ibid, Sch 10, para 2(2).
[3]   Under LRA 2002, Schs 1 and 3.
[4]   LPA 1925, s 44(1), as amended by LPA 1969, s 23.
[5]   Ibid, s 44(2).
[6]   LRA 2002, Sch 11, para 2(4), inserting a new LPA 1925, s 44(12).
[7]   Namely, LRA 1925, s 44(2)–(4).
[8]   LRA 2002, Sch 11, para 2(2), inserting a new LPA 1925, s 44(4A).

enabling him to be registered with absolute title.[1] That is, of course, the intention of the provision. However, this is only a default position, and the parties are free to provide otherwise if they so wish.[2]

COVENANTS FOR TITLE

6.8   The LRA 2002 does not make any substantial change to the way in which covenants for title operate in relation to registered land. The law governing covenants for title was substantially reformed by Part 1 of the Law of Property (Miscellaneous Provisions) Act 1994 (LP(MP)A 1994). There was therefore no reason for any fundamental reappraisal of the operation of such covenants in relation to registered land. The LRA 2002 does, however, make the provisions which govern such covenants rather easier to understand. In particular, the principle that a person making a disposition of an interest in land the title to which was registered, is not liable in relation to certain of the covenants implied by the LP(MP)A 1994 in respect of matters entered in the register of title of that interest,[3] is no longer a matter for rules.[4] The LRA 2002 inserts a new s 6(4) into the LP(MP)A 1994 to give effect to this principle.[5] Other matters relating to the application of covenants for title to registered land will continue to be dealt with in rules as they were under the LRA 1925.[6]

---

[1]   Cf Standard Conditions of Sale (SCS), c 8.2.4, which creates a similar default position in relation to the grant of a new lease for more than 21 years.

[2]   LPA 1925, s 44(11).

[3]   See LP(MP)A 1994, s 6.

[4]   As it was: see LRR 1925, r 77A(2).

[5]   LRA 2002, Sch 11, para 31(2). Strictly speaking, this alteration changes the law. However, the changes are unlikely to be of any significance: see (2001) Law Com No 271, para 12.19.

[6]   See LRA 2002, Sch 10, para 3.

CHAPTER 7

ELECTRONIC CONVEYANCING

THE MAIN FEATURES AT A GLANCE

7.1 The most significant single feature of the LRA 2002 is that it introduces a wholly new system of electronic conveyancing (e-conveyancing). These provisions are found in Part 8 of and Sch 5 to the Act. The main elements of the new system are as follows.

– A principal aim of e-conveyancing is to enable dispositions of registered land to be made and registered simultaneously. This can only happen if conveyancers have authority to make changes to the register.
– E-conveyancing will be conducted through a secure electronic network. Access will be regulated by network access agreements made between the registrar and those authorised to have access to the network. Rules will prescribe the way in which e-conveyancing is to be conducted. Such rules will override any obligations that a conveyancer might otherwise owe to his client.
– All stages of a conveyancing transaction will be conducted electronically and the Registry will become involved in a transaction at a much earlier stage than at present.
– The LRA 2002 provides how electronic documents are to be made. Such documents that are made in accordance with the Act will be deemed to comply with common law and statutory requirements as to form.
– It is likely that, in the early days of e-conveyancing, conveyancers will authenticate electronic documents on behalf of their clients, who are unlikely to have their own electronic signatures. The LRA 2002 makes provision that will ensure that conveyancers can do this.
– It is intended that there will be a system of electronic settlement to ensure that all financial aspects of a transaction are dealt with on completion.

7.2   Although e-conveyancing has been singled out for specific comment, it must be stressed that it is merely one example of e-commerce and should be seen in that context. It is not unique and it will not develop in a vacuum. Many of the concerns that have been raised in relation to e-conveyancing apply equally to all or many other forms of e-commerce. There are likely to be common solutions. Certain forms of e-commerce have been operating very successfully for some time now, such as the electronic trading of shares on the London Stock Exchange.[1]

7.3   E-conveyancing will not come about as soon as the LRA 2002 comes into force in the latter part of 2003. It is proposed to introduce it gradually over the following 4 or 5 years. The first step towards an electronic system is likely to be the electronic registration of registered charges, which could be introduced within one year. Electronic lodgement of notices and restrictions are also probable candidates for early introduction. These are, however, a far cry from the system of e-conveyancing that the Act seeks to create. Much of the detail as to the workings of e-conveyancing is necessarily left to rules and those rules will not be made prior to the coming into force of the Act. HM Land Registry has recently launched a major consultation on the form of e-conveyancing as it is to be developed and this provides an insight into the Registry's thinking.[2]

7.4   One particular concern that is frequently voiced about e-conveyancing – and indeed about all forms of e-commerce – is about the level of security that it offers and the extent to which it can provide protection from fraud. It should in fact be possible to create an electronic system of conveyancing that is *more* secure than the present paper-based one, where forgery and fraud are commonplace. HM Land Registry has a strong incentive to minimise the risk of fraud, given that it guarantees registered title and may have to pay indemnity if the register is fraudulently altered.

WHAT IS E-CONVEYANCING?

7.5   At present, conveyancing is paper-based. Although it is now possible to have direct access to the register[3] in order to view its

---

[1]   Known as CREST.
[2]   See *E-Conveyancing: A Land Registry Consultation*, May 2002.
[3]   Under the Land Registry's Direct Access Service.

contents and to make certain applications to the Registry,[1] contracts, transfers and grants are all made using written documents. Those documents then have to be submitted to the Registry for registration. It is already possible for a mortgage lender to notify the Registry electronically of the discharge of a registered charge.[2] The intention of the LRA 2002 is to bring about a change whereby all dealings are conducted in dematerialised form. It would have been possible to create an e-conveyancing system under which changes to the register were made, as now, by HM Land Registry on application, but where those applications were made electronically. However, the Act goes much further than that: the system of e-conveyancing that will be created under the powers which it confers, changes the way in which land registration is conducted. It will no longer be the Registry alone that makes changes to the register, whether on application, to give effect to a court order or on the registrar's own volition. The registrar will still make changes to the register in appropriate circumstances. However, when there are dealings with registered land, the register will be changed automatically to give effect to them as a result of electronic documents and applications created by solicitors and licensed conveyancers acting for the parties to the transaction.[3] Although such dealings will be subject to prior scrutiny by the Registry, it will no longer be the Registry that makes the change. This system is dictated by the fundamental aim of the LRA 2002 to bring about a conclusive register.[4] It is intended that, when e-conveyancing is fully functional, dealings with registered land will not have any effect unless they are simultaneously registered.[5] In this way, the so-called 'registration gap' that presently exists between the making of a disposition of registered land and its registration following application to the Registry will disappear. Although it is the objective of a conclusive register that has driven the policy of the Act in this regard, the elimination of the registration gap will bring many advantages with it. In particular, it will eliminate any risk that a disposition might be made between the making of the transfer or grant and its registration.[6]

---

[1]   The applications in question are for various office copies, to inspect and copy register entries, for an official search of the Index Map and Parcels Index, and an enquiry as to discharge of a charge by electronic means. See Notice 4A of the Chief Land Registrar: Direct Access Office Copy Service; see also Ruoff and Roper *Registered Conveyancing*, F-06.

[2]   LRR 1925, r 151A.

[3]   See (2001) Law Com No 271, para 2.57.

[4]   See para **1.7**.

[5]   See paras **7.53–7.54**.

[6]   Cf *Brown & Root Technology Ltd v Sun Alliance and London Assurance Co Ltd* [2001] Ch 733.

7.6   The system of e-conveyancing that the LRA 2002 creates is concerned only with dealings with registered land and with those aspects of conveyancing that involve registration. That is only one part of the conveyancing process. The Land Register will provide an intending purchaser with information about the title. However, there are many other searches that an intending purchaser of land may wish to make, such as a local authority search, an environmental search, or, in certain parts of the country, a Coal Authority search. The process for making these 'parallel' searches electronic is under way through the NLIS, which also provides a portal to access the Land Register. It is not just a conclusive Land Register that is required. If an effective e-conveyancing system is to be constructed, these other sources of data must be readily and speedily accessible on line.[1]

7.7   There are no precedents for creating an e-conveyancing system under which dealings with registered land are simultaneously registered.[2] The LRA 2002 has therefore had to proceed from first principles. The questions that arise are as follows.

–   What formal requirements will apply to contracts and dealings with registered land that are made in electronic form?
–   What mechanisms will be in place to protect the integrity of the register, given that solicitors and licensed conveyancers will be able to make changes to it?
–   How will e-conveyancing be made compulsory?
–   What other steps are needed to ensure that e-conveyancing operates as smoothly as possible?

FORMAL REQUIREMENTS

Introduction

7.8   As a consequence of a number of statutory provisions, many dealings with both land and interests in land have to comply with prescribed formal requirements of signed writing or of a deed. It was therefore necessary for the LRA 2002 to ensure that electronic documents that effected such dealings would not be invalidated by these formal requirements. Section 91 of the LRA 2002 provides a

---

[1]   There is a particular concern that local authorities are not computerising their local searches either at all or too slowly.
[2]   E-conveyancing of some kind or another has been introduced in other jurisdictions, such as Ontario.

uniform system for creating electronic documents in relation to specified dispositions of estates, rights and interests in registered land. Section 91 does not apply to contracts for the sale or other disposition of an interest in land. This is because such contracts were to be dealt with in another way.

7.9 Under s 8 of the Electronic Communications Act 2000 (ECA 2000), the appropriate Minister is given power to modify by order made by statutory instrument the provisions of any enactment in such manner as he may think for the purpose of authorising or facilitating the use of electronic communications or electronic storage. In March 2001, some months prior to the introduction of the Land Registration Bill, the Lord Chancellor's Department issued for consultation a draft Order to be made under s 8.[1] Part of that draft Order was concerned with dispositions of registered land and s 91 of the LRA 2002 is an extended version of that provision.[2] The draft Order also contained a proposed new s 2A of the LP(MP)A 1989 that specified the formalities that would be required to make a contract for the sale of an interest in electronic form.[3] The new section would have applied to contracts relating to both registered and unregistered land. The LRA 2002 is limited by its scope to registered land and does not replicate the proposed s 2A, even in relation to contracts concerning registered land. It has not yet been decided whether any such Order will be required to introduce the proposed s 2A.[4] Indeed, there is now some doubt as to whether such an Order is needed at all, because it has now been suggested that an electronic document can satisfy any statutory requirements of writing and signature.[5] However, it is not clear how s 2 of the LP(MP)A 1989 could apply in its present form to contracts made electronically.[6] The practice of conveyancers influenced the requirements of s 2[7] and, in particular, its recognition of the custom of exchanging contracts.[8] Exchange of contracts makes no sense in relation to electronic documents and the draft Order recognised this fact. In particular, it would require that all the terms which the parties

---

[1]   Electronic Conveyancing, a draft Order under s 8 of the ECA 2000.
[2]   An Order under s 8 can only amend *statutory* requirements and not common law rules. Section 91 amends certain rules of common law as well.
[3]   In place of the requirements of LP(MP)A 1989, s 2.
[4]   An analysis of the responses to the draft Order was published by the Lord Chancellor's Department in December 2001: CP(R) 05/2001.
[5]   See *Electronic Commerce: Formal Requirements in Commercial Transactions: Advice from the Law Commission* (December 2001), chapter 3. This Advice is not in one of the usual Law Commission series.
[6]   A point acknowledged in *E-Conveyancing: A Land Registry Consultation*, para 2.3.3.
[7]   See (1987) Law Com No 164, paras 4.6, 4.15.
[8]   See LP(MP)A 1989, s 2(1).

had expressly agreed were incorporated in the document (whether by being set out in it or by reference to some other document), and that the contract would take effect at the date and time specified in that document.

The statutory requirements

The function of LRA 2002, s 91

7.10 The effect of s 91 of the LRA 2002 is that, if an electronic document is made in accordance with its provisions, it is to be regarded as made by signed writing and to satisfy any statutory requirements of a deed.[1] Section 91 is a remarkably concise and subtle provision. It was the subject of much comment – and misunderstanding – during the passage of the LRA 2002 through Parliament. It is *only* concerned with the formal requirements for making a disposition in electronic form.

Dispositions within LRA 2002, s 91

7.11 The section will apply to three classes of disposition.[2] The first is a disposition of a registered estate or charge. The second is something of a novelty. It is a disposition of an interest which is the subject of a notice in the register, such as an equitable charge or an option. The LRA 2002 visualises that it will become possible to transfer electronically certain interests that are only protected by a notice and are not registered with their own titles. This is a notable extension of the principles of registration. The third class of disposition is a disposition of unregistered land which triggers the requirement of registration contained in s 4 of the Act.[3] In addition to falling into one of these three categories, the disposition must be of a kind specified by rules. It is envisaged that, eventually, all possible dispositions will be specified by rules.[4] However, the need to specify in rules dispositions that can be made electronically means that e-conveyancing can be extended on a transaction-by-transaction basis over a period of time. The more difficult transactions, such as sales of part only of an existing registered title, are likely to be amongst the last to be brought within the e-conveyancing system.

The four conditions to be satisfied

7.12 It is not enough that the disposition falls within the requirements

---

[1] See further, para **7.17**.
[2] LRA 2002, s 91(2).
[3] See paras **2.12** et seq.
[4] (2001) Law Com No 271, para 13.12.

of para **7.11**. To have the effect mentioned in para **7.10**, it must meet four conditions.[1]

7.13 The first condition is that the electronic document must make provision for the time and date when it takes effect.[2] There has to be some mechanism for fixing the moment at which an electronic document takes effect. Any concept of delivery, such as applies to deeds, is inappropriate for electronic documents for at least three reasons. First, s 91 covers cases where the statutory requirements of form are for signed writing rather than a deed. Secondly, as explained below, an electronic document that complies with the requirements of the section is not in fact a deed but is merely to be regarded as one for the purposes of the section.[3] Thirdly, it is not clear how the technical concept of delivery could apply to an electronic document, because it involves words or acts by which the maker indicates that the deed binds him.[4] It follows, therefore, that some other means had to be found for fixing the moment at which an electronic document will take effect. The means adopted – the fixing of a date and time – gives the parties as much flexibility as they presently enjoy. That date and time could be inserted into the document at a late stage, just before the transaction is to be completed.

7.14 The second condition is that the document has the electronic signature of each person by whom it purports to be authenticated.[5] An electronic signature is the means by which a person authenticates an electronic document as his own.[6] There are various different forms of electronic signature presently available[7] and each has its protagonists and its detractors. With some forms of electronic signature, the recipient of the signed message can tell whether a hacker has interfered with that message. It is unlikely that any one form of electronic signature will be prescribed. What will matter will be the level of security that each offers. It will be noted that the electronic document must be signed electronically by 'every person by whom it purports to

---

[1]   LRA 2002, s 91(3).

[2]   Ibid, s 91(3)(a).

[3]   Ibid, s 91(5); see also para **7.19**.

[4]   Cf *Vincent v Premo Enterprises (Voucher Sales) Ltd* [1969] 2 QB 609, at p 619.

[5]   LRA 2002, s 91(3)(b).

[6]   For the purposes of s 91, 'electronic signature' has the meaning given to it by ECA 2000, s 7(2): see LRA 2002, s 91(10).

[7]   These include, for example, 'public' or 'dual' key cryptography, and iris recognition. The Land Registry's present working assumption is that some form of public key infrastructure will be employed: see *E-Conveyancing: A Land Registry Consultation*, para 8.2.2.

be authenticated'. Sometimes the disponees as well as the disponor may execute a document. This *should* happen when there is a disposition of registered land in favour of joint proprietors (although, in practice, it often does not) because the transfer form sets out the trusts upon which the land is to be held by the disponees[1] and, if it is signed by them, that document will satisfy the formal requirements for an enforceable declaration of a trust respecting any land.[2]

7.15 The third condition is related to the second and it is that each electronic signature should be certified.[3] Certification is the means by which an electronic signature is itself authenticated.[4] If an electronic document is signed with Joan Smith's electronic signature, there has to be a way of ensuring that that signature really is Joan Smith's and not that of some other person who fraudulently holds herself out to be Joan Smith. What in practice will probably happen is that the certifying authority will actually *provide* Joan Smith with her electronic signature,[5] but only when it has satisfied itself of her identity. Certification is therefore likely to be an integral part of the process by which a person obtains his or her own electronic signature.[6]

7.16 The fourth condition is that such other conditions as rules may provide are met.[7] It is likely that, as e-commerce develops, it will be necessary to introduce other requirements to ensure the security or smooth working of the system. It may, for example, be necessary to require transactions to meet a specified level of security. Indeed, this may be an early requirement.[8]

The effect of compliance

7.17 Section 91 does not disapply the various statutory or common law requirements for signed writing or a deed.[9] Instead, it deems compliance with them if an electronic document is made in accordance

---

1   See, eg, Form TR1 under the present LRR 1925, Sch 1.
2   See LPA 1925, s 53(1)(b).
3   LRA 2002, s 91(3)(c).
4   For the purposes of s 91, 'certification' has the meaning given to it by ECA 2000, s 7(3): see LRA 2002, s 91(10).
5   Perhaps in the form of a swipe card, but that is not the only possible method.
6   Where a person has an electronic signature, it will still be necessary to be sure that he is whom he claims to be, and that he is not impersonating the person whose electronic signature he has stolen.
7   LRA 2002, s 91(3)(d).
8   Cf para **7.14**.
9   Not all formal requirements are statutory. For example, some significant categories of corporation can only execute a document under the corporate seal. That is a common law and not a statutory requirement.

with the requirements set out above. Indeed, s 91 contains no less than four such deeming provisions.

7.18 First, a document that is made in accordance with the requirements explained in paras **7.11–7.16** is to be regarded as in writing and signed by each individual and sealed by each corporation whose electronic signature it has.[1] The provision makes no reference to *statutory* requirements of signed or sealed writing. This is important because it will enable any corporation to have an electronic signature, even if it is one that can only execute a document under its corporate seal because it has no statutory powers of execution.

7.19 Secondly, a document that is made in accordance with the requirements of s 91 is to be regarded for the purposes of any enactment as a deed.[2] It is important to stress that the document is *not* a deed. It is merely to be regarded as a deed for the purposes set out. This means, for example, that the rule that an agent cannot execute a deed on behalf of his principal unless he is authorised to do so by a deed,[3] is inapplicable. The requirements of s 91 do in fact differ markedly from the statutory requirements for a deed. For example, an electronic document under the section does not have to state that it is a deed.[4] Nor, if it is made by an individual, does it have to be attested.[5]

7.20 Thirdly, if a document that is made in accordance with the requirements of s 91 is authenticated by a person as agent, it is to be regarded for the purposes of any enactment as authenticated by him under the written authority of his principal.[6] The purpose of this provision is to deal with a minor technical point. Under some statutory provisions, an agent can only make certain disposition on behalf of his principal if he has been authorised by that principal in writing. The most important example is the LPA 1925, s 53(1)(a), by which 'no interest in land can be created or disposed of except by writing signed by the person creating or conveying the same, or his agent thereunto lawfully authorised in writing …'. The result of the deeming provision in s 91 is that where an agent makes a disposition in electronic form on behalf of his principal, he is deemed to comply with the formal

---

[1] LRA 2002, s 91(4).
[2] Ibid, s 91(5).
[3] See, eg, *Powell v London and Provincial Bank* [1893] 2 Ch 555, at p 563.
[4] Cf LP(MP)A 1989, s 1(2).
[5] Cf ibid, s 1(3).
[6] LRA 2002, s 91(6).

requirement that he should have the *written* authority of his principal. As a consequence, the other party or parties to the transaction cannot require him to prove that his authority to authenticate the electronic document was given in writing. It would rather defeat the point of having e-conveyancing if they could. It should be stressed that this provision does *not* deem the agent to have authority where he has none.[1] All it does is to deem him, for the purposes of any enactment, to have authenticated the electronic document under the *written* authority of his principal.

7.21 Fourthly, if notice of an assignment is made by means of a document to which s 91 applies and is given in electronic form in accordance with the rules, it is to be regarded for the purposes of any enactment as given in writing.[2] The reason for this provision is as follows. It has been explained in para **7.11** that it is intended that it will become possible to make electronic dispositions of certain interests that are not registered with their own titles, but are merely protected by a notice on the register. By s 136(1) of the LPA 1925, where there is an assignment of a debt or legal chose in action, it is necessary to give 'express notice in writing' to the debtor or other contracting party. The provision mentioned above is intended to meet this point. It means that if there is an electronic assignment of a debt or legal chose in action – such as an option or other estate contract – under the provisions of s 91 of the LRA 2002, notice of that assignment can be given electronically to the debtor or contracting party. Such notice will be regarded as complying with s 136(1) of the LPA 1925.

Execution by corporations

7.22 The manner in which a corporation may execute a document depends upon the type of corporation. While there are statutory provisions applicable to certain types of corporation, the common law rules on execution apply to others. First, any corporation can execute a document by affixing its common seal, whether by statute[3] or at common law. Secondly, by statute, certain corporations do not have to have a common seal.[4] Such corporations have statutory powers to

---

1   See also LRA 2002, Sch 5, para 8, which is explained at para **7.49**, and which is concerned with an agent's lack of implied authority to contract or make a disposition on behalf of his principal.

2   LRA 2002, s 91(7).

3   See, eg, Companies Act 1985, s 36A(2) (which applies to corporations that are companies for the purposes of the Companies Act 1985 and certain other corporations); Friendly Societies Act 1992, Sch 6, para 2 (friendly societies); Charities Act 1993, s 60(2) (incorporated charities).

4   See, eg, Companies Act 1985, s 36A; Friendly Societies Act 1992, Sch 6, para 2; Charities Act 1993, s 60.

execute documents in other ways by the signatures of their officers or
trustees. Thirdly, all corporations may appoint an agent to execute
instruments on their behalf, whether by power of attorney[1] or
otherwise.

7.23 How then can a corporation execute a document under s 91 of
the LRA 2002? First, the section permits every corporation to have an
electronic signature (s 91(4)(b)). It will not be possible for the
corporation's signature to be incorporated into or otherwise logically
associated with an electronic document unless this was done at the
direction of an authorised officer or trustee of that corporation.[2]
Secondly, where a statute permits officers of a corporation to sign a
document on its behalf, those officers will be able to sign a document
electronically under s 91. Thirdly, a duly authorised agent will also be
able to sign a document electronically on behalf of a corporation under
s 91.

7.24 Under s 36A(4) of the Companies Act 1985, where a document
has been signed by a director and the secretary of a company, or by two
directors of a company, and is expressed (in whatever form) to be
executed by the company, it has the same effect as if it were executed
under the common seal of the company. There is a statutory
presumption in favour of a purchaser that a document is deemed to
have been duly executed by a company if it purports to be signed by a
director and the secretary of the company, or by two directors of the
company.[3] That presumption is carried forward into e-conveyancing
and will apply to a document signed electronically.[4]

Rights of a purchaser as to execution

7.25 Section 75 of the LPA 1925 provides that, although on a sale a
purchaser is not entitled to require that a conveyance to him should be
executed in his (or his solicitor's) presence, he is entitled to have the
conveyance attested by some person appointed by him, who may be his

---

[1]   See Powers of Attorney Act 1971, s 7; LPA 1925, s 74(3).
[2]   See (2001) Law Com No 271, para 13.26. In other words, the person or persons who could affix the
      company's seal to a document could also direct the use of the company's electronic signature.
[3]   Companies Act 1985, s 36A(6). This can be important. The presumption will protect purchasers in
      cases where, for example, the directors were not authorised, or were acting other than as a board of
      directors. In these cases, there is no protection under the provisions of Part III of the Companies Act
      1985.
[4]   LRA 2002, s 91(9).

solicitor.[1] This right does not apply to documents to which s 91 applies[2] because attestation is inappropriate to e-conveyancing.[3]

THE LAND REGISTRY NETWORK

Introduction: a typical transaction in electronic form

7.26 The second of the four questions that have been raised at para **7.7** concerns the mechanisms that will be required to protect the integrity of the register, in a world in which solicitors and licensed conveyancers[4] will be able to make changes to it. This question necessarily underpins the whole structure of e-conveyancing. The system of e-conveyancing will be built around a secure electronic network operated by or for HM Land Registry.[5] The manner in which this network will be used in conveyancing transactions will be regulated in some detail. The framework for that regulation is found in Sch 5 to the LRA 2002. The detail will be contained in rules made under that Schedule or under general rule-making powers contained in Sch 10 to the Act.

7.27 To understand the provisions of the LRA 2002 that govern the network, it is necessary to have a picture of how HM Land Registry envisages that a typical conveyancing transaction may operate under the electronic system.[6] This will depend upon whether or not the transaction is a 'linked' transaction – in other words whether or not it is part of a chain.

7.28 If the transaction is free-standing, the sequence of events as presently visualised is likely to be as follows.

7.29 First, the seller agrees in principle to sell the property to the buyer and both parties instruct conveyancers to act on their behalf. It may be that the pre-contractual information that is then supplied by the seller to the buyer will already have been prepared. This will certainly be the

---

1   The section was passed to deal with a specific difficulty that had arisen from certain judicial decisions.
2   LRA 2002, s 91(8).
3   Cf (2001) Law Com No 271, para 13.31.
4   Referred to for convenience in this chapter as 'conveyancers'.
5   Referred to for convenience in this chapter as 'the network'.
6   For the Registry's latest thinking, see *E-Conveyancing: A Land Registry Consultation*, Part 6.

case if, as seems likely, some form of the 'seller's pack' is resurrected.[1] The pre-contractual information could be supplied electronically to the intending buyer using the network whether or not there is requirement for such a pack.

7.30 Secondly, the draft contract will be prepared in electronic form by the seller's conveyancer. Before the draft is transmitted to the buyer's conveyancer, it will be subject to some form of automatic validation by HM Land Registry.[2] This will be some form of computerised check to ensure that, for example, the seller's name, the address and the title number of the property correspond with the details held by the Registry. In this way, common mistakes can be eliminated at the outset. It also means that the Registry can begin to build up the information about the transaction that will enable the register to be changed on completion. What will happen is that, during the course of the conveyancing process, the Registry will construct a 'notional register' – in other words, a version of the register as it will be when the transaction is completed.

7.31 Thirdly, the draft contract will be transmitted to the buyer's conveyancer for consideration. Any enquiries, such as local searches, that have not already been made by the buyer will be undertaken electronically.[3] The buyer will, in many cases, be seeking a mortgage offer. It is likely that this process itself may in future be conducted on line where the buyer has the necessary internet and e-mail facilities. The extent to which any mortgage offer will be communicated in a form that will automatically generate entries on the notional register has not yet been decided.[4]

7.32 Fourthly, the parties will proceed to the making of the contract. As has been indicated above,[5] there will be no 'exchange of contracts' in e-conveyancing. What is visualised is that there will be one electronic document which will be signed by or on behalf of each of the parties. The contract will then be 'released' by each of them and will take effect

---

[1]   See *E-Conveyancing: A Land Registry Consultation*, para 4.4. The provisions on the 'seller's pack' contained in the Homes Bill (which was lost as a result of the 2001 General Election) were wholly inappropriate to a system of e-conveyancing. It is to be hoped that any new legislation will take account of both the LRA 2002 (particularly in relation to title: see paras **6.3–6.6**) and the intention to dematerialise the conveyancing process.

[2]   See *E-Conveyancing: A Land Registry Consultation*, para 6.2.3.

[3]   Cf para **7.6**.

[4]   See *E-Conveyancing: A Land Registry Consultation*, para 6.2.5.

[5]   See para **7.9**

on the time and date agreed. Although individuals are likely to have
their own electronic signatures in due course, it is probable that initially
it will be their respective conveyancers who sign electronic documents
on their behalf. As is explained below, there are obstacles that would
preclude conveyancers from signing conveyancing documents as agents
for their clients, and the LRA 2002 contains provisions that overcome
these difficulties.[1] As the contract is made, a notice will simultaneously
and automatically be entered on the register. This will have two
consequences:[2] first, it will protect the priority of the estate contract;[3]
and secondly, it will create a priority period in the same manner as a
priority search.[4] Any entry made during that priority period will be
postponed to the application to register the disposition which is the
subject of the estate contract.[5]

7.33 Once contracts have been made, the parties will proceed in the
usual way to completion. All the draft documentation for completion
will be prepared in electronic form, including not only the transfer, but
also any charge that is to be executed by the buyer on completion. All
of this information will be communicated electronically to the Registry
so that the 'notional register' can be built up. Completion will take place
at the time and date agreed by the parties.[6] Again, it is likely that, at least
initially, the conveyancing documents will be signed electronically by
the parties' conveyancers on their behalf.

7.34 On completion, it is intended that the following should
simultaneously occur.

- The transfer and any charge take effect.
- The register is changed in accordance with the final version of the
  'notional register' to record the changes that have occurred. The
  new owner is registered as proprietor and, if there is a charge, that
  too is registered. If any easements are granted or reserved or any
  restrictive covenants are taken, the appropriate entries will appear
  on the register.

---

[1]   See paras **7.48–7.49**.
[2]   LRA 2002, s 72; see also para **5.33**.
[3]   Ibid, s 32; see also para **3.46**.
[4]   See para **5.34**.
[5]   LRA 2002, s 72(2).
[6]   Ibid, s 91(3)(a); see also para **7.13**.

– The consideration passes under the proposed electronic funds transfer system,[1] and stamp duty[2] and Land Registry fees are paid.

7.35 One of the striking features of the new system is that the transaction is concluded in all respects on completion.[3] At present, the Registry may (and often does) raise requisitions after completion when a transfer has been submitted for registration. That cannot happen under the proposed system: everything must be resolved before completion. Some commercial transactions are concluded within a very short time, with contract and completion on the same day. Furthermore, deals are often concluded outside office hours. It has been accepted by HM Land Registry that, to meet this need, it will have to offer a service that is available '24 hours a day, 7 days a week, 52 weeks a year'.[4]

7.36 Where there are linked transactions, typically in a chain of domestic sales, the Registry is proposing that there should be a 'linked transaction matrix'.[5] This would enable conveyancers within the chain to know of the progress of all the other transactions in the chain, and what steps each had still to take.[6] It could also be used to synchronise the making of contracts and the subsequent completion of transactions. The extent to which it will be necessary or desirable to have a 'chain manager' and who any such manager might be, are matters on which the Land Registry is seeking views. Conveyancers might be under obligations to provide information to the Registry about transactions in which they had been instructed to enable such linked transactions to be identified.[7] The Registry might, therefore, be involved in a proposed transaction at an even earlier stage than will be the case where the transaction is free-standing.

---

1   See para **7.57**.
2   The Inland Revenue is presently consulting on a system of stamp duty that would be payable on dematerialised transactions: see *Modernising Stamp Duty on land and buildings in the UK*, April 2002.
3   In this one respect it resembles unregistered conveyancing.
4   *E-Conveyancing: A Land Registry Consultation*, para 8.16.
5   See ibid, para 6.3.
6   To protect confidentiality, the names of the clients would not be known. Transactions would probably be recorded by reference to the name of the firm of conveyancers acting for a party and that firm's reference.
7   See further, para **7.41**.

The provisions of the LRA 2002

The electronic communications network

7.37 The provisions of the LRA 2002 reflect the model of e-conveyancing that is set out above. Under s 92(1), the registrar may provide, or arrange for the provision of, an electronic communications network. This network is to be used for such purposes as the registrar sees fit relating to registration or the carrying on of transactions which involve registration and are capable of being effected electronically. Those purposes are necessarily wide and, as will be apparent from what has been said in paras **7.28–7.36**, they are intended to cover the entire life of a conveyancing transaction from the stage when a property is put on the market to the completion of its sale. The network might therefore be used:

 — for the provision of information by a party to a transaction that had to be completed by registration[1] either to another party or to the registrar;
 — for the preparation and communication of conveyancing documents; and
 — for the purpose of registering any disposition.

As a necessary adjunct to the creation of the electronic communications network and the system of e-conveyancing that it will support, there are specific rule-making powers to make provision about the communication of documents in electronic form to the registrar and for their electronic storage.[2]

Network access agreements

7.38 A person who is not a member of the Land Registry will only be able to access the network if he enters into a network access agreement made with the registrar.[3] That agreement may authorise access for one or more of the following purposes:

(a) the communication, posting or retrieval of information;

---

[1] This might include a disposition of unregistered land that was subject to the requirement of compulsory registration. It remains to be seen how far e-conveyancing will come to be used in relation to first registrations. First registration is not a straightforward matter in many cases and it is likely that it will have to remain the responsibility of the Registry except perhaps in relation to the grant of certain short leases that have to be registered.

[2] LRA 2002, s 95.

[3] Ibid, Sch 5, para 1(1).

(b) the making of changes to the register of title[1] or to the cautions register;[2]
(c) the issue of official search certificates;
(d) the issue of official copies;[3] or
(e) such other conveyancing purposes as the registrar thinks fit.[4]

There is no reason why the level of access should be the same for all professionals. For example, whereas a conveyancer might be authorised to have access for all five of the purposes listed above, an estate agent might only require access for the first of them. The second, third and fourth of the purposes listed above are functions that are presently performed by the registrar, and the fifth might include such functions. Subject to provision in rules,[5] the authority conferred by a network access agreement may include the performance of the registrar's functions.[6] Indeed, it is difficult to see how e-conveyancing as it is presently visualised could be carried out by conveyancers unless they could carry out functions that are vested in the registrar. For example, parties to a conveyancing transaction will wish to make an official search of the register and obtain official copies of documents referred to in it.

7.39 The criteria which have to be met by an applicant for a network access agreement will be laid down in rules.[7] If the applicant meets those criteria, the registrar *must* enter into a network access agreement with him.[8] In making rules as to the relevant criteria, the Lord Chancellor is required to have regard to, in particular, the need to secure:

(a) the confidentiality of private information kept on the network;
(b) competence in relation to the use of the network (in particular for the making of changes); and

---

1   See para **5.48**.
2   See para **5.63**.
3   See para **5.20**.
4   LRA 2002, Sch 5, para 1(2).
5   The Lord Chancellor is required to consult before he makes such rules: LRA 2002, Sch 5, para 11(1), (2). Such rules are made by statutory instrument and are subject to affirmative resolution, the most stringent form of scrutiny that there is for statutory instruments: see LRA 2002, s 128(5).
6   LRA 2002, Sch 5, para 1(3).
7   Once again, the Lord Chancellor can only make such rules after consultation (LRA 2002, Sch 5, para 11(1), (2)) and they are then subject to affirmative resolution procedure (LRA 2002, s 128(5)).
8   LRA 2002, Sch 5, para 1(4).

(c)   the adequate insurance of potential liabilities in connection with the use of the network.[1]

It is not difficult to see what underlies these requirements. The Land Registry guarantees the register and the registrar must pay indemnity where loss is suffered as a result of a mistake in the register.[2] Under the system of e-conveyancing that will be established under the LRA 2002, it will be conveyancers who initiate changes to the register for the future. It is therefore important that the proper steps are taken to minimise the risk that mistakes may be made. To the same end, the Act specifically empowers the registrar to provide, or to arrange for the provision of, education and training in relation to the use of the network.[3] This will, presumably, take the form of online training packages.

Terms of access

The general principle

7.40 The LRA 2002 makes provision as to the terms upon which access to the network will be permitted. The general principle is that the terms on which access to the network is authorised will be such as the registrar thinks fit, and, in particular, may include charges for access.[4] That general principle is subject to a number of qualifications, which are set out in the following paragraphs.

The purposes for which the power to authorise may be exercised

7.41 The LRA 2002 specifies the purposes for which access may be authorised.

(1)   The first is for regulating the use of the network.[5] This is the principal purpose for which access will be given.

(2)   The second is for securing that the person who is granted access uses the network to carry out such 'qualifying transactions' as may be specified in, or under, the agreement.[6] A 'qualifying transaction' is a transaction that involves registration and is capable of being effected electronically.[7] In consequence of this

---

1   LRA 2002, Sch 5, para 11(3).
2   See para **5.67**.
3   LRA 2002, Sch 5, para 10.
4   Ibid, para 2(1).
5   Ibid, para 2(2).
6   Ibid, para 2(2)(a).
7   Ibid, para 12.

provision, the terms of access may *require* the person authorised to conduct all of a particular type or types of transaction electronically. It would not be open to him to carry them out in paper form. The object is to ensure a speedy transition from a paper-based system of conveyancing to one that is wholly electronic. The period during which the paper-based and electronic systems exist side by side has to be kept as short as possible because of the difficulties to which it will give rise, particularly in chain transactions. It is to be noted that, in consequence of this provision, conveyancers who have network access agreements will have to conduct the specified transactions electronically before the power to make electronic conveyancing compulsory[1] is exercised.

(3) The third is for such other purposes relating to the carrying on of qualifying transactions as rules may provide.[2] As a result of this provision, it will be possible to provide that a person authorised must use the network for purposes such as providing official search certificates and obtaining official copies.

(4) The fourth is for enabling network transactions to be monitored.[3] The intention of this provision is that those who are authorised to use the network may have to provide the registrar (or whoever has responsibility for the matter) with information about linked transactions. This will enable chains to be managed in the way explained in para **7.36**.[4]

The obligation to comply with network transaction rules

7.42 It is to be a condition of a network access agreement that the person granted access complies with the network transaction rules that are in force for the time being.[5] The network transaction rules will make provision about 'how to go about network transactions'.[6] These rules will tell conveyancers how to conduct e-conveyancing and, in particular, they may include provision about the procedure to be followed and the supply of information, including information about unregistered interests.[7] It has been explained elsewhere that, under s 71 of the LRA 2002, there is a duty imposed on a person applying for first registration

---

1 Contained in LRA 2002, s 93; see also para **7.53**.
2 LRA 2002, Sch 5, para 2(2)(b).
3 Ibid, Sch 5, para 2(2)(c).
4 See further, para **7.50**.
5 LRA 2002, Sch 5, para 2(3).
6 Ibid, Sch 5, para 5(1).
7 Ibid, Sch 5, para 5(2).

or to register a registrable disposition to disclose any unregistered interest which overrides either first registration or a registrable disposition.[1] It is likely that network transaction rules will require authorised conveyancers to disclose such interests so that they can be protected on the register.[2] This will be so, even if the conveyancer's client does not want the interest disclosed.[3] It is also probable that network transaction rules will provide for the simultaneous registration of dispositions of registered land even before that is made compulsory under s 93.[4] For the purposes of the LRA 2002, network transaction rules are land registration rules.[5] As such they will be made by the Lord Chancellor with the advice and assistance of the Rules Committee.[6]

Terms of access regulated by rules

7.43 The LRA 2002 provides that rules may regulate the terms on which access to the network is authorised.[7] It is thought that such rules may prescribe terms that will be contained in all network access agreements, although these terms are likely to vary according to the level of access that is granted.[8]

Termination of access

7.44 The LRA 2002 makes provision for the termination of a network access agreement both by the person authorised and by the registrar. As regards the former, the person authorised may terminate the agreement at any time by notice to the registrar.[9] By contrast, the circumstances in which the registrar may terminate such an agreement are much more limited. The matter will be governed by rules, which may make provision about:

–   the grounds of termination;
–   the procedure to be followed in relation to termination; and
–   the suspension of termination pending any appeal.[10]

---

1   See paras **2.51**, **3.109**.
2   The policy underlying this is the fundamental principle on which the LRA 2002 rests of achieving a conclusive register: see para **1.7**.
3   Cf LRA 2002, Sch 5, para 6; see also para **7.47**
4   For ibid, s 93, see para **7.53**.
5   See ibid, s 132(1).
6   Ibid, s 127. See paras **11.4–11.6**.
7   Ibid, Sch 5, para 2(4). The Lord Chancellor can only make such rules after consultation (Sch 5, para 11(1), (2)) and they are then subject to affirmative resolution procedure (s 128(5)).
8   See (2001) Law Com No 271, para 13.54; see also para **7.38**.
9   LRA 2002, Sch 5, para 3(1).
10 Ibid, Sch 5, para 3(2). The Lord Chancellor can only make such rules after consultation (Sch 5, para 11(1), (2)) and they are then subject to affirmative resolution procedure (s 128(5)).

Those rules may, in particular, authorise the registrar to terminate a network access agreement, if the person granted access:

— fails to comply with the terms of the agreement;
— ceases to be a person with whom the registrar would be required to enter into a network access agreement conferring the authority which the agreement confers; or
— does not meet such conditions as those rules may provide.[1]

7.45 Termination of access by the registrar will be a very serious matter and a remedy of last resort. As all conveyancing will be e-conveyancing within a comparatively short time, termination of access will prevent a person from acting as a conveyancer. A network access agreement will normally be a contract,[2] and the registrar will, therefore, have contractual remedies that he can pursue rather than terminating access.

7.46 In any event, the LRA 2002 makes provision for appeals by a person aggrieved by a decision of the registrar:

— not to enter into a network access agreement;[3] or
— to terminate an existing network access agreement.[4]

The appeal will be to the Adjudicator.[5] It is the one occasion under the Act in which he may hear an appeal from a decision of the registrar.[6] An appeal to the Adjudicator is likely to be quicker, cheaper and more informal than any appeal to a court. In any event, as has been explained in para **7.44**, rules are likely to make provision for the termination of an agreement to be suspended pending an appeal. The Adjudicator will be able to substitute his own decision for that of the registrar and give the necessary directions accordingly.[7] A further appeal lies from the Adjudicator to the High Court, but only on a point of law.[8]

---

1   LRA 2002, Sch 5, para 3(3).
2   It will not be a contract in cases where the body given authority is another emanation of the Crown. The Crown is one and indivisible and cannot contract with itself.
3   In other words, where the registrar takes the view that the applicant does not satisfy the criteria for entry into such an agreement: see para **7.39**.
4   LRA 2002, Sch 5, para 4(1).
5   Ibid. For the office of Adjudicator, see para **9.10**. Rules may make provision about such appeals: LRA 2002, Sch 5, para 4(3).
6   Ibid, s 108(1)(b). See also para **9.12**.
7   Ibid, Sch 5, para 4(2).
8   Ibid, s 111(2).

Overriding nature of network access obligations

7.47 It will be apparent from what has been said above that there could be a conflict between a conveyancer's obligations to the registrar under a network access agreement and his obligations to his client. For example, a client might not want the conveyancer to disclose the fact that the land which he was purchasing was subject to an unregistered interest that overrode a registered disposition.[1] Indeed, the situation might be more extreme: the client might not wish the transaction to be conducted in electronic form at all.[2] The LRA 2002 provides that the obligation under the network access agreement prevails and discharges the other obligation to the extent that the two conflict.[3] Such cases are unlikely to be common in practice. It is plainly very important that a conveyancer should so far as possible respect his client's wishes and, in particular, observe his obligations of confidentiality to his client.[4] However, when the overriding objectives of the Act, namely to secure an effective system of e-conveyancing and to ensure that the register is as conclusive as it can be made, conflict with a client's wishes, the latter must yield to the former. Furthermore, in those circumstances, the conveyancer must be protected against any claim that could otherwise be brought against him by his client.

Presumption of authority

7.48 When e-conveyancing is first introduced, it seems likely that conveyancers will execute electronic documents on behalf of their clients. This is because it is not thought that many individuals will have their own electronic signatures at that stage.[5] However, a conveyancer has no implied authority to sign a contract on behalf of his client.[6] If, therefore, a conveyancer is to sign on behalf of his client, he must have actual authority to do so. This means that he must obtain his client's written authority. However, if no provision were made in the LRA 2002, the other party's conveyancer would be entitled to see that authority before he was prepared to enter into the contract. It would rather defeat the purposes of e-conveyancing if the parties had to

---

1   See para **7.42**.

2   In such a case, a conveyancer who had entered into a network access agreement would in practice have to decline to act.

3   LRA 2002, Sch 5, para 6.

4   It is clear that the Land Registry is well aware of this point: see *E-Conveyancing: A Land Registry Consultation*, para 6.3.

5   See paras **7.32–7.33**.

6   'A solicitor has no ostensible or apparent authority to sign a contract on behalf of a client so as to bind him when there is no contract in fact': *H Clark (Doncaster) Ltd v Wilkinson* [1965] Ch 694, at p 702, *per* Lord Denning MR.

exchange copies of the written authority given to them by their respective clients.

7.49 The way in which this problem is to be addressed is as follows. First, it is intended to provide under network transaction rules that a conveyancer should obtain the written authority of his client to sign any electronic documents on that client's behalf.[1] The need for such authority might, for example, be explained in a conveyancer's standard client care letter. Secondly, the LRA 2002 creates a presumption of authority in certain cases where a conveyancer authenticates an electronic document on behalf of his client. It applies where a person who is authorised under a network access agreement to use the network to make either a disposition or contract, purports to do so as agent. In favour of any other party, that person will be deemed to be acting with the authority of his or her principal if the document which purports to effect the disposition or to be a contract:

- purports to be authenticated by him or her as agent; and
- contains a statement to the effect that he is acting under the authority of his or her principal.[2]

Concerns have been expressed that this power could enable a dishonest conveyancer to defraud his client of his property. However, a conveyancer would be acting very foolishly if he authenticated an electronic document which explicitly stated that he had his client's authority when in fact he had not obtained it. One feature of the proposed e-conveyancing system is that the Registry will be able to identify the source of any entry on the register.[3] The source of any fraud would therefore be readily apparent.

Management of network transactions

7.50 It has been explained above that it is envisaged that the electronic system should provide some means for managing linked transactions.[4] The objective is to try to facilitate chains of domestic sales, in an attempt to ensure that fewer such chains 'break'. One aspect of the strategy has already been mentioned. Under the terms of a network access agreement, a conveyancer may be obliged to provide monitoring

---

1   See (2001) Law Com No 271, para 13.62.
2   LRA 2002, Sch 5, para 8.
3   On this 'audit trail', see *E-Conveyancing: A Land Registry Consultation*, para 4.1.5.
4   See para **7.36**.

information.[1] The LRA 2002 goes further than that. It empowers the registrar – or the person to whom he has delegated his 'chain management' functions[2] – to use such monitoring information[3] for the purposes of managing network transactions.[4] He is specifically authorised to disclose such information to persons authorised to use the network, and may authorise further disclosure, if he considers it necessary or desirable to do so.[5] This will mean that the registrar (or whoever is authorised to manage such transactions) can disclose to other parties in the chain the state of progress of the other transactions in the chain.[6] The Registry is consulting on the extent to which such chain management should, for example, involve the chain manager in a more pro-active role rather than just providing information about the state of the chain.[7]

Do-it-yourself conveyancing

7.51 Once there is a network, the LRA 2002 imposes a duty on the registrar to provide such assistance as he thinks appropriate for the purpose of enabling persons engaged in qualifying transactions who wish to do their own conveyancing to do so by means of the network.[8] The registrar is not allowed to provide legal advice.[9] It is presently envisaged that such 'DIY conveyancers' would be allowed to use dedicated terminals at District Land Registries to conduct e-conveyancing, where their identities could be checked and they could be given advice on the use of the electronic system.[10]

MAKING E-CONVEYANCING COMPULSORY

7.52 The third of the four issues raised in para **7.7** concerns how e-conveyancing may be made compulsory. It is inevitable that it will have to be made compulsory because many of the benefits of e-conveyancing will be lost if paper and electronic dispositions can subsist side by side for any length of time. For example, where there is a

---

1   See para **7.41**(4).
2   See LRA 2002, Sch 5, para 9(2).
3   See ibid, Sch 5, para 9(3).
4   Ibid, Sch 5, para 9(1).
5   Ibid, Sch 5, para 9(1).
6   As has been explained at para **7.36**, the names of the parties in the chain would not be disclosed. It would only be the names of the conveyancers acting and the file reference that would be made known.
7   See *E-Conveyancing: A Land Registry Consultation*, para 8.8.
8   LRA 2002, Sch 5, para 7(1).
9   Ibid, Sch 5, para 7(2).
10 See *E-Conveyancing: A Land Registry Consultation*, para 8.17.

chain of sale, the chain moves at the speed of the slowest link. The potential to speed up such linked transactions by means of e-conveyancing would be defeated if paper-based links could continue.

7.53 Section 93 of the LRA 2002 contains provisions for making e-conveyancing compulsory. First, the section applies to dispositions of:

– a registered estate or charge; or
– an interest which is the subject of a notice in the register,

where that disposition is of a description specified in rules.[1] Because the transactions can be specified by rules, it will be possible to introduce compulsory e-conveyancing on a disposition-by-disposition basis. Indeed, that seems likely. The potential range of dispositions is substantial: it includes, quite expressly, an agreement between chargees that the respective priorities of their charges be changed.[2] It also includes dispositions of interests that are protected by the entry of a notice, such as equitable charges, or the benefit of an option or other estate contract. It has been explained above that it is not at present possible to register transfers of such interests, but it is intended that it should become so when they can be made electronically.[3]

7.54 Secondly, the section defines the nature of compulsory e-conveyancing. It embodies the essential principle in the LRA 2002 that the making of the disposition and its registration should be simultaneous. This is an important part of the strategy of making the register conclusive at any given time by eliminating the 'registration gap'.[4] A disposition that is required to be made electronically, or a contract to make such a disposition will only have effect if it is made by means of a document in electronic form, is electronically communicated to the registrar, and the relevant registration requirements are met.[5] The relevant registration requirements are, in the case of registrable dispositions, those that are prescribed in Sch 2 to the LRA 2002.[6] In the case of any other disposition, or a contract to make a disposition, the registration requirements will be prescribed by rules.[7] Under s 27(1) of the Act, a disposition of a registered estate does not

---

[1]   LRA 2002, s 93(1).
[2]   Ibid, s 93(6). See also para **4.10**.
[3]   See para **7.11**.
[4]   See paras **1.8**, **7.5**.
[5]   LRA 2002, s 93(2).
[6]   Ibid, s 93(3)(a). For Sch 2, see paras **3.12** et seq.
[7]   Ibid, s 93(3)(b).

operate at law until the registration requirements of Sch 2 are met.[1] As an electronic disposition under s 93 will have no effect at all except on registration, s 27(1) is disapplied in relation to such dispositions.[2]

OTHER STEPS TO FACILITATE E-CONVEYANCING

7.55 The final issue raised in para **7.7** concerns the other steps that are needed to ensure that e-conveyancing operates as smoothly as possible. Two matters require comment in this regard.

Stamp duty

7.56 First, it has already been mentioned that stamp duty legislation will have to be changed to accommodate e-conveyancing, and that the Inland Revenue is in the process of consulting on its proposals.[3]

Electronic settlement

7.57 Secondly, the most important change that is needed concerns the system of settlement when a conveyancing transaction is completed. If dispositions are to be registered simultaneously, the necessary payments must also be made at the same time. The LRA 2002 provides that the registrar may take such steps as he thinks fit for the purpose of securing the provision of a system of electronic settlement in relation to transactions involving registration.[4] As is explained below,[5] the registrar also has power under the Act, if he considers it expedient, to form, or participate in the formation of, a company, or purchase, or invest in, a company in connection with this system of electronic settlement.[6] These provisions, which were added at a late stage in the passage of the LRA 2002 through Parliament,[7] ensure that the registrar has all the necessary powers that he might need to provide an effective system of electronic settlement. In particular, it means that there can be no doubt as to his ability to enter into a collaborative venture with a private sector partner to develop such a system. The present system of settlement is not adequate for an effective e-conveyancing system.[8] The

---

[1]   See paras **3.12** et seq.
[2]   LRA 2002, s 93(4).
[3]   See para **7.34**.
[4]   LRA 2002, s 94.
[5]   See para **10.9**.
[6]   LRA 2002, s 106.
[7]   Namely at Report and Third Reading in the House of Commons.
[8]   See the criticisms in *E-Conveyancing: A Land Registry Consultation*, paras 7.2, 7.3.

Land Registry has set out what it will require of any system of electronic settlement.[1] In particular, it wants to see an integrated e-conveyancing and payments system, so that all monies can be dealt with simultaneously on completion of any transaction, including the payment of Stamp Duty and Land Registry fees. The Registry has suggested various options as to how this might be achieved, including an electronic transfer system, a real-time settlement system (akin to CREST, which is used in relation to dealings in shares at the London Stock Exchange), or an escrow bank.

---

[1]   See *E-Conveyancing: A Land Registry Consultation*, Part 7.

CHAPTER 8

ADVERSE POSSESSION

THE MAIN CHANGES AT A GLANCE

8.1   One of the most striking features of the LRA 2002 is that it disapplies the present law of adverse possession in relation to registered land. In its place it substitutes a new scheme that reflects the principles underlying registered conveyancing. Although these changes are fundamental, the relevant provisions of the Act consist of just the three sections that make up Part 9 of the Act together with Sch 6.[1]

8.2   The new system is intended to reflect the fact that, in relation to registered land, the basis of title is primarily registration rather than possession. The system is also intended to strike a fairer balance between landowner and squatter,[2] by shifting that balance in favour of the registered owner. There is little doubt that the principles of adverse possession have been abused. During the passage of the Bill, Baroness Scotland of Asthall, the Parliamentary Secretary in the Lord Chancellor's Department, made it clear that the Government's intention was to strengthen the position of registered proprietors and made no apology for doing so. She explained that, every year, the Land Registry received over 20,000 applications for registration based in whole or in part on adverse possession. In about 15,000 of those cases, the applicant was successful. Many cases were disputed and had to be resolved either by the courts or in hearings before the Solicitor to HM Land Registry. About three-quarters of the hearings before the Solicitor involved squatters, and in approximately 60 per cent of the cases, the squatter succeeded in whole or in part.[3] In practice, the new provisions are likely to provide a strong incentive to all owners of unregistered

---

[1]   See (2001) Law Com No 271, paras 2.69–2.74 and Part XIV.
[2]   Ibid, para 14.4. The proposals for change were supported in principle by 60 per cent of those who responded to (1998) Law Com No 254 on the issue.
[3]   *Hansard* (HL), 30 October 2001, vol 627, col 1332.

land to register their titles, and indeed, it is clear that the Government intended this to be the case.[1]

8.3   The main changes made by the LRA 2002 are as follows.

– The Act replaces the previous 12-year limitation period with a scheme under which there is no limitation period as such. A squatter's adverse possession, however long, will not of itself bar the registered proprietor's title to a registered estate.
– A squatter will be able to apply to be registered as proprietor after 10 years' adverse possession.
– If the application is not opposed by any of those whom the registrar is required to notify, the squatter will be registered as proprietor of the land.
– If any of those notified do oppose the application it will be refused, unless the squatter can bring himself within one of three limited exceptions.
– If the application for registration is refused, but the squatter remains in adverse possession for a further 2 years, he will be entitled to make a new application for registration, and, on this occasion, will be registered as proprietor regardless of any objection.
– Where the registered proprietor commences proceedings to recover possession from a squatter, those proceedings will succeed unless the squatter can make out one of a number of limited defences.
– Effect of registration.

The Act contains transitional provisions to protect the rights of squatters who have barred the rights of the registered proprietor prior to the commencement of the Act.

THE AIMS OF THE SCHEME

8.4   The new scheme recognises that, while the present law of adverse possession is both appropriate and necessary for unregistered land, it is much harder to justify in relation to registered land. The basis of title to registered land is the fact of registration not possession. However, although it is a fundamental theme of the LRA 2002 that registration should, of itself, protect the registered proprietor, this is subject to

---

[1]   See the comments of Baroness Scotland of Asthall: *Hansard* (HL), 30 October 2001, vol 627, col 1379.

certain qualifications. Adverse possession has some limited justification even in relation to registered land.[1] In particular, it is necessary to ensure that land remains marketable where, for example, the registered proprietor has disappeared, or where he has been given the opportunity to vindicate his rights but has failed to do so. Furthermore, the register may be conclusive as to the ownership of a registered estate, but is not normally conclusive as to boundaries, because of the general boundaries rule and the fact that the power to fix boundaries is seldom exercised.[2] The protection given by the Act is not absolute, but recognises that adverse possession does have a limited role to play even in relation to registered land.

8.5   The new scheme could not apply to unregistered land, not only because there would not be any administrative framework within which it could operate, but also because the principles of adverse possession are essential to a system of unregistered conveyancing. Proof of title to unregistered land involves proof of a suitable root of title that is at least 15 years old and an unbroken chain of title linking that root to the landowner who is conveying the land.[3] The period prescribed by law for the root of title has always been directly linked to the limitation period applicable to possession actions.[4] It follows that, without principles of limitation and adverse possession, it would never be possible to deduce title to unregistered land. It would not be possible to be sure that any adverse claims to the land had been barred. The fact that the new scheme could not apply to unregistered land is not regarded as a reason for leaving the existing law in place for registered land, even though it could lead to anomalies.[5] One of the guiding principles of the LRA 2002 is that the rational development of registered land cannot be constrained because the principles applicable to unregistered land are different.[6] This is particularly so given the aim to eliminate unregistered land as soon as possible.[7]

---

[1]   See (1998) Law Com No 254, paras 10.11–10.16; (2001) Law Com No 271, para 2.72.

[2]   See LRA 2002, s 60; see also paras **5.7, 5.8**.

[3]   LPA 1925, s 44(1); LPA 1969, s 23.

[4]   Presently 12 years in most cases: see LA 1980, s 15(1). For the link between the limitation period and the length of title required, see Martin Dockray, 'Why do we need adverse possession?' [1985] Conv 272.

[5]   As, for example, where a squatter is in adverse possession of land that includes both registered and unregistered titles.

[6]   See para **1.6**.

[7]   See (2001) Law Com No 271, paras 1.6, 2.9. Many other Commonwealth countries which have title registration systems have either abolished adverse possession in relation to registered titles, or have restricted it.

8.6   The LRA 2002 makes provision to cover three situations.

(1)   Where a squatter applies to be registered as proprietor.
(2)   Where a squatter could have applied to be registered as proprietor but, before he did so, he was evicted by the registered proprietor (or person claiming under him).
(3)   Where the registered proprietor (or person claiming under him) takes proceedings to recover possession from a squatter.

The principles laid down in the Act are intended to ensure that the outcome will be the same whichever of these three situations occurs.

THE EFFECT OF THE LRA 2002

The general principle: no limitation period for the recovery of a registered estate or rentcharge

8.7   The governing principle of the new scheme is that where an estate or rentcharge is registered with its own title:

–   in relation to an action to recover land, no period of limitation under the LA 1980[1] runs against *any person other than a chargee;*[2]
–   in relation to a claim to redeem a charge against a chargee in possession, no period of limitation under the LA 1980[3] runs against *any person.*[4]

As a result, as there is no applicable period of limitation, a registered proprietor's title can never be extinguished under the LA 1980, s 17.[5] Ironically, this may be good news for squatters. As Lord Goodhart explained during the Second Reading Debate on the Bill in the House of Lords: 'this change will help rather than hinder squatters because unless and until squatters in a particular building serve an application for title to that building under Schedule 6, the owner will not be under any pressure to remove them'.[6]

---

1   See LA 1980, s 15.
2   LRA 2002, s 96(1). For the reason for the exception in relation to chargees, see para **8.8**.
3   See LA 1980, s 16.
4   LRA 2002, s 96(2). See further, para **8.9**.
5   Ibid, s 96(3).
6   *Hansard* (HL), 3 July 2001, vol 626, col 792.

The application of the principle to registered estates and rentcharges

8.8   The limitation periods for the recovery of land are disapplied *only* in relation to registered estates in land and registered rentcharges, because the register is conclusive as to ownership of such estates and rentcharges. The limitation periods laid down in the LA 1980 will continue to apply in the following circumstances where there has been adverse possession of registered land:

–   where there has been adverse possession against a leasehold estate where the lease was granted for 21 years or less prior to the coming into force of the LRA 2002, and which, consequently, took effect as an overriding interest;[1] and
–   where the claim for possession is not brought by a registered proprietor but by a licensee or tenant at will.[2]

The limitation period will also continue to apply to a right of re-entry as where:

–   a lease has become liable to forfeiture for breach of a covenant or condition in the lease; or
–   that right of re-entry has become exercisable in respect of a fee simple for breach of condition or on the occurrence of a specified event.

These rights are not estates in land, and the LA 1980 therefore continues to apply in relation to them.

Mortgagors in possession

8.9   The LRA 2002 does not change the law in relation to mortgagors in possession. Under the Act, where a mortgagor is in possession, the mortgagee's rights to recover possession or to foreclose remain subject to the provisions of LA 1980.[3] As a chargee's right to possession is tied directly to its rights to recover monies under the charge, the two rights

---

1   LRA 1925, s 70(1)(k). Such a lease is not a registered estate and is generally treated in the same way as unregistered land. This type of case will disappear within 21 years of the LRA 2002 coming into force as the only leases that will take effect as overriding interests are leases for 7 years or less.
2   This might happen where a squatter ousted a licensee or tenant at will and the ousted occupier sought to recover possession from that squatter.
3   LRA 2002, s 96(1). The limitation period is 12 years: LA 1980, ss 15(1), 20(4).

should be linked. If the right to recover the money is time-barred,[1] the chargee's remedies to enforce its security should be as well.[2]

Mortgagees in possession

8.10 Under s 16 of the LA 1980, once a mortgagee has been in possession of land for 12 years, the mortgagor loses his right to redeem the mortgage and his title is extinguished, with the result that the mortgagee becomes the owner of the land. The Law Commission criticised this rule as anomalous. It over-protected mortgagees and could no longer be justified.[3] The LRA 2002 therefore disapplies s 16 of the LA 1980 in relation to an estate in land or a rentcharge registered under the LRA 2002.[4]

THE RIGHT TO APPLY FOR REGISTRATION

The general position

8.11 A person may apply to be registered as the proprietor of a registered estate in land if he has been in adverse possession of the estate for the period of 10 years ending on the date of the application.[5] As now, the applicant will have to prove to the registrar that he has been in adverse possession for the relevant period.[6] It will not be presumed.[7]

8.12 It is not necessary for the estate to have been registered throughout the period of adverse possession.[8] If, for example, the squatter commenced adverse possession when the title was unregistered, and the title was voluntarily registered by the owner 6 years later, the squatter would be able to apply to be registered after 4 more years of adverse possession.

---

[1]   It is subject to a 12-year limitation period: see LA 1980, s 20(1).
[2]   See (2001) Law Com No 271, paras 14.12–14.14.
[3]   See ibid, paras 14.15–14.18.
[4]   LRA 2002, s 96(2).
[5]   Ibid, Sch 6, para 1(1). For the reasons why a period of 10 rather than 12 years was chosen, see (2001) Law Com No 271, para 14.19.
[6]   For the present law, see LRA 1925, s 75.
[7]   If an applicant was registered under the scheme provided by the LRA 2002 and it then transpired that he had not in fact been in adverse possession for 10 years, his registration would be a mistake, and there would, therefore, be grounds for an application for rectification of the register: see LRA 2002, Sch 4, paras 2(1)(a), 5(a). See paras **5.51**, **5.58**.
[8]   LRA 2002, Sch 6, para 1(4).

8.13 It is provided that rules may be made to govern the procedure to be followed pursuant to an application under Sch 6 to the LRA 2002.[1]

The meaning of 'adverse possession'

8.14 A person is in adverse possession of an estate in land for the purposes of the LRA 2002 if, but for s 96 of the Act, a period of limitation under s 15 of the LA 1980 would run in his favour in relation to the estate.[2] A person is also to be regarded as having been in adverse possession of an estate in land:

– where he is the successor in title to an estate in the land, during any period of adverse possession by a predecessor in title to that estate, or
– during any period of adverse possession by another person which comes between, and is continuous with, periods of adverse possession of his own.[3]

8.15 It is not, therefore, necessary for the applicant for registration to show that he has himself been in adverse possession for the whole of the 10-year period required under the LRA 2002. It will be sufficient for him to show that he is the successor in title to an earlier squatter from whom he acquired the land, and that, together, the two periods of adverse possession total 10 years. It will also be sufficient if the applicant demonstrates that he has been in adverse possession, has himself been dispossessed by a second squatter, and has then recovered the land from that second squatter, and that, taken together, the periods of adverse possession total 10 years.

8.16 If, however, the applicant for registration is a second squatter who has evicted a previous squatter, the second squatter will not be a successor in title of the first squatter. He will not, therefore, be able to add the first squatter's period of adverse possession to his own in order to demonstrate 10 years' adverse possession. In such circumstances, the second squatter will not be able to apply to be registered until he can show 10 years' adverse possession himself.[4]

---

[1]   LRA 2002, Sch 6, para 15.
[2]   Ibid, Sch 6, para 11(1). The law requires both factual possession and an intention to possess. In the recent decision of *JA Pye (Oxford) Ltd v Graham* [2002] UKHL 30 (4 July 2002), unreported, the House of Lords affirmed the classic statement as to the requirements of intention set out in Slade J in his judgment in *Powell v McFarlane* (1977) 38 P&CR 452.
[3]   LRA 2002, Sch 6, para 11(2).
[4]   See (2001) Law Com No 271, para 14.21.

8.17 The 10-year period of adverse possession must be continuous. If Squatter A abandoned land after several years' adverse possession of it, and, at some later date, Squatter B took adverse possession of it, Squatter B could not consolidate the two periods of adverse possession. The 10-year period would start again from the date when Squatter B took adverse possession.

8.18 The LRA 2002 qualifies the basic principle that adverse possession has the same meaning as it does for the purposes of s 15 of the LA 1980[1] in two respects. First, in determining whether a period of limitation would run under s 15 of the LA 1980, the commencement of any legal proceedings is to be disregarded.[2] Prior to the implementation of the LRA 2002, the commencement of proceedings stopped time running under the LA 1980 for the purposes of that particular action.[3] As the right of recovery is never barred by mere lapse of time under the new statutory scheme, this principle is necessarily inapplicable. Secondly, the Act disapplies a technical rule found in para 6 of Sch 1 to the LA 1980 about the adverse possession of a reversion.[4]

An extended right to apply for registration

8.19 Once a squatter has been in adverse possession for 10 years, the right to apply to be registered will not necessarily be lost if he is evicted. The LRA 2002 provides that a person may apply to be registered as the proprietor of a registered estate in land if he has been evicted by the registered proprietor or a person claiming under that proprietor other than pursuant to a judgment for possession. To be able to make such application he must:

— make his application to be registered within 6 months of his eviction; and
— have been entitled to apply to be registered under the principles explained at para **8.11** on the day before he was evicted.[5]

The rationale for this provision is that it would be wrong, in principle, for the registered proprietor to be able to defeat a squatter's right to apply to be registered by resorting to self-help.[6] Although an objection

---

[1] See para **8.14**.
[2] LRA 2002, Sch 6, para 11(3)(a).
[3] *Markfield Investments Ltd v Evans* [2001] 1 WLR 1321.
[4] LRA 2002, Sch 6, para 11(3)(b).
[5] Ibid, Sch 6, para 1(2).
[6] Cf para **8.6**.

to an application for registration by the registered proprietor will normally be successful, the Act does specify certain limited circumstances in which a squatter has a right to be registered even if the registered proprietor objects to his application.[1] But for this provision, therefore, a registered proprietor could deprive a squatter of his right to be registered.

Circumstances where no valid application can be made

8.20 The LRA 2002 sets out four circumstances in which a squatter cannot make a valid application to be registered as registered proprietor despite 10 years of adverse possession.

(1) Where the squatter is a defendant in proceedings which involve asserting a right to possession of the land.[2] The reason for this limitation is to protect the registered proprietor's right to apply for possession without having to fight off an application for registration at the same time.[3]

(2) Where judgment for possession of the land has been given against the squatter in the last 2 years.[4]

(3) During any period in which the existing registered proprietor is for the purposes of the Limitation (Enemies and War Prisoners) Act 1945 an enemy, or detained in enemy territory, or within 12 months of the end of any such period.[5]

(4) During any period in which the existing registered proprietor is unable because of mental disability to make decisions about issues of the kind to which such an application would give rise,[6] or unable to communicate such decisions because of mental disability or physical impairment.[7] For these purposes 'mental disability' means a disability or disorder of the mind or brain, whether permanent or temporary, which results in an impairment or disturbance of mental functioning.[8]

8.21 As regards the situation in para **8.20**(4), the provisions are

---

[1] See paras **8.29–8.37**. See also, in relation to possession proceedings, para **8.53**.

[2] LRA 2002, Sch 6, para 1(3)(a).

[3] Such an application could otherwise be used tactically by a squatter to harass the registered proprietor.

[4] LRA 2002, Sch 6, para 1(3)(b). Cf LRA 2002, s 98(2); see also para **8.55**.

[5] Ibid, Sch 6, para 8(1)(a) and (b). This provision is necessary to provide equivalent protection to that which is given by the Limitation (Enemies and War Prisoners) Act 1945, s 1.

[6] Ibid, Sch 6, para 8(2)(a).

[7] Ibid, Sch 6, para 8(2)(b).

[8] Ibid, Sch 6, para 8(3).

designed to protect the registered proprietor against the possibility that an application to register may otherwise be successful because the registrar's notice of the application to the registered proprietor goes unanswered. The protection under the LRA 2002 goes beyond what is presently given by s 28 of the LA 1980 in two respects. First, the relevant time at which a person has to be suffering from a disability is at the date that the squatter applies to be registered.[1] Secondly, the protection extends to persons suffering from a physical as well as a mental disability that prevents them from communicating their decisions.

8.22 Where it appears to the registrar that either of the situations described in para **8.20**(3) or (4) applies in relation to an estate in land, he may include a note to that effect in the register.[2]

NOTIFICATION OF THE APPLICATION

The persons to be notified

8.23 Once a valid application has been made under the LRA 2002, the registrar must give notice of the application to those persons who would be prejudiced if the squatter's application was to be successful:

– the proprietor of the estate to which the application relates;[3]
– the proprietor of any registered charge on the estate;[4]
– where the estate is leasehold, the proprietor of any superior registered estate;[5]
– any person who is registered in accordance with rules as a person to be notified;[6] and

---

[1]   As opposed to the date when the adverse possession commenced and the cause of action accrued.
[2]   LRA 2002, Sch 6, para 8(4). In practice, the registrar is unlikely to know that a registered proprietor suffers from a physical or mental disability. It is likely, therefore, that the squatter's application to be registered would, therefore, be successful because the registered proprietor would be unable to propose it. If, in consequence, the squatter is registered as proprietor, that will be a mistake. In those circumstances, the person under a disability will be entitled to apply for rectification of the register: see Sch 4, paras 2(1)(a), 5(a). See also paras **5.51**, **5.58**. He will either recover his land or, at very least, an indemnity for his loss.
[3]   Ibid, Sch 4, para 2(1)(a).
[4]   Ibid, Sch 4, para 2(1)(b).
[5]   Ibid, Sch 4, para 2(1)(c).
[6]   Ibid, Sch 4, para 2(1)(d). A category likely to comprise persons who can satisfy the registrar that they have some estate, right or interest in the land that would or might be prejudicially affected if a squatter was to acquire it, for example, an equitable chargee or a rent charge owner: (2001) Law Com No 271, para 14.33(4).

– such other persons as rules may provide.[1]

What links the persons in that list is that they have the ability to do one or more of the following:

– to take possession proceedings against the squatter;[2]
– to negotiate the grant of a lease or a licence to the squatter in order to regularise his occupation; or
– to take steps to ensure that proceedings are commenced against the squatter by the person who has the immediate right to possession.

The content of the notice

8.24 The notice must inform the recipient of three matters:

– the squatter's application for registration;[3]
– that the recipient can serve a counter-notice on the registrar within such period as may be prescribed by the rules, requiring the registrar to reject the application unless the squatter can satisfy one of three conditions which will entitle him or her to be registered;[4] and
– that if such a counter-notice is not served by at least one of those persons notified of the application, the registrar must enter the applicant as the new proprietor of the registered estate.[5]

8.25 Given the importance of the consequences that flow from the notice procedure, it will be of the greatest importance that the registered proprietor and any registered chargee should maintain their current address for service on the register. This is a matter that practitioners will wish to raise with their clients.

---

[1] LRA 2002, Sch 6, para 2(1)(e). This might include those bodies or persons with a supervisory role in relation to property, such as the Charity Commissioners in relation to land held on charitable trusts, the Church Commissioners as regards benefices, and trustees in bankruptcy in respect of land registered in the bankrupt's name: (2001) Law Com No 271, para 14.33(5).
[2] Both the registered proprietor and the proprietor of a registered charge can take such possession proceedings.
[3] LRA 2002, Sch 6, para 2(1).
[4] Ibid, Sch 6, para 3.
[5] Ibid, Sch 6, paras 2(2), 4.

THE TREATMENT OF THE APPLICATION

If a counter-notice is served

8.26 A person who has received notice of an application for registration may give the registrar a counter-notice before the end of the period prescribed by rules,[1] requiring the registrar to deal with the application under para 5 of Sch 6 to the LRA 2002.[2] The effect of para 5 is explained at paras **8.29–8.37**.

8.27 Once such a counter-notice has been served, the registrar *must* reject the squatter's application for registration unless he can establish that he satisfies one of the three conditions set out in para 5 of Sch 6 to the Act.[3]

If no counter-notice is served

8.28 If no counter-notice is given, the applicant is entitled to be registered as the new proprietor of the estate.[4]

The procedure following service of a counter-notice

8.29 If a counter-notice is served, the squatter is only entitled to be registered as the new proprietor of the estate if he can demonstrate that one of three express exceptional conditions is satisfied.[5] The first condition is intended to embody the equitable principles of proprietary estoppel. The second condition applies where the squatter was otherwise entitled to the land. The third condition applies where the squatter is the owner of adjacent property and has been in adverse possession of the land in question under the mistaken but reasonable belief that he is the owner of it.

8.30 The Law Commission considered that where any one of these conditions was established, the balance of fairness lay with the squatter, and he should, therefore, prevail over the registered proprietor. The first two conditions are not true 'exceptions' in that, even if the LRA 2002 were silent, a squatter could assert his claims to the land in court proceedings. The reason why they are included is procedural. If a squatter claims that he satisfies one of the three conditions, then unless

---

1   LRA 2002, Sch 6, para 3(2).
2   Ibid, Sch 6, para 3(1).
3   Ibid, Sch 6, para 5(1). For those conditions, see para **8.29**.
4   Ibid, Sch 6, para 4.
5   Ibid, Sch 6, para 5(1).

the dispute can be resolved by agreement between the squatter and the registered proprietor, it will have to be referred to the Adjudicator for resolution.[1] That is likely to be cheaper, quicker and less formal than court proceedings.[2]

The first condition: estoppel

8.31 The first condition embodies in statutory form the equitable principles of proprietary estoppel. It is applicable if:

- it would be unconscionable for the registered proprietor to seek to dispossess the applicant, and
- the circumstances are such that the applicant ought to be registered as the proprietor.[3]

In order to show that such an equity by estoppel has arisen in his favour, the applicant will have to prove that he acted to his detriment, in the belief, encouraged or acquiesced in by the registered proprietor, that he owned the land in question.[4] The circumstances will have to be such that it would be unconscionable for the proprietor to deny the applicant that ownership. Cases of this kind will be rare. Usually a person claiming an equity by estoppel such that he or she should be entitled to the land itself will not be in adverse possession, but will be on the land with the consent of the registered proprietor. However, such a situation could arise, as where a person builds a garage or other building on land which he believes to be his own but which, in fact, belongs to another, and where that other person realises the mistake, but acquiesces in it.[5]

8.32 An equity is an inchoate right. It merely gives the claimant a right to apply to the court for relief and the court has a discretion, exercisable according to equitable principles, as to how to give effect to that equity. The court will 'analyse the minimum equity to do justice' to the claimant and will grant relief accordingly.[6] The case may be such

---

[1] See LRA 2002, ss 73(1), (7), 108(1); see also paras **5.38, 9.12**.

[2] See (2001) Law Com No 271, para 14.37. Under the present law, where a person falls within one of the first two categories and has also been in adverse possession for 12 years, he is entitled to apply to be registered on the ground of adverse possession alone, and can do so under LRA 1925, s 75. The registrar *may* refer the matter to the court but, in the alternative, it may be resolved by the Solicitor to HM Land Registry.

[3] LRA 2002, Sch 6, para 5(2).

[4] See Harpum, *Megarry & Wade's Law of Real Property* (Sweet & Maxwell, 6th edn, 2000), ch 13.

[5] See (2001) Law Com No 271, para 14.42.

[6] *Crabb v Arun District Council* [1976] Ch 179, at p 198, *per* Scarman LJ.

that the equity can only be satisfied by a transfer of the owner's freehold or leasehold title to the claimant. But in many other cases, some lesser relief will be appropriate. This might take the form of the grant of some less extensive right over the land, an order for the payment of monetary compensation or merely the grant of an injunction to restrain the defendant from enforcing his strict legal rights against the claimant.[1]

8.33 The Adjudicator will, similarly, have to exercise his discretion as to the relief to be granted when a squatter claims that he is entitled to be registered because an equity by estoppel has arisen in his favour.[2] The LRA 2002 expressly empowers the Adjudicator in such a case to grant the applicant some less extensive form of relief than that he should be registered as proprietor.[3] On any appeal from the Adjudicator's decision to the court,[4] the court has a similar power.[5]

The second condition: some other right to the land

8.34 The second condition is that the applicant is, for some other reason, entitled to be registered as the proprietor of the estate.[6] In other words, this is intended to cover the case where the squatter has a right to the land that would entitle him to be registered as proprietor irrespective of his adverse possession. Such cases may include:

— where the claimant is entitled to the land under the will or intestacy of the deceased proprietor but is on the land without the consent of the deceased's personal representatives; or

— where the claimant contracted to buy the land and paid the purchase price, but where the legal estate was never transferred to him.[7]

Such cases are likely to be rare.

---

1   See Harpum, *Megarry & Wade's Law of Real Property* (Sweet & Maxwell, 6th edn, 2000), para 13-020; (2001) Law Com No 271, para 14.40.
2   LRA 2002, s 110(4).
3   Ibid, s 110(4).
4   Under ibid, s 111(1).
5   Ibid, s 111(3).
6   Ibid, Sch 6, para 5(3).
7   In this second example, the squatter-beneficiary is a beneficiary under a bare trust, and can, therefore, be in adverse possession: see (2001) Law Com No 271, para 14.43 and *Bridges v Mees* [1957] Ch 475.

The third condition: reasonable mistake as to boundary

8.35 The third condition is the most important.[1] Of the three conditions it is the only one which entitles a squatter to be registered *solely* because of his adverse possession. It is, however, narrowly drawn, and to fall within it four matters have to be established:

– the land to which the application relates is adjacent to land belonging to the applicant;
– the exact line of the boundary between the two has not been determined under rules under s 60(3) of the LRA 2002;[2]
– for at least 10 years of the period of adverse possession ending on the date of the application, the applicant (or any predecessor in title) reasonably believed that the land to which the application relates belonged to him;[3] and
– the estate to which the application relates was registered more than one year prior to the date of the application.

8.36 The third condition reflects the fact that, as a consequence of the general boundaries rule found in s 60 of the LRA 2002, the register is not normally conclusive as to boundaries. There is, therefore, a case for permitting a squatter to acquire title within certain tightly drawn limits where he has acted in good faith and has not attempted to 'steal' his neighbour's land. This third condition is intended to meet the common situation where the boundaries as they appear on the ground and as they appear on the register do not coincide. Typically this may happen because the physical features suggest that the boundaries are in one place when in fact they are in another, or because of some mistake in the erection of the fences or walls when a new estate is laid out otherwise than in accordance with the plan.[4] Adverse possession provides a useful "curative" method of dealing with cases of this kind.

---

[1]   LRA 2002, Sch 6, para 5(4).

[2]   See para **5.8**. If the boundary has been 'fixed', the boundary will not be a general boundary within LRA 2002, s 60(1), the register will be conclusive about the boundary, and the exception is, therefore, irrelevant.

[3]   Where a squatter has been ousted by the registered proprietor or some persons claiming under him (see para **8.19**), the relevant date will not be the date of the application, but the day before the date of the applicant's eviction: see LRA 2002, Sch 6, para 5(5).

[4]   According to the Parliamentary Secretary, Lord Chancellor's Department, Baroness Scotland of Asthall, *Hansard* (HL), 17 July 2001, vol 626, cols 1622–1623, the Land Registry had found it 'very common indeed' for there to be small differences between the legal boundaries of an estate and those laid out on the ground. Problems were particularly marked in relation to new estates, where it was said to be 'rare' for properties to be exactly in the same spot marked on the original plan, the result being that a developer may build a whole estate some 3 or 4 inches in the wrong place, causing considerable potential difficulties when the new owners of individual houses naturally assume that their garden fence marks their boundary, and plan their gardens accordingly, without reference to the original plan.

8.37 Something must be said of the four requirements (listed in para **8.35**) that have to be met to establish the third condition.

–   The first requirement is factual. The applicant must own adjacent land.[1] The third condition is therefore restricted to disputes about the location of the boundary between two properties.
–   The second requirement is to show the necessary mental element. Adverse possession has a mental element. The squatter has to show that, for the limitation period, he had an intention to exclude the world including the true owner. One way in which he may show this intention is by proving that he believed he was the owner of the land which he claims.[2] If the squatter has been in possession of land for a period in excess of 10 years, in circumstances where the physical boundaries of the land suggest that it belongs to him, those facts are likely to raise a presumption that the squatter had the necessary intention required to establish this exception. It will then be incumbent on the registered proprietor to show that the squatter knew or ought to have known that the land did not belong to him, for example, by proving that he had told the squatter that the land was not the squatter's.[3]
–   The third requirement is that the boundary must be a general and not a fixed boundary. The whole justification for the third condition is the fact that the register is not normally conclusive as to boundaries. However, it is possible to fix boundaries so that the general boundaries rule does not apply.[4] Where that has been done, the third condition will not apply. Landowners who fear encroachment on their land in cases where the boundaries are not clear on the ground can, therefore, exclude any possibility that the third condition might apply.[5]
–   The provision that the land to which the application relates was registered more than one year prior to the date of the application is necessary as, under the LRA 2002, the third condition can be established after 10 years' adverse possession. By contrast, title to unregistered land can usually only be acquired after 12 years' adverse possession. In the absence of this fourth requirement, if an

---

[1]   There is no requirement that his title should be registered.
[2]   See, eg, *Prudential Assurance Co Ltd v Waterloo Real Estate Inc* [1999] 2 EGLR 85.
[3]   See (2001) Law Com No 271, para 14.52.
[4]   LRA 2002, s 60(1), (3); see also para **5.8**.
[5]   There is a power to make rules which require a boundary to be fixed in particular circumstances: see LRA 2002, s 60(3)(a). It is likely that rules will require a successful applicant under this third condition to have the boundary with the remaining land of the registered proprietor fixed to prevent any further applications: see (2001) Law Com No 271, para 9.13; see also para **5.8**.

owner applied to register his title at a time when a squatter had been in adverse possession of unregistered land for more than 10 years but less than 12 years, and the requirements of the third exception were otherwise fulfilled, the squatter could apply immediately for registration as proprietor, and the owner would have no opportunity to evict him.

The squatter's right to make further application

8.38 The new scheme is intended to produce a definite result. The LRA 2002 therefore provides for the steps that may be taken by both the squatter and the registered proprietor following the rejection of a squatter's application to be registered after service of a counter-notice and in circumstances where none of the special exceptions were fulfilled.

8.39 Where a squatter's application to be registered is rejected, he may make a further application to be registered as the proprietor of the estate if he remains in adverse possession of the estate from the date of the application until 2 years after the date of its rejection.[1]

8.40 The effect of this provision is that a proprietor of a registered estate or charge will usually have one chance to remove the squatter by taking possession proceedings against him or by agreeing to grant him a lease or licence (so that he ceases to be in adverse possession). But if he fails to take such steps within 2 years of the rejection of the squatter's action he stands to lose his land. If the registered proprietor *does* bring possession proceedings within that 2-year period, the squatter will have no defence and the registered proprietor will be able to seek summary judgment.

8.41 The squatter will not be able to make a new application to be registered as proprietor in three situations.[2]

- The first is where he is a defendant in proceedings which involve asserting a right to possession of the land.
- The second is where a judgment for possession of the land has been given against him in the last 2 years.

---

[1] LRA 2002, Sch 6, para 6(1).
[2] Ibid, Sch 6, para 6(2).

- The third is where he has been evicted from the land pursuant to a judgment for possession.

Subject to these exceptions, if a squatter makes a new application, he is entitled to be entered as the new proprietor of the estate.[1]

8.42 It follows from what is said in the previous paragraph that the squatter *will* be entitled to be registered in the following situations.

- The first is where the registered proprietor obtains a judgment for possession against the squatter in proceedings commenced within 2 years of the rejection of the latter's application to be registered, but then fails to enforce that judgment within 2 years. The LRA 2002 expressly provides that, in those circumstances, the proprietor's judgment for possession ceases to be enforceable.[2]
- The second is where the registered proprietor of the estate or charge commences proceedings against the squatter within 2 years of the rejection of the latter's application, but they are discontinued or struck out after the 2-year period has elapsed. Provided that the squatter has remained in adverse possession throughout, he is then entitled to make a new application to be registered.[3]

In other words, it is not enough for the registered proprietor to commence proceedings within 2 years of the rejection of the squatter's application to be registered. The proprietor must both obtain judgment and then enforce it.

The status of the squatter's right to be registered

8.43 There will be five situations in which a squatter will acquire an indefeasible statutory right to be registered as proprietor in place of the registered proprietor. They are:

- where no counter-notice is served in response to the squatter's application to be registered;
- where the squatter establishes that one of the three exceptional conditions applies;

---

[1]   LRA 2002, Sch 6, para 7.

[2]   Ibid, s 98(4). In the absence of this provision, the registered proprietor of the estate or charge would have 6 years either to bring an action on the judgment for possession (LA 1980, s 24(1)), or to execute the judgment without leave of the court (Civil Procedure Rules 1998 (CPR 1998), SI 1998/3132, Sch 1, r 46.2(a)).

[3]   This follows from LRA 2002, Sch 6, para 6(2).

- where the squatter becomes entitled to re-apply to be registered;
- where the squatter has a defence to possession proceedings;[1] or
- where the squatter had barred the rights of the registered proprietor prior to the commencement of the LRA 2002.

This right to be registered is necessarily a proprietary right.[2] As such, the squatter may assert it against the registered proprietor. It will also bind any third party to whom the registered proprietor makes a registered disposition of the land, provided that the squatter was in actual occupation of the land.[3] The Act does not give effect to the squatter's right to be registered by means of a trust, as does the present law,[4] given the criticisms of that device.[5]

The effect of registration

The general principle

8.44 Where a squatter's application is successful and a person is registered as the proprietor of an estate in land against which he had adversely possessed, the title by virtue of adverse possession which he had at the time of the application is extinguished.[6] As a result, the squatter is the successor in title to the previously registered proprietor. This means that in most cases the squatter will be registered with absolute title because the former registered owner will have been registered with absolute title. The squatter will only be registered with possessory title on the rare occasion when the former registered owner was registered with possessory title.

8.45 Where the estate acquired is a lease which was granted after 1995, the registration of the squatter as the new proprietor will operate as an 'excluded assignment' under s 11 of the Landlord and Tenant (Covenants) Act 1995. As a result, the former tenant will remain liable on the covenants in the lease.

8.46 The registration of the squatter will extinguish any claims that the former registered proprietor might have had against the squatter for

---

1   See paras **8.53–8.57**.
2   It is a statutory right for the squatter to have a legal estate vested in him.
3   The squatter's unregistered interest would, therefore, override the registered disposition under LRA 2002, Sch 3, para 2.
4   See LRA 1925, s 75(1).
5   For these criticisms, see (2001) Law Com No 271, paras 14.67, 14.70.
6   LRA 2002, Sch 6, para 9(1).

damages for trespass or rent. Following registration, the former registered proprietor is no longer entitled to possession, and cannot make any claim that is dependent upon such a state of affairs. This is consistent with the rule,[1] applicable where title to land is extinguished by adverse possession under s 17 of the LA 1980, that rights which that title carried must be also extinguished.[2]

8.47 Subject to the exception in relation to charges explained in para **8.48**, the registration of a squatter as the proprietor of an estate in land does not affect the priority of any interest affecting the estate.[3] The squatter will, therefore, step into the previous registered proprietor's shoes and will take the land subject to the same estates, rights and interests that bound the land previously.

The effect of registration on registered charges

8.48 As an exception to the general rule that registration will not affect the priority of any interest affecting the registered estate, where a squatter is registered as the proprietor of an estate, the estate will be vested in him free of any registered charge affecting the estate immediately before his registration,[4] *unless* the squatter has obtained title under one of the three exceptional conditions.[5] The principle behind this provision is as follows. Under the LRA 2002 the registered chargee will receive notice of the application to be registered. Because the chargee has a right to possession it is entitled to take proceedings against the squatter to recover the land even if the registered proprietor does not. The chargee can, therefore, prevent the squatter acquiring title just as much as can the registered proprietor. If the chargee fails to take such proceedings, the squatter should, in principle, take the land free of the charge.[6] As a result, the chargee cannot assert its charge in circumstances where the registered proprietor has lost his estate. The squatter can then deal with the land as he chooses.[7]

---

[1]   See *Re Jolly; Gathercole v Norfolk* [1900] 2 Ch 616.

[2]   *Mount Carmel Investments Ltd v Peter Thurlow Ltd* [1988] 1 WLR 1078, at p 1089 *per* Nicholls LJ.

[3]   LRA 2002, Sch 6, para 9(2).

[4]   Ibid, Sch 6, para 9(3).

[5]   Ibid, Sch 6, para 9(4).

[6]   Under the present law, it is probably the case that a successful squatter whose adverse possession pre-dates the registered charge is not bound by it. If, however, the charge pre-dates the adverse possession, it will be binding on a squatter who acquires title to the registered estate by adverse possession. See LA 1980, s 15(4); *Thornton v France* [1897] 2 KB 143; *Ludbrook v Ludbrook* [1901] 2 KB 96; *Carroll v Maneck* (1999) 79 P&CR 173. The point cannot be regarded as finally settled, however.

[7]   See (2001) Law Com No 271, para 14.75. This promotes one of the aims of the LRA 2002, namely, that the land should remain in commerce whether title to the land is retained by the registered proprietor or acquired by the squatter.

8.49 The squatter *will* be bound by a registered charge notwithstanding the service of a counter-notice by the registered proprietor or chargee, if the facts fall within one of the three exceptional conditions contained in Sch 6, para 5 to the LRA 2002.[1] The squatter will also be bound by any equitable charges, such as any charging order.[2] In both cases it is, however, possible that the squatter's independent right that justifies his registration as proprietor will take priority over the charge so that he will take free of it. This will often be the case if that right arose prior to the charge and (in the case of a registered charge) the squatter was in actual occupation at the time that the charge was created so that his rights overrode the disposition.[3]

Apportionment and discharge of charges

8.50 It follows from what has been said above that there may be occasions where a squatter who is registered as proprietor will be bound by either a registered charge or an equitable charge. Sometimes the land acquired by the squatter will comprise only part – perhaps only a small part – of the property subject to the charge. Where this situation occurs under the present law, the squatter has to redeem the whole charge if he wishes to sell his land free of it.[4] In practice, he may not be able to do this and cannot therefore sell the land. As one of the aims of the LRA 2002 is to ensure that land remains in commerce, it makes provision by which a squatter who finds himself in this situation can require the chargee to apportion the amount secured by the charge. The apportionment is made at the time when the squatter seeks it and according to the respective values of the land acquired by the squatter and the remainder of the land subject to the charge.[5]

8.51 The person requiring the apportionment is entitled to a discharge of his estate from the charge on payment of the amount apportioned to the estate together with the costs incurred by the chargee as a result of

---

[1] For the three exceptional cases, see paras **8.29–8.30**.

[2] Equitable chargees do not have a right to possession of the property charged, although they can obtain it in court proceedings: see Harpum, *Megarry & Wade's Law of Real Property* (Sweet & Maxwell, 6th edn, 2000), para 19-087.

[3] LRA 2002, Sch 3, para 2. In the case of an equitable charge, the squatter's right to be registered would always take priority if it pre-dated the charge: see LRA 2002, s 28.

[4] *Hall v Heward* (1886) 32 ChD 430; *Carroll v Maneck* (1999) 79 P&CR 173. He would then be subrogated to the rights of the chargee in relation to the other land of the mortgagor: see *Ghana Commercial Bank v Chandiram* [1960] AC 732, at p 745. In practice, many lenders do not insist upon their strict rights and, particularly if the squatter has only established title to a small portion of the land charge, will agree to release their charge in relation to the squatter's part.

[5] LRA 2002, Sch 6, para 10(1).

the apportionment.[1] On a discharge, the liability of the chargor to the chargee is reduced by the amount apportioned to the estate.[2] The details of the apportionment process will be prescribed in rules.[3]

POSSESSION PROCEEDINGS

The general rule

8.52 The LRA 2002 ensures that the position of the squatter in possession proceedings brought by the registered proprietor or registered chargee to recover the land mirrors that which prevails on an application by the squatter for registration. Under the new scheme the rights of the proprietor are not barred by lapse of time, and the general rule is, therefore, that if the registered proprietor or registered chargee brings possession proceedings, those proceedings will succeed however long the squatter has been in possession. To this general rule there are defences that accord with the principles, explained above, as to when a squatter may be registered as proprietor, even if the existing registered proprietor objects to his application.

Exceptions to the general rule: defences

Reasonable mistake as to boundary

8.53 It is a defence to an action for possession for the squatter to show that, the day before the possession proceedings were brought:

– he would have been entitled to make an application to be registered as proprietor under para 1 of Sch 6 in accordance with the principles explained in para **8.11**; and
– if he had made such an application, he would have established that he would have satisfied the third condition in para 5(4) of Sch 6 (reasonable mistake as to boundary),[4] explained in paras **8.35–8.37**.

When a squatter has a right to make further application for registration

8.54 A squatter will have a defence to possession proceedings if:

---

1   LRA 2002, Sch 6, para 10(2).
2   Ibid, Sch 6, para 10(3).
3   Ibid, Sch 6, para 10(4). Rules may, in particular, make provision about procedure, valuation, calculation of costs payable and payment by the squatter of any costs incurred by the chargor.
4   Ibid, s 98(1).

- he had been in adverse possession for 10 years;
- he had made an application for registration that had been rejected; and
- on the day before the proceedings were commenced he was entitled to make a further application to be registered under the provisions of para 6 of Sch 6 that have been explained at paras **8.38–8.42**.[1]

When a judgment for possession ceases to be enforceable

8.55 A theme that runs through the provisions of the LRA 2002 on adverse possession is that they are designed to achieve finality and to do so expeditiously. One aspect of this is that, if a registered proprietor obtains a judgment for possession against a squatter who would have been entitled to apply to be registered in accordance with the principles in para 1 of Sch 6,[2] that judgment ceases to be enforceable after a mere 2 years and not (as at present) after 6 years.[3]

8.56 A judgment for possession obtained against a squatter ceases to be enforceable 2 years after it was given if the following conditions are satisfied:

- the squatter had been in adverse possession for 10 years;
- he had made an application for registration that had been rejected; and
- he was entitled to make a further application to be registered under the provisions of para 6 of Sch 6 that have been explained at paras **8.38–8.42**.[4]

8.57 Where the court determines in any possession proceedings that the squatter is entitled to a defence under the LRA 2002, or that a judgment for possession has ceased to be enforceable, the court must order the registrar to register the squatter as the proprietor of the estate in relation to which he is entitled to make an application for registration as proprietor.[5]

Other defences

8.58 The statutory defences listed above are additional to any other

---

[1]   LRA 2002, s 98(3).
[2]   See para **8.11**.
[3]   LRA 2002, s 98(2).
[4]   Ibid, s 98(4).
[5]   Ibid, s 98(5).

defences that the squatter may have apart from the LRA 2002.[1] The squatter will, therefore, be able to raise any defence available to him in the possession proceedings, such as an equity arising by proprietary estoppel or that the land was held on bare trust for him.

SPECIAL CASES

Rentcharges

8.59 Under the LA 1980,[2] the rights of an owner of a rentcharge are barred if no rent has been paid for 12 years, or where the rent has been paid to a third party for 12 years.[3] The LRA 2002 does not state how its provisions are to apply to the adverse possession of a registered rentcharge. The matter is left to rules, in relation to both applications for registration[4] and actions for the recovery of rent due under a rentcharge.[5]

Trusts

Adverse possession of land held in trust

8.60 A person is not to be regarded as being in adverse possession of an estate for the purposes of the LRA 2002 at any time when the estate is subject to a trust, unless the interest of each of the beneficiaries in the estate is an interest in possession.[6] Thus, for example, where land is held in trust for A for life, thereafter for B for life, thereafter for C absolutely, a squatter will only be able to apply to be registered under the Act if he can show that he has been in adverse possession for at least 10 years since C became entitled in possession. In this regard, the LRA 2002 follows the present law and aims to protect the interests of beneficiaries who are not yet entitled in possession.[7]

---

[1]   LRA 2002, s 98(6).

[2]   LA 1980, s 38(8), Sch 1, Part 1, para 8(3)(a).

[3]   See Harpum, *Megarry & Wade's Law of Real Property* (Sweet & Maxwell, 6th edn, 2000), para 21-034.

[4]   LRA 2002, Sch 6, para 14.

[5]   Ibid, s 98(7).

[6]   Ibid, Sch 6, para 12.

[7]   The policy of the LRA 2002 was criticised in Parliament by Lord Goodhart, who considered that such protection was no longer needed. If the trustees failed to oppose a squatter's application to be registered, the beneficiaries could sue the trustees for breach of trust. However, a claim for breach of trust is not a substitute for the land formerly held in trust.

Adverse possession by a trustee or beneficiary of land held in trust

8.61   Neither a trustee nor a beneficiary will be entitled to apply to be registered as proprietor on the basis of adverse possession, or to resist proceedings for possession under the provisions in the LRA 2002. Neither is in adverse possession for the purposes of the definition of adverse possession contained in the Act.[1]

Crown foreshore

8.62   It was explained in Chapter 2[2] that the LRA 2002 makes provision by which the Crown can grant itself a fee simple out of land held in demesne in order to register it. Most of the foreshore is held by the Crown in demesne, and it is anticipated that much of this land will be registered to protect it from adverse possession by squatters. Such adverse possession is common, as, for example, where an owner of land adjoining the foreshore builds a jetty, slipway or pipe across the foreshore out into the sea.

8.63   Under the LA 1980, the limitation period for the recovery of the foreshore by the Crown is 60 years or, where land has ceased to be foreshore but remains in the ownership of the Crown, either 60 years from the date of accrual of the cause of action, or 30 years from the date on which the land ceased to be foreshore, whichever period expires first.[3] The extended limitation period reflects the difficulty that the Crown faces monitoring the large areas of the foreshore that it holds. The LRA 2002 follows this approach. It provides that, where a person is in adverse possession of an estate in land, the estate belongs to the Crown or one of the Royal Duchies,[4] and the land consists of foreshore, a squatter must be in adverse possession for 60 years before he may apply to be registered as the proprietor of a registered estate.[5]

8.64   For these purposes, land is to be treated as foreshore if it has been foreshore at any time in the previous 10 years.[6] 'Foreshore' means the shore and bed of the sea and of any tidal water, below the line of the medium high tide between the spring and neap tides.[7]

---

[1]   This follows from the LRA 2002, Sch 6, para 11(1), and is similar in effect to LA 1980, s 21(1)(b) and Sch 1, para 9.

[2]   See para **2.61**.

[3]   LA 1980, Sch 1, Part 2, para 11.

[4]   That is, Cornwall or Lancaster.

[5]   LRA 2002, Sch 6, para 13(1).

[6]   Ibid, Sch 6, para 13(2).

[7]   Ibid, Sch 6, para 13(3).

TRANSITIONAL PROVISIONS

8.65   The provisions of the LRA 2002 are to be brought into force by order, and they may be brought into force at different dates.[1] It is proposed to bring the 'boundary dispute' provisions of Sch 6, para 5(4) into force one year after the rest of Sch 6.[2] This is to enable registered proprietors to use that one-year period either to take proceedings for possession against, or to regularise the position with, any squatter who might otherwise be able to take advantage of the exceptional condition in Sch 6, para 5(4) of the Act.[3]

8.66   The LRA 2002 also preserves the rights of those who are entitled to be registered prior to the coming into force of the Act. Where a registered proprietor holds his estate on trust for a squatter under s 75 of the LRA 1925 immediately before the LRA 2002 comes into force,[4] the squatter is entitled to be registered.[5] As that entitlement will be a proprietary right, the squatter will be able to protect it against third parties as an overriding interest, provided that he is in actual occupation.[6] The squatter will also be able to rely on this right to be registered as a defence to any possession proceedings.[7]

---

[1]   LRA 2002, s 136(2).
[2]   See para **8.35**.
[3]   See (2001) Law Com No 271, paras 14.102–14.103.
[4]   Such trusts are abolished by the repeal without replication of LRA 1925, s 75: see para **8.43**.
[5]   LRA 2002, Sch 12, para 18(1).
[6]   Ibid, Sch 3, para 2: see para **3.96**.
[7]   Ibid, Sch 12, para 18(2).

CHAPTER 9

ADJUDICATION AND OFFENCES

THE MAIN CHANGES AT A GLANCE

9.1 Part 11 of the LRA 2002 contains the judicial provisions applicable to adjudication.[1] The offences created by the Act are found in Part 12.[2]

9.2 The main changes made by the LRA 2002 are as follows.

- It creates a new office of Adjudicator to HM Land Registry, which is wholly independent of HM Land Registry.
- It permits a person to apply directly to the Adjudicator to rectify or set aside conveyancing documents, so saving the need for some references to court.
- It creates three new offences relating to registration, which reflect the changes that will come about with the introduction of electronic conveyancing.

THE NEW APPROACH TO ADJUDICATION

9.3 The Adjudicator is to determine objections that are made to any application to the registrar that cannot be resolved by agreement between the parties; a function that was performed by the Solicitor to the Land Registry under the LRA 1925. As the Solicitor to the Land Registry is the senior lawyer within the Land Registry, the new office of Adjudicator has been created as a matter of principle. This is to avoid any perception of partiality in circumstances where, for example, a

---

[1]   See (2001) Law Com No 271, Part XVI.
[2]   Ibid.

dispute between parties involves consideration of decisions made by Land Registry officials.[1]

9.4 The Adjudicator will be under the supervision of the Council on Tribunals[2] and will in consequence have to comply with the requirements of the Tribunals and Inquiries Act 1992.[3]

9.5 At present, the determinations by the Solicitor to HM Land Registry provide an inexpensive, speedy and informal means of dealing with disputes that arise out of applications to the Registry, without the need to have recourse to court proceedings. It is intended that dispute resolution by the Adjudicator should fulfil the same function. Indeed, there are provisions of the Act that are specifically intended to enable persons with claims to registered land to take advantage of the procedure before the Adjudicator, rather than compelling them to have recourse to the courts.[4]

THE POWERS OF THE REGISTRAR

9.6 The powers of the registrar to make determinations are defined both negatively (by conferring jurisdiction on the Adjudicator) and positively (by making express provision for certain specific functions to be carried out by the registrar). First, the general right for anyone to object to an application[5] to the registrar has already been explained.[6] The registrar must notify the applicant of any objection to an application and may not determine the application until the application has been disposed of.[7] Where the registrar is satisfied that the application is not groundless[8] and it is not possible to dispose of the objection by agreement, the registrar *must* refer the matter to the Adjudicator for resolution. He cannot deal with it himself.[9]

9.7 Secondly, subject to the provisions relating to disputed

---

1   See Art 6.1 of the European Convention on Human Rights, which provides that, 'In the determination of his civil rights and obligations … everyone is entitled to a fair and public hearing within a reasonable time by an independent and impartial tribunal established by law'.
2   LRA 2002, Sch 9, para 8. The Solicitor to HM Land Registry is presently not under such supervision.
3   These requirements include the giving of reasons for the decision, if requested, under s 10 of that Act.
4   See, eg, in relation to adverse possession, LRA 2002, Sch 6, para 5(2), (3); see also para **8.30**.
5   Cf LRA 2002, s 132(3)(c).
6   Ibid, s 73; see also paras **5.38–5.40**.
7   Ibid, s 73(5).
8   See ibid, s 73(6).
9   Ibid, s 73(7).

applications, the registrar will, however, determine many matters, whether they arise on application or otherwise. Examples given by the Law Commission[1] include where the registrar:

- examines the title of an applicant for first registration;[2] or
- exercises his powers to alter the register so as to bring it up to date or to remove a spent entry.[3]

9.8 In any proceedings before him, the registrar is given specific powers by the Act:

- to require a person to produce a document for the purposes of those proceedings;[4] and
- to make orders about costs in relation to those proceedings.[5]

9.9 In each case, the registrar's requirement or order is enforceable as an order of the court,[6] and a person who is aggrieved by the registrar's requirement or order has a right to appeal to a county court which may make any order which appears appropriate.[7] With the exception of these specific matters, any other challenge to a decision of the registrar, of whatever kind, must be by way of an application for judicial review.

THE OFFICE OF ADJUDICATOR

9.10 The Adjudicator is to be appointed by the Lord Chancellor.[8] To be qualified for appointment as Adjudicator, a person must have a 10-year general qualification as defined in s 71 of the Courts and Legal Services Act 1990 (CLSA 1990).[9] The LRA 2002 contains provisions about the resignation and removal from office of the Adjudicator, for his remuneration, the payment of his pension and (in special circumstances) compensation.[10] He will also be disqualified from

---

[1] (2001) Law Com No 271, para 16.11.
[2] Cf LRA 2002, s 14(b).
[3] Ibid, Sch 4, para 5(b).
[4] Ibid, s 75(1). The power is subject to rules: s 75(2).
[5] Ibid, s 76(1). The power is subject to rules: see s 76(2), (3), indicating some of the matters that may be addressed by such rules.
[6] Ibid, ss 75(3), 76(4).
[7] Ibid, ss 75(4), 76(5).
[8] Ibid, s 107(1).
[9] Ibid, s 107(2). Under CLSA 1990, s 71(3)(c) a person will have such a general qualification if he has a right of audience in relation to any class of proceedings in any part of the Supreme Court, or in all proceedings in county courts or magistrates' courts.
[10] LRA 2002, Sch 9, paras 1, 2.

serving as a Member of Parliament or as a Member of the Northern Ireland Assembly.[1]

9.11 Under the LRA 2002, the Adjudicator may appoint such staff as he thinks fit.[2] Given the likely volume of work that will fall on the Adjudicator, the Act permits him to delegate any functions to those members of his staff as are authorised for that purpose.[3] However, in the case of any functions which are not of an administrative character, such as the determination of cases, an authorised member of staff must, like the Adjudicator himself, have a 10-year general qualification within the meaning of s 71 of the CLSA 1990.[4]

THE JURISDICTION OF THE ADJUDICATOR

9.12 The Adjudicator has two principal functions.

– The first is to determine matters referred to him by the registrar under s 73(7) of the LRA 2002 in circumstances where an objection to an application to the registrar cannot be disposed of by agreement between the parties.[5] The registrar may either refer the whole of the disputed application to the Adjudicator or, if only one or more issues are in contention between the parties, those specific issues.[6]
– The second is to determine appeals under para 4 of Sch 5 by a person – likely to be a solicitor or licensed conveyancer – who is aggrieved by a decision of the registrar with respect to entry into, or termination of, a network access agreement.[7]

The second of these two matters is the only case under the LRA 2002 in which there is an appeal from a decision of the registrar to the Adjudicator. In any other case, if a person is dissatisfied with a decision

---

[1] LRA 2002, Sch 9, para 9.
[2] Ibid, Sch 9, para 3(1). The terms and conditions on which they are appointed must be approved by the Minister for the Civil Service: para 3(2).
[3] Ibid, Sch 9, para 4(1).
[4] Ibid, Sch 9, para 4(2).
[5] LRA 2002, s 108(1)(a). For the general right to object to an application under s 73, see para **5.38**.
[6] See (2001) Law Com No 271, para 16.6.
[7] LRA 2002, s 108(1)(b). In other words, the situation will be where the registrar either refuses to enter into a network access agreement with a solicitor or licensed conveyancer (or is prepared to do so only on terms that the solicitor or licensed conveyancer considers unacceptable) or terminates an existing agreement. See further LRA 2002, Sch 5; see also paras **7.44–7.46**.

of the registrar, he can only challenge it by an application for judicial review.[1]

9.13 In addition to the two matters mentioned in para **9.12**, the Adjudicator also has limited jurisdiction, on application, to make any order which the High Court could make for the rectification or setting aside of a document which falls into any one of three categories.

(1) The first is an instrument which is used to make either a registrable disposition or a disposition that creates an interest which may be the subject of a notice in the register.[2] Examples of the instruments that could be rectified would therefore include a transfer or grant of a legal estate and an instrument creating a restrictive covenant.[3]

(2) The second is a contract to make a disposition of the kind mentioned in (1).[4]

(3) The third is an instrument that is used to make a transfer of an interest which is the subject of a notice in the register.[5] An example would be a transfer of a *profit à prendre* in gross, such as fishing or shooting rights, that was noted on the register but not registered with its own title, and where there was an error in that conveyance.[6]

9.14 This power is new. Under the present law, the registrar has no power to rectify or set aside a document.[7] On occasions, he has had to refer a matter to the High Court so that an instrument could be rectified. This is expensive for the party involved and inevitably delays the relevant application before the registrar. The new power given by the Act to the Adjudicator, although restricted in its scope,[8] overcomes these difficulties. Application for rectification by the Adjudicator is made directly to him: it is not made to the registrar.[9] The general law about the effect of an order of the High Court for the rectification or setting aside of a document applies to any order made by the Adjudicator.[10] This means, for example, that the rectification has

---

[1] Cf para **9.9**.
[2] LRA 2002, s 108(2)(a), (3).
[3] See (2001) Law Com No 271, para 16.8.
[4] LRA 2002, s 108(2)(b).
[5] Ibid, s 108(2)(c).
[6] See (2001) Law Com No 271, para 16.8.
[7] Ibid, para 16.9.
[8] It only applies to conveyancing documents.
[9] This follows from LRA 2002, s 108(2).
[10] Ibid, s 108(4).

retrospective effect, and the instrument is thereafter to be read as if it had been drafted in its rectified form.[1]

THE PROCEDURE BEFORE THE ADJUDICATOR

General

9.15 The Adjudicator may either determine matters referred to him on the papers submitted to him by the parties or may hold a hearing.[2] Hearings before the Adjudicator are to be held in public, except where the Adjudicator is satisfied that exclusion of the public is just and reasonable.[3] The Lord Chancellor is empowered to make rules to regulate the practice and procedure to be followed and in relation to matters incidental to or consequential upon such proceedings.[4] He may also prescribe fees to be paid in respect of hearings before the Adjudicator and make provisions about their payment.[5] Any requirement made of a party by the Adjudicator is enforceable as an order of the court.[6]

Proceedings on a reference under s 73(7) of the LRA 2002

9.16 The LRA 2002 makes further provision in relation to proceedings before the Adjudicator on a reference under s 73(7).

9.17 First, the Adjudicator may, instead of deciding a matter himself, direct a party to the proceedings to commence proceedings within a specified time within the High Court or the county court for the purpose of obtaining the court's decision on the matter.[7] This may be appropriate where:

- the application raises a difficult legal point;
- there is a complex factual dispute between the parties;
- there are other issues between the parties before the court; or

---

[1]   See (2001) Law Com No 271, para 16.10.
[2]   As with determinations by the Solicitor to HM Land Registry under the present law and practice, a hearing will not be necessary in all cases. See (2001) Law Com No 271, para 16.15.
[3]   LRA 2002, s 109(1).
[4]   Ibid, ss 109(2), (3), 114.
[5]   Ibid, s 113.
[6]   Ibid, s 112.
[7]   Ibid, s 110(1).

— the court has powers which are not available to the Adjudicator, such as the power to award damages.[1]

The Adjudicator may refer the whole of the proceedings to the court or merely one or more specific issues.

9.18 Secondly, the Act provides that rules may be made by the Lord Chancellor about the reference of matters to the court.[2] These may, in particular, make provision about the adjournment of the proceedings before the Adjudicator pending the court's decision, and the powers of the Adjudicator if a party fails to make the directed application to the court.

9.19 Thirdly, as has been explained above, the issues referred to the Adjudicator may only be in respect of certain specific issues raised on an application to the registrar and not the whole of that application.[3] It is therefore necessary to make provision as to what the Adjudicator may do in such a case. Under the LRA 2002, this is to be a matter for rules.[4] These may, in particular, make provision enabling the Adjudicator to determine or give directions about the determination of:

— the application to which the reference relates; or
— such other present or future application to the registrar as the rules may provide.

The reason for the second of these two points is that it will enable the Adjudicator to give a ruling or general directions on a point that could be applied in other unconnected applications, whether pending or which might arise at some future date.[5]

9.20 Fourthly, one technical matter that may arise on an application under s 73(7) of the LRA 2002 has already been mentioned.[6] Where a squatter has applied to be registered as proprietor after more than 10 years' adverse possession, he may be registered as proprietor in three limited circumstances even if a counter-notice is served by the registered proprietor (or by some other person entitled to do so).[7] One

---

[1] For example under LRA 2002, s 77 (duty to act reasonably); see also para **5.40**.
[2] LRA 2002, s 110(2).
[3] See para **9.12**.
[4] LRA 2002, s 110(3).
[5] See (2001) Law Com No 271, para 16.18.
[6] See paras **8.31–8.33**.
[7] LRA 2002, Sch 6, para 5.

of these exceptional cases is where it would be unconscionable, because of an equity arising by estoppel, for a registered proprietor to seek to dispossess the applicant.[1] If, however, on a reference in such a case where an equity by estoppel is alleged, the Adjudicator determines that it would be unconscionable for the registered proprietor to seek to dispossess the applicant, but the circumstances are not such that the applicant ought to be registered as proprietor, the Adjudicator has jurisdiction to determine how that equity should be satisfied.[2] He may for that purpose make any order that the High Court could make in the exercise of its equitable jurisdiction.[3]

APPEALS FROM THE ADJUDICATOR

9.21   If a party is aggrieved by a decision of the Adjudicator in relation to an application made under s 73(7), that party has a right of appeal to the High Court on a point of fact or law.[4]

9.22   If a party is aggrieved by a decision of the Adjudicator on an appeal under para 4 of Sch 5 to the LRA 2002, only an appeal to the High Court on a point of law is possible, as the appeal is a second appeal.[5]

9.23   The LRA 2002 makes special provision for one case where a party appeals to the High Court from a decision of the Adjudicator relating to an application by a squatter to be registered under para 1 of Sch 6 to the Act. There may be cases where the Court determines that it would be unconscionable because of an equity by estoppel for the registered proprietor to seek to dispossess the applicant.[6] If, however, it also decides that the circumstances are not such that the applicant ought to be registered as proprietor, it must then determine how best to satisfy the applicant's equity.[7]

---

[1]   LRA 2002, Sch 6, para 5(2).
[2]   Ibid, s 110(4)(a).
[3]   Ibid, s 110(4)(b).
[4]   Ibid, s 111(1). There is no appeal to the county court. The right of appeal conferred by s 111(1) is subject to any rules of court that may be made under ATJA 1999, s 54, by which any right of appeal may only be exercised with permission. Although CPR 1998, Part 52 limits second appeals, there are at present no such rules requiring leave for a first appeal.
[5]   Ibid, s 111(2).
[6]   Cf para **9.20**.
[7]   LRA 2002, s 111(3).

OFFENCES

9.24 Under the LRA 1925, there are three offences, although these have seldom been charged. The first relates to the suppression of deeds and evidence, the second deals with the fraudulent procurement of changes to the register, and the third with disobedience to an order of the registrar.[1] The LRA 2002 replaces the first two of these offences with three new ones. The third offence under the 1925 Act is not replicated because any requirement of the registrar or Adjudicator will be enforceable as an order of the court.[2] The three offences under the Act are as follows.

Suppression of information

9.25 It is an offence for a person to suppress information in the course of proceedings relating to registration if he does so with the intention either of concealing a person's right or claim or of substantiating a false claim.[3] For these purposes 'proceedings' will include both 'judicial' proceedings before the Adjudicator and any procedure relating to an application before the registrar. On conviction on indictment, a person will be liable to imprisonment for a term not exceeding 2 years or to an unlimited fine.[4] On summary conviction, a person is liable to imprisonment for a term not exceeding 6 months or to a fine not exceeding the statutory maximum, or to both.[5]

Improper alteration of the registers

9.26 The two new offences described in paras **9.27** and **9.28** relate to improper alteration of the registers. They have been enacted against the background of the introduction of e-conveyancing. When that happens, persons other than the registrar will be given authority to change the registers[6] and there is, therefore, an increased risk that an improper alteration might be made.

---

[1]   See LRA 1925, ss 115, 116, 117, 128(3).
[2]   See paras **9.9**, **9.15**. Non-compliance with an order of the registrar or Adjudicator would, therefore, be punishable as contempt.
[3]   LRA 2002, s 123(1).
[4]   Ibid, s 123(2)(a).
[5]   Ibid, s 123(2)(b). For the maximum fine that can be imposed on summary conviction, see Magistrates' Courts Act 1980 (MCA 1980), s 32(2), (9).
[6]   See para **7.5**.

9.27 First, it will be an offence if a person dishonestly induces another either:

(a) to change the register of title or the cautions register; or
(b) to authorise such a change.[1]

The reference to changing the register includes changing a document referred to in it.[2] The offence in (a) is very much like the present offence of fraudulently procuring a change to the register.[3] It will be committed where, for example, a person intentionally makes a false statement in an application. The offence in (b) might be committed where, after the introduction of e-conveyancing, a person dishonestly persuades the Registry to approve in advance a change to the register that he then makes.[4]

9.28 Secondly, it will be an offence for a person intentionally or recklessly to make an unauthorised change in the register of title or cautions register.[5] This offence can be committed in either of two ways. The first is where the person making the change does so knowing that he is not entitled to do so, or is reckless as to that fact. The second is where a person, having authority to make specific changes to the register intentionally or recklessly makes some other unauthorised alteration.

9.29 A person guilty of an offence relating to improper alteration of the register is liable, on conviction on indictment, to imprisonment for a term not exceeding 2 years or to a fine.[6] On summary conviction, a person is liable to imprisonment for a term not exceeding 6 months or to a fine not exceeding the statutory maximum, or to both.[7]

Privilege against self-incrimination

9.30 In relation to the privilege against self-incrimination, the LRA 2002 replicates the position under the LRA 1925.[8] Insofar as it relates

---

1   LRA 2002, s 124(1).
2   Ibid, s 124(4).
3   LRA 1925, s 116.
4   For the anticipated procedure in e-conveyancing, see paras **7.29–7.34**.
5   LRA 2002, s 124(2). Once again, the reference to a change in the register of title includes the changing of any document referred to in that register: s 124(4).
6   Ibid, s 124(3)(a).
7   Ibid, s 124(3)(b).
8   LRA 1925, s 119(2).

to offences under the Act, the privilege against self-incrimination does not entitle a person to refuse to answer any question or produce any document or thing in any legal proceedings other than criminal proceedings.[1] No evidence obtained in such a way under the Act will be admissible in any criminal proceedings under the Act either against the person from whom it was obtained or his or her spouse.[2]

---

[1]   LRA 2002, s 125(1).
[2]   Ibid, s 125(2).

CHAPTER 10

THE LAND REGISTRY

THE MAIN FEATURES AT A GLANCE

10.1 This chapter is concerned with the provisions of Part 10 of and Sch 7 to the LRA 2002 that concern HM Land Registry.[1] The changes that are made by these parts of the Act to the workings of the Land Registry are not likely to impinge much on practitioners. However, as has been explained,[2] there will be dramatic changes to the way in which conveyancing is conducted once e-conveyancing has been introduced. It will be the provisions governing e-conveyancing, rather than the specific provisions of the LRA 2002 on the Land Registry, that will define the radically different relationship that will exist between conveyancing practitioners and the Registry. One other change that will affect practitioners in their dealings with the Registry has also been explained. Disputes arising out of applications to the Registry will no longer be resolved by the Solicitor to HM Land Registry, but will be referred for a resolution to the new independent Adjudicator to HM Land Registry.[3] The post of Solicitor to HM Land Registry will necessarily disappear when the LRA 2002 comes into force.[4]

10.2 The main changes made by the LRA 2002 are as follows.

– The Registry is given express powers to publish information about land in England and Wales, to provide or arrange for the provision of consultancy or advisory services about the registration of land,

---

1   For the provisions on indemnity found in Sch 8 to the Act, see para **5.66**.
2   See para **7.5**.
3   See para **9.12**.
4   The Solicitor to HM Land Registry is a registrar who is nominated by the Chief Land Registrar to deal with the matters specified in the Schedules to the Land Registration (Conduct of Business) Regulations 2000, SI 2000/2212. The matters specified are the judicial or quasi-judicial functions that are vested in the Chief Land Registrar under LRA 1925 and LRR 1925. Prior to the CLA 1990, the Chief Land Registrar was required to be a barrister or solicitor of 10 years' standing.

and to form, acquire or invest in a company for a number of specified purposes.

– The power to determine fees is placed on a much more flexible basis and need not be fixed by reference to the value of the land registered.

THE LAND REGISTRY AND ITS STAFF

10.3 The LRA 2002, like the LRA 1925 before it,[1] makes provision for the continuance of the Land Registry.[2] It consists of the Chief Land Registrar as its head and the staff appointed by him.[3] The Lord Chancellor must appoint the Chief Land Registrar.[4] As now, no member of the Land Registry is liable for any act or omission in the discharge, actual or purported, of any function relating to land registration, unless it is shown that the act or omission was in bad faith.[5] However, a person who suffers loss as a result of any erroneous act or omission by any member of the Registry will normally be able to claim indemnity from the Chief Land Registrar under the provisions of Sch 8 to the LRA 2002 that have already been explained.[6]

THE CONDUCT OF BUSINESS

10.4 The functions conferred on the Chief Land Registrar by the LRA 2002 and the rules that will be made under it may be carried out by any member of the Land Registry who is authorised for the purpose by the Chief Land Registrar.[7] As under the present Act,[8] the Chief Land Registrar is given power to prepare and publish such forms and

---

1   LRA 1925, s 126(1).
2   LRA 2002, s 99(1).
3   Ibid, s 99(2). The Chief Land Registrar may appoint such staff as he thinks fit: Sch 7, para 3(1). However, the terms and conditions on which they are appointed must be approved by the Minister for the Civil Service: para 3(2). Under LRA 1925, s 126(1), the appointment of the staff of the Land Registry is a matter for the Lord Chancellor rather than for the Chief Land Registrar.
4   LRA 2002, s 99(3). The Act contains provisions about the resignation and removal from office of the Chief Land Registrar (Sch 7, para 1), for his remuneration, the payment of his pension and (in special circumstances) compensation (Sch 7, para 2). The Chief Land Registrar will, for the first time, be disqualified from serving as a Member of Parliament or as a Member of the Northern Ireland Assembly (Sch 7, para 7).
5   LRA 2002, Sch 7, para 4. For the present provision, see LRA 1925, s 131.
6   See para **5.66**.
7   LRA 2002, s 100(1). The Lord Chancellor may make regulations for the carrying out of the registrar's functions during any vacancy in that office: LRA 2002, s 100(2). For the present regulations (made under LRA 1925, s 126(6)): see Land Registry Regulations 1926, SR&O 1926/240.
8   LRA 1925, s 127.

directions as he considers necessary or desirable for facilitating the conduct of the business of registration under the Act.[1]

10.5 The LRA 2002, unlike the LRA 1925,[2] does not make express provision for district land registries. However, it is clear that district registries will continue under the Act. Thus the Act specifically empowers the Lord Chancellor by order to designate a particular office of the Land Registry as the proper office for the receipt of applications or a specified description of application.[3]

10.6 There is a statutory obligation on the Chief Land Registrar to make an Annual Report on the business of land registration to the Lord Chancellor[4] and to publish it in such manner as he thinks fit.[5] The Lord Chancellor must lay copies of the Annual Report before Parliament.[6]

MISCELLANEOUS POWERS

10.7 The LRA 2002 confers certain miscellaneous powers on the registrar. First, he is given express authority to publish information about land in England and Wales if it appears to him to be information in which there is legitimate public interest.[7]

10.8 Secondly, the LRA 2002 makes express provision for the registrar to provide or arrange for the provision of consultancy or advisory services about the registration of land, whether in England and Wales or elsewhere.[8]

---

[1] LRA 2002, s 100(4). For the present directions, see Ruoff & Roper, *Registered Conveyancing*, App F. There have been directions on a number of matters, including the telephone office copy service and Direct Access.

[2] See LRA 1925, s 132.

[3] LRA 2002, s 100(3). There are a number of situations in which it might be appropriate to exercise this power. For example, when e-conveyancing is introduced, certain district registries might be designated for 24-hour working to ensure that transactions could be simultaneously registered at whatever time they were concluded: cf para **7.35**.

[4] LRA 2002, s 101(1).

[5] Ibid, s 101(2). Thus the registrar could publish the report on the internet (as indeed he already does).

[6] Ibid, s 101(3).

[7] Ibid, s 104. The registrar already publishes information on property prices. As more commercial leases become registrable, it is possible that information about trends in rents and the average length of registrable leases might be made available.

[8] Ibid, s 105(1). The terms upon which such services are provided, including payment, will be such as the registrar thinks fit: s 105(2). Charges will not be prescribed by fee order as will those that apply to fees in relation to dealings with land: s 102(a).

10.9 Thirdly, the LRA 2002 makes provision for the registrar to form or participate in the formation of a company, or to purchase or invest in a company.[1] The registrar may do this in relation to the provision of:

- information about the history of a registered title under s 69 of the LRA 2002;[2]
- an electronic communications network under s 92 of the LRA 2002;[3]
- a system of electronic settlement under s 94 of the LRA 2002;[4]
- consultancy or advisory services under s 105 of the LRA 2002;[5] or
- education and training in relation to the use of a land registry network under Sch 5, para 10 to the LRA 2002.[6]

10.10 These powers were a late addition to the LRA 2002, having been introduced by way of government amendment at Third Reading in the House of Commons.[7] They were added to give effect to recommendations contained in the Quinquennial Review of the Land Registry.[8] While such powers were probably not strictly necessary because the registrar has them by necessary implication,[9] the provision puts the matter beyond doubt and is intended to provide reassurance to those who might be interested in joint ventures with the Land Registry.

FEE ORDERS

10.11 At present, many fees payable for registration are calculated on an *ad valorem* basis as prescribed by the LRA 1925.[10] The provisions of the LRA 2002 on fees are much simpler. They provide that the Lord Chancellor, with the advice and assistance of the Rules Committee[11] and the consent of the Treasury, may by order[12] prescribe fees to be paid in respect of dealings with the Land Registry and make provision

---

1   LRA 2002, s 106(1). For the definition of 'company' and 'invest', see s 106(2).
2   See para **5.29**.
3   See para **7.37**.
4   See para **7.57**.
5   See para **10.8**.
6   See para **7.39**.
7   *Hansard* (HC), 11 February 2002, vol 380, col 23.
8   By Mr Andrew Edwards, June 2001, para 14.4.
9   The LRA 2002 makes it clear that s 106 is without prejudice to any powers of the registrar otherwise than by virtue of that section: s 106(3).
10   LRA 1925, s 145.
11   For the Rules Committee, see LRA 2002, s 127, para **11.6**.
12   The power to make orders is exercisable by statutory instrument: see LRA 2002, s 128(2).

about the payment of prescribed fees.[1] The power to make such orders carries with it a power to make different provision for different cases.[2] It is likely that the present method of assessing fees will be replaced with a new method.[3]

---

[1]   LRA 2002, s 102. The power to prescribe fees does not apply in two cases: see s 102(a). The first is where historical information about a title is provided not by the registrar but by a person authorised by him under s 69(3). The second, which has been mentioned at para **10.8**, is where the registrar provides or arranges for the provision of consultancy or advisory services.

[2]   LRA 2002, s 128(1).

[3]   See (2001) Law Com No 271, para 15.10.

CHAPTER 11

RULES AND MISCELLANEOUS PROVISIONS

THE MAIN CHANGES AT A GLANCE

11.1   This chapter is concerned with the powers conferred by the LRA 2002 to make rules, regulations and orders.[1] All rules, regulations and orders under the Act are made by the Lord Chancellor.[2] That power is exercisable by statutory instrument.[3] At the time of going to press, no rules have been made under the Act, although a draft set of rules exists and is likely to be published for consultation by HM Land Registry in the near future.

11.2   The main changes that the LRA 2002 makes in relation to rules, regulations and orders are as follows.

–   Rules will generally be made under specific rule-making powers rather than (as now) under the residual rule-making power.
–   Rules are subject to a higher degree of Parliamentary scrutiny than at present.
–   The composition of the Rules Committee is enlarged to include persons who will represent the interests of licensed conveyancers, chartered surveyors and consumers.

RULES UNDER THE LRA 1925

11.3   Rules have been an essential feature of the workings of the land registration system under the LRA 1925. The use of rules has enabled land registration to develop because it is much easier to change them

---

[1]   See (2001) Law Com No 271, Part XVII.
[2]   LRA 2002, s 128(1).
[3]   Ibid, s 128(2).

than it is to obtain amending legislation.[1] Not only are the existing rules numerous[2] but they also contain some of the fundamental concepts of the present system, such as the general boundaries rule[3] and the system of official searches.[4] Indeed, what is in primary legislation and what is in rules sometimes appears arbitrary. Three other features of the present law may be mentioned. The first is that land registration rules are subject to no effective parliamentary scrutiny. They are merely required to be laid.[5] Secondly, the rule-making powers are contained in one section – s 144 of the LRA 1925. They do not arise in context in the Act. Thirdly, in practice, despite the long list of rule-making powers in s 144(1), for many years almost all rules have been made under the residual rule-making power found in s 144(1)(xxxi).[6]

RULES UNDER THE LRA 2002

11.4 The approach to rules under the LRA 2002 is very different. First, in general, rule-making powers are found where they arise in the Act, although certain miscellaneous and general rule-making powers are found in Sch 10 to the Act.[7] Although the LRA 2002 does contain a residual rule-making power,[8] it is just that. In the great majority of cases, rules will be made pursuant to a specific power. This means that it will be possible to read the rules, when made, in conjunction with the provisions of the Act. This should make it easier to operate the new legislation. Secondly, considerable attention has been paid by the draftsman in deciding upon the allocation of material between the Act and the rules to be made under it. Thirdly, the degree of parliamentary scrutiny will, at least in theory, be greater. Following a recommendation by the Delegated Powers Scrutiny Committee of the House of Lords, the Bill was amended in its passage through Parliament so that the great majority of rules made under the Act will be subject to annulment in

---

1   Within the lifetime of LRA 1925, registered conveyancing has moved from a system, used by few, that had to be conducted by personal attendance at HM Land Registry to one that is the norm and where certain applications can be lodged electronically. That change has been achieved by changes in the rules.

2   The main set of rules are found in LRR 1925, but there are also others, such as LROSR 1993.

3   See LRR 1925, r 278.

4   See LROSR 1993.

5   LRA 1925, s 144(3).

6   'For regulating any matter to be prescribed or in respect of which rules are to or may be made under this Act and any other matter or thing, whether similar or not to those above mentioned, in respect of which it may be expedient to make rules for the purpose of carrying this Act into execution.'

7   See LRA 2002, s 126. For the rule-making powers under Sch 10, see paras **2.26**, **5.37**, **5.44**, Chapter 6 and para **11.7**.

8   See LRA 2002, Sch 10, para 8.

pursuance of a resolution of either House of Parliament.[1] Certain rules connected with e-conveyancing are subject to an even higher degree of scrutiny. Rules that are made under s 93 (by which e-conveyancing may be made compulsory for specific dispositions)[2] and the first three paragraphs of Sch 5 (network access agreements)[3] are subject to affirmative resolution procedure.[4] In other words, they will have to be laid before and approved by resolution of each House of Parliament. It should also be noted that some rules can only be made after prior consultation by the Lord Chancellor.[5]

11.5 Not all the rules, regulations and orders that can be made under the LRA 2002 are land registration rules.[6] Land registration rules are those that explain how land registration is to be conducted. Thus, for example, rules about adjudication and the forwarding to the registrar of companies of applications relating to certain registered charges are not land registration rules.[7] Orders (such as fee orders[8] and orders made in connection with the bringing into force of the Act[9]) and regulations (such as regulations about the carrying out of functions of the registrar or Adjudicator in any vacancy in the office[10]) are clearly not land registration rules.

THE RULES COMMITTEE

11.6 Whatever may be the position in relation to parliamentary scrutiny, the LRA 2002, like the LRA 1925 before it, provides that the Lord Chancellor can only exercise his power to make land registration rules with the advice and assistance of the Rules Committee.[11] Under the LRA 2002, the composition of the Rules Committee is wider than it

---

[1] LRA 2002, s 128(4). Whether this will lead to greater parliamentary scrutiny is questionable if the treatment of the Bill itself is anything to go by. During the course of Report and Third Reading in the House of Commons – the only stages of the Bill that were discussed on the floor of the House of Commons – the number of Members of Parliament present was in single figures.

[2] See paras **7.53**, **7.54**.

[3] See paras **7.38–7.44**.

[4] LRA 2002, s 128(5).

[5] See, eg, ibid, ss 93(5) (power to require dispositions to be made electronically with simultaneous registration), 118(3) (power to reduce length of registrable leases), Sch 5, para 11(1) (power to make network access rules).

[6] See ibid, s 132(1), and the definition of 'land registration rules'.

[7] See ibid, Part 11 and s 121 respectively.

[8] Ibid, s 102.

[9] Ibid, ss 134(1), 136(2).

[10] See ibid, s 100(2), Sch 9, para 5.

[11] Ibid, s 127(1). In relation to other rules, the Lord Chancellor will no doubt seek the views of the Rules Committee even though he is not required to do so.

has been under the LRA 1925.[1] Indeed, its composition was widened during the parliamentary passage of the legislation. As now, the Committee will be chaired by a judge of the Chancery Division of the High Court, nominated by the Lord Chancellor.[2] As now, it will also include the Chief Land Registrar,[3] and a person nominated by each of the General Council of the Bar and the Council of the Law Society.[4] It will no longer include a person nominated by DEFRA.[5] For the first time, there will also be a person nominated by each of the Council of Mortgage Lenders, the Council of Licensed Conveyancers and the Royal Institution of Chartered Surveyors,[6] together with a person with experience in, and knowledge of, consumer affairs.[7] As now, the Lord Chancellor may nominate to be a member of the Rules Committee, any person who appears to him to have qualifications or experience which would be of value to the Committee in considering any matter with which it is concerned.[8] The Rules Committee has, over the years, proved itself to be a very effective and critical scrutinising body and it is to be hoped that it will continue to be so.

GENERAL RULE-MAKING POWERS

11.7 As has been explained above, most of the rule-making powers in the LRA 2002 are found in the context in which they arise. However, there are a number of miscellaneous and general rule-making powers that are collected in Sch 10 to the Act. The miscellaneous powers have already been explained in various parts of this book. Of the four general rule-making powers contained in Part 2 of Sch 10:

–   the power to make rules in relation to applications[9] has been explained in Chapter 5;[10]
–   the residual rule-making power[11] has been mentioned above;[12]

---

[1]   LRA 2002, s 127(2).
[2]   Ibid, s 127(2)(a). It is presently Mr Justice Blackburne.
[3]   Ibid, s 127(2)(b).
[4]   Ibid, s 127(2)(c), (d).
[5]   Formerly MAFF. This was at the request of the Department.
[6]   LRA 2002, s 127(2)(e)–(g).
[7]   Ibid, s 127(2)(f).
[8]   Ibid, s 127(2)(g).
[9]   Ibid, Sch 10, para 6.
[10]   See para **5.37**.
[11]   LRA 2002, Sch 10, para 8.
[12]   See para **11.4**.

- there is a power to make rules about the form, content and service of notices under the Act;[1] and
- there is a power to make rules about the form of any statement required under an enactment to be included in an instrument effecting a registrable disposition or a disposition which triggers a requirement of registration.[2]

The last power is required because, by statute, some dispositions of land have to contain certain particulars. Examples of such cases include:

- certain dispositions by charities;[3] and
- a vesting deed in favour of a tenant for life under the SLA 1925.[4]

---

[1]   LRA 2002. Sch 10, para 5. In particular, the rules may require that an address for service be supplied and for its entry in the register. They may also make provision about the time for the service of notices, the way in which service is made, and when service is regarded as having taken place: Sch 10, para 5(2).

[2]   Ibid, Sch 10, para 7.

[3]   Charities Act 1993, ss 37, 39.

[4]   SLA 1925, s 5.

APPENDIX

LAND REGISTRATION ACT 2002

1   Register of title

(1)   There is to continue to be a register of title kept by the registrar.

(2)   Rules may make provision about how the register is to be kept and may, in particular, make provision about –

    (a)   the information to be included in the register,

    (b)   the form in which information included in the register is to be kept, and

    (c)   the arrangement of that information.

2   Scope of title registration

This Act makes provision about the registration of title to –

    (a)   unregistered legal estates which are interests of any of the following kinds –

        (i)   an estate in land,

        (ii)   a rentcharge,

        (iii)   a franchise,

        (iv)   a profit a prendre in gross, and

        (v)   any other interest or charge which subsists for the benefit of, or is a charge on, an interest the title to which is registered; and

    (b)   interests capable of subsisting at law which are created by a disposition of an interest the title to which is registered.

3   When title may be registered

(1)   This section applies to any unregistered legal estate which is an interest of any of the following kinds –

    (a)   an estate in land,

    (b)   a rentcharge,

    (c)   a franchise, and

    (d)   a profit a prendre in gross.

(2)   Subject to the following provisions, a person may apply to the registrar to be registered as the proprietor of an unregistered legal estate to which this section applies if –

    (a)   the estate is vested in him, or

    (b)   he is entitled to require the estate to be vested in him.

(3)   Subject to subsection (4), an application under subsection (2) in respect of a leasehold estate may only be made if the estate was granted for a term of which more than seven years are unexpired.

(4)   In the case of an estate in land, subsection (3) does not apply if the right to possession under the lease is discontinuous.

(5)   A person may not make an application under subsection (2)(a) in respect of a leasehold estate vested in him as a mortgagee where there is a subsisting right of redemption.

(6)   A person may not make an application under subsection (2)(b) if his entitlement is as a person who has contracted to buy under a contract.

(7)   If a person holds in the same right both –

    (a)   a lease in possession, and

    (b)   a lease to take effect in possession on, or within a month of, the end of the lease in possession,

then, to the extent that they relate to the same land, they are to be treated for the purposes of this section as creating one continuous term.

Compulsory registration

4   When title must be registered

(1)   The requirement of registration applies on the occurrence of any of the following events –

    (a)   the transfer of a qualifying estate –

        (i)   for valuable or other consideration, by way of gift or in pursuance of an order of any court, or

        (ii)   by means of an assent (including a vesting assent);

    (b)   the transfer of an unregistered legal estate in land in circumstances where section 171A of the Housing Act 1985 applies (disposal by landlord which leads to a person no longer being a secure tenant);

    (c)   the grant out of a qualifying estate of an estate in land –

        (i)   for a term of years absolute of more than seven years from the date of the grant, and

        (ii)   for valuable or other consideration, by way of gift or in pursuance of an order of any court;

    (d)   the grant out of a qualifying estate of an estate in land for a term of years absolute to take effect in possession after the end of the period of three months beginning with the date of the grant;

(e)   the grant of a lease in pursuance of Part 5 of the Housing Act 1985 (the right to buy) out of an unregistered legal estate in land;

(f)   the grant of a lease out of an unregistered legal estate in land in such circumstances as are mentioned in paragraph (b);

(g)   the creation of a protected first legal mortgage of a qualifying estate.

(2)   For the purposes of subsection (1), a qualifying estate is an unregistered legal estate which is –

(a)   a freehold estate in land, or

(b)   a leasehold estate in land for a term which, at the time of the transfer, grant or creation, has more than seven years to run.

(3)   In subsection (1)(a), the reference to transfer does not include transfer by operation of law.

(4)   Subsection (1)(a) does not apply to –

(a)   the assignment of a mortgage term, or

(b)   the assignment or surrender of a lease to the owner of the immediate reversion where the term is to merge in that reversion.

(5)   Subsection (1)(c) does not apply to the grant of an estate to a person as a mortgagee.

(6)   For the purposes of subsection (1)(a) and (c), if the estate transferred or granted has a negative value, it is to be regarded as transferred or granted for valuable or other consideration.

(7)   In subsection (1)(a) and (c), references to transfer or grant by way of gift include transfer or grant for the purpose of –

(a)   constituting a trust under which the settlor does not retain the whole of the beneficial interest, or

(b)   uniting the bare legal title and the beneficial interest in property held under a trust under which the settlor did not, on constitution, retain the whole of the beneficial interest.

(8)   For the purposes of subsection (1)(g) –

(a)   a legal mortgage is protected if it takes effect on its creation as a mortgage to be protected by the deposit of documents relating to the mortgaged estate, and

(b)   a first legal mortgage is one which, on its creation, ranks in priority ahead of any other mortgages then affecting the mortgaged estate.

(9)   In this section –

'land' does not include mines and minerals held apart from the surface;

'vesting assent' has the same meaning as in the Settled Land Act 1925.

5   Power to extend section 4

(1)   The Lord Chancellor may by order –

(a)   amend section 4 so as to add to the events on the occurrence of which the requirement of registration applies such relevant event as he may specify in the order, and

(b)   make such consequential amendments of any provision of, or having effect under, any Act as he thinks appropriate.

(2)   For the purposes of subsection (1)(a), a relevant event is an event relating to an unregistered legal estate which is an interest of any of the following kinds –

(a)   an estate in land,

(b)   a rentcharge,

(c)   a franchise, and

(d)   a profit a prendre in gross.

(3)   The power conferred by subsection (1) may not be exercised so as to require the title to an estate granted to a person as a mortgagee to be registered.

(4)   Before making an order under this section the Lord Chancellor must consult such persons as he considers appropriate.

6   Duty to apply for registration of title

(1)   If the requirement of registration applies, the responsible estate owner, or his successor in title, must, before the end of the period for registration, apply to the registrar to be registered as the proprietor of the registrable estate.

(2)   If the requirement of registration applies because of section 4(1)(g) –

(a)   the registrable estate is the estate charged by the mortgage, and

(b)   the responsible estate owner is the owner of that estate.

(3)   If the requirement of registration applies otherwise than because of section 4(1)(g) –

(a)   the registrable estate is the estate which is transferred or granted, and

(b)   the responsible estate owner is the transferee or grantee of that estate.

(4)   The period for registration is 2 months beginning with the date on which the relevant event occurs, or such longer period as the registrar may provide under subsection (5).

(5)   If on the application of any interested person the registrar is satisfied that there is good reason for doing so, he may by order provide that the period for registration ends on such later date as he may specify in the order.

(6)   Rules may make provision enabling the mortgagee under any mortgage falling within section 4(1)(g) to require the estate charged by the mortgage to be registered whether or not the mortgagor consents.

7   Effect of non-compliance with section 6

(1)   If the requirement of registration is not complied with, the transfer, grant or creation becomes void as regards the transfer, grant or creation of a legal estate.

(2)   On the application of subsection (1) –

(a)   in a case falling within section 4(1)(a) or (b), the title to the legal estate reverts to the transferor who holds it on a bare trust for the transferee, and

(b)   in a case falling within section 4(1)(c) to (g), the grant or creation has effect as a contract made for valuable consideration to grant or create the legal estate concerned.

(3)   If an order under section 6(5) is made in a case where subsection (1) has already applied, that application of the subsection is to be treated as not having occurred.

(4)   The possibility of reverter under subsection (1) is to be disregarded for the purposes of determining whether a fee simple is a fee simple absolute.

8   Liability for making good void transfers etc

If a legal estate is retransferred, regranted or recreated because of a failure to comply with the requirement of registration, the transferee, grantee or, as the case may be, the mortgagor –

(a)   is liable to the other party for all the proper costs of and incidental to the retransfer, regrant or recreation of the legal estate, and

(b)   is liable to indemnify the other party in respect of any other liability reasonably incurred by him because of the failure to comply with the requirement of registration.

Classes of title

9   Titles to freehold estates

(1)   In the case of an application for registration under this Chapter of a freehold estate, the classes of title with which the applicant may be registered as proprietor are –

(a)   absolute title,

(b)   qualified title, and

(c)   possessory title;

and the following provisions deal with when each of the classes of title is available.

(2)   A person may be registered with absolute title if the registrar is of the opinion that the person's title to the estate is such as a willing buyer could properly be advised by a competent professional adviser to accept.

(3)   In applying subsection (2), the registrar may disregard the fact that a person's title appears to him to be open to objection if he is of the opinion that the defect will not cause the holding under the title to be disturbed.

(4)   A person may be registered with qualified title if the registrar is of the opinion that the person's title to the estate has been established only for a limited period or subject to certain reservations which cannot be disregarded under subsection (3).

(5)   A person may be registered with possessory title if the registrar is of the opinion –

(a)   that the person is in actual possession of the land, or in receipt of the rents and profits of the land, by virtue of the estate, and

(b)   that there is no other class of title with which he may be registered.

10   Titles to leasehold estates

(1)   In the case of an application for registration under this Chapter of a leasehold estate, the classes of title with which the applicant may be registered as proprietor are –

(a)   absolute title,

(b)   good leasehold title,

(c)   qualified title, and

(d)   possessory title;

and the following provisions deal with when each of the classes of title is available.

(2)   A person may be registered with absolute title if –

(a)   the registrar is of the opinion that the person's title to the estate is such as a willing buyer could properly be advised by a competent professional adviser to accept, and

(b)   the registrar approves the lessor's title to grant the lease.

(3)   A person may be registered with good leasehold title if the registrar is of the opinion that the person's title to the estate is such as a willing buyer could properly be advised by a competent professional adviser to accept.

(4)   In applying subsection (2) or (3), the registrar may disregard the fact that a person's title appears to him to be open to objection if he is of the opinion that the defect will not cause the holding under the title to be disturbed.

(5)   A person may be registered with qualified title if the registrar is of the opinion that the person's title to the estate, or the lessor's title to the reversion, has been established only for a limited period or subject to certain reservations which cannot be disregarded under subsection (4).

(6)   A person may be registered with possessory title if the registrar is of the opinion –

(a)   that the person is in actual possession of the land, or in receipt of the rents and profits of the land, by virtue of the estate, and

(b)   that there is no other class of title with which he may be registered.

Effect of first registration

11   Freehold estates

(1)   This section is concerned with the registration of a person under this Chapter as the proprietor of a freehold estate.

(2)   Registration with absolute title has the effect described in subsections (3) to (5).

(3)   The estate is vested in the proprietor together with all interests subsisting for the benefit of the estate.

(4)   The estate is vested in the proprietor subject only to the following interests affecting the estate at the time of registration –
  (a)   interests which are the subject of an entry in the register in relation to the estate,
  (b)   unregistered interests which fall within any of the paragraphs of Schedule 1, and
  (c)   interests acquired under the Limitation Act 1980 of which the proprietor has notice.

(5)   If the proprietor is not entitled to the estate for his own benefit, or not entitled solely for his own benefit, then, as between himself and the persons beneficially entitled to the estate, the estate is vested in him subject to such of their interests as he has notice of.

(6)   Registration with qualified title has the same effect as registration with absolute title, except that it does not affect the enforcement of any estate, right or interest which appears from the register to be excepted from the effect of registration.

(7)   Registration with possessory title has the same effect as registration with absolute title, except that it does not affect the enforcement of any estate, right or interest adverse to, or in derogation of, the proprietor's title subsisting at the time of registration or then capable of arising.

12   Leasehold estates
(1)   This section is concerned with the registration of a person under this Chapter as the proprietor of a leasehold estate.

(2)   Registration with absolute title has the effect described in subsections (3) to (5).

(3)   The estate is vested in the proprietor together with all interests subsisting for the benefit of the estate.

(4)   The estate is vested subject only to the following interests affecting the estate at the time of registration –
  (a)   implied and express covenants, obligations and liabilities incident to the estate,
  (b)   interests which are the subject of an entry in the register in relation to the estate,
  (c)   unregistered interests which fall within any of the paragraphs of Schedule 1, and
  (d)   interests acquired under the Limitation Act 1980 of which the proprietor has notice.

(5)   If the proprietor is not entitled to the estate for his own benefit, or not entitled solely for his own benefit, then, as between himself and the persons beneficially

entitled to the estate, the estate is vested in him subject to such of their interests as he has notice of.

(6)   Registration with good leasehold title has the same effect as registration with absolute title, except that it does not affect the enforcement of any estate, right or interest affecting, or in derogation of, the title of the lessor to grant the lease.

(7)   Registration with qualified title has the same effect as registration with absolute title except that it does not affect the enforcement of any estate, right or interest which appears from the register to be excepted from the effect of registration.

(8)   Registration with possessory title has the same effect as registration with absolute title, except that it does not affect the enforcement of any estate, right or interest adverse to, or in derogation of, the proprietor's title subsisting at the time of registration or then capable of arising.

Dependent estates

13   Appurtenant rights and charges
Rules may –
- (a)   make provision for the registration of the proprietor of a registered estate as the proprietor of an unregistered legal estate which subsists for the benefit of the registered estate;
- (b)   make provision for the registration of a person as the proprietor of an unregistered legal estate which is a charge on a registered estate.

Supplementary

14   Rules about first registration
Rules may –
- (a)   make provision about the making of applications for registration under this Chapter;
- (b)   make provision about the functions of the registrar following the making of such an application, including provision about –
  - (i)   the examination of title, and
  - (ii)   the entries to be made in the register where such an application is approved;
- (c)   make provision about the effect of any entry made in the register in pursuance of such an application.

Chapter 2
Cautions against First Registration

15   Right to lodge
(1)   Subject to subsection (3), a person may lodge a caution against the registration of title to an unregistered legal estate if he claims to be –
- (a)   the owner of a qualifying estate, or
- (b)   entitled to an interest affecting a qualifying estate.

(2) For the purposes of subsection (1), a qualifying estate is a legal estate which –

    (a)   relates to land to which the caution relates, and

    (b)   is an interest of any of the following kinds –

        (i)   an estate in land,

        (ii)   a rentcharge,

        (iii)   a franchise, and

        (iv)   a profit a prendre in gross.

(3) No caution may be lodged under subsection (1) –

    (a)   in the case of paragraph (a), by virtue of ownership of –

        (i)   a freehold estate in land, or

        (ii)   a leasehold estate in land granted for a term of which more than seven years are unexpired;

    (b)   in the case of paragraph (b), by virtue of entitlement to such a leasehold estate as is mentioned in paragraph (a)(ii) of this subsection.

(4) The right under subsection (1) is exercisable by application to the registrar.

16   Effect

(1) Where an application for registration under this Part relates to a legal estate which is the subject of a caution against first registration, the registrar must give the cautioner notice of the application and of his right to object to it.

(2) The registrar may not determine an application to which subsection (1) applies before the end of such period as rules may provide, unless the cautioner has exercised his right to object to the application or given the registrar notice that he does not intend to do so.

(3) Except as provided by this section, a caution against first registration has no effect and, in particular, has no effect on the validity or priority of any interest of the cautioner in the legal estate to which the caution relates.

(4) For the purposes of subsection (1), notice given by a person acting on behalf of an applicant for registration under this Part is to be treated as given by the registrar if –

    (a)   the person is of a description provided by rules, and

    (b)   notice is given in such circumstances as rules may provide.

17   Withdrawal

The cautioner may withdraw a caution against first registration by application to the registrar.

18   Cancellation

(1) A person may apply to the registrar for cancellation of a caution against first registration if he is –

    (a)   the owner of the legal estate to which the caution relates, or

    (b)   a person of such other description as rules may provide.

(2)   Subject to rules, no application under subsection (1)(a) may be made by a person who –

> (a)   consented in such manner as rules may provide to the lodging of the caution, or
>
> (b)   derives title to the legal estate by operation of law from a person who did so.

(3)   Where an application is made under subsection (1), the registrar must give the cautioner notice of the application and of the effect of subsection (4).

(4)   If the cautioner does not exercise his right to object to the application before the end of such period as rules may provide, the registrar must cancel the caution.

19   Cautions register

(1)   The registrar must keep a register of cautions against first registration.

(2)   Rules may make provision about how the cautions register is to be kept and may, in particular, make provision about –

> (a)   the information to be included in the register,
>
> (b)   the form in which information included in the register is to be kept, and
>
> (c)   the arrangement of that information.

20   Alteration of register by court

(1)   The court may make an order for alteration of the cautions register for the purpose of –

> (a)   correcting a mistake, or
>
> (b)   bringing the register up to date.

(2)   An order under subsection (1) has effect when served on the registrar to impose a duty on him to give effect to it.

(3)   Rules may make provision about –

> (a)   the circumstances in which there is a duty to exercise the power under subsection (1),
>
> (b)   the form of an order under that subsection, and
>
> (c)   service of such an order.

21   Alteration of register by registrar

(1)   The registrar may alter the cautions register for the purpose of –

> (a)   correcting a mistake, or
>
> (b)   bringing the register up to date.

(2)   Rules may make provision about –

> (a)   the circumstances in which there is a duty to exercise the power under subsection (1),
>
> (b)   how the cautions register is to be altered in exercise of that power,
>
> (c)   applications for the exercise of that power, and

(d)   procedure in relation to the exercise of that power, whether on application or otherwise.

(3)   Where an alteration is made under this section, the registrar may pay such amount as he thinks fit in respect of any costs reasonably incurred by a person in connection with the alteration.

22   Supplementary

In this Chapter, 'the cautioner', in relation to a caution against first registration, means the person who lodged the caution, or such other person as rules may provide.

PART 3
Dispositions of Registered Land

Powers of disposition

23   Owner's powers

(1)   Owner's powers in relation to a registered estate consist of –
(a)   power to make a disposition of any kind permitted by the general law in relation to an interest of that description, other than a mortgage by demise or sub-demise, and
(b)   power to charge the estate at law with the payment of money.

(2)   Owner's powers in relation to a registered charge consist of –
(a)   power to make a disposition of any kind permitted by the general law in relation to an interest of that description, other than a legal sub-mortgage, and
(b)   power to charge at law with the payment of money indebtedness secured by the registered charge.

(3)   In subsection (2)(a), 'legal sub-mortgage' means –
(a)   a transfer by way of mortgage,
(b)   a sub-mortgage by sub-demise, and
(c)   a charge by way of legal mortgage.

24   Right to exercise owner's powers

A person is entitled to exercise owner's powers in relation to a registered estate or charge if he is –
(a)   the registered proprietor, or
(b)   entitled to be registered as the proprietor.

25   Mode of exercise

(1)   A registrable disposition of a registered estate or charge only has effect if it complies with such requirements as to form and content as rules may provide.

(2)   Rules may apply subsection (1) to any other kind of disposition which depends for its effect on registration.

26   Protection of disponees

(1)   Subject to subsection (2), a person's right to exercise owner's powers in relation to a registered estate or charge is to be taken to be free from any limitation affecting the validity of a disposition.

(2)   Subsection (1) does not apply to a limitation –
    (a)   reflected by an entry in the register, or
    (b)   imposed by, or under, this Act.

(3)   This section has effect only for the purpose of preventing the title of a disponee being questioned (and so does not affect the lawfulness of a disposition).

Registrable dispositions

27   Dispositions required to be registered

(1)   If a disposition of a registered estate or registered charge is required to be completed by registration, it does not operate at law until the relevant registration requirements are met.

(2)   In the case of a registered estate, the following are the dispositions which are required to be completed by registration –
    (a)   a transfer,
    (b)   where the registered estate is an estate in land, the grant of a term of years absolute –
        (i)   for a term of more than seven years from the date of the grant,
        (ii)   to take effect in possession after the end of the period of three months beginning with the date of the grant,
        (iii)   under which the right to possession is discontinuous,
        (iv)   in pursuance of Part 5 of the Housing Act 1985 (the right to buy), or
        (v)   in circumstances where section 171A of that Act applies (disposal by landlord which leads to a person no longer being a secure tenant),
    (c)   where the registered estate is a franchise or manor, the grant of a lease,
    (d)   the express grant or reservation of an interest of a kind falling within section 1(2)(a) of the Law of Property Act 1925, other than one which is capable of being registered under the Commons Registration Act 1965,
    (e)   the express grant or reservation of an interest of a kind falling within section 1(2)(b) or (e) of the Law of Property Act 1925, and
    (f)   the grant of a legal charge.

(3)   In the case of a registered charge, the following are the dispositions which are required to be completed by registration –
    (a)   a transfer, and
    (b)   the grant of a sub-charge.

(4)   Schedule 2 to this Act (which deals with the relevant registration requirements) has effect.

(5)   This section applies to dispositions by operation of law as it applies to other dispositions, but with the exception of the following –
  (a)   a transfer on the death or bankruptcy of an individual proprietor,
  (b)   a transfer on the dissolution of a corporate proprietor, and
  (c)   the creation of a legal charge which is a local land charge.

(6)   Rules may make provision about applications to the registrar for the purpose of meeting registration requirements under this section.

(7)   In subsection (2)(d), the reference to express grant does not include grant as a result of the operation of section 62 of the Law of Property Act 1925.

Effect of dispositions on priority

28   Basic rule
(1)   Except as provided by sections 29 and 30, the priority of an interest affecting a registered estate or charge is not affected by a disposition of the estate or charge.

(2)   It makes no difference for the purposes of this section whether the interest or disposition is registered.

29   Effect of registered dispositions: estates
(1)   If a registrable disposition of a registered estate is made for valuable consideration, completion of the disposition by registration has the effect of postponing to the interest under the disposition any interest affecting the estate immediately before the disposition whose priority is not protected at the time of registration.

(2)   For the purposes of subsection (1), the priority of an interest is protected –
  (a)   in any case, if the interest–
      (i)   is a registered charge or the subject of a notice in the register,
      (ii)   falls within any of the paragraphs of Schedule 3, or
      (iii)   appears from the register to be excepted from the effect of registration, and
  (b)   in the case of a disposition of a leasehold estate, if the burden of the interest is incident to the estate.

(3)   Subsection (2)(a)(ii) does not apply to an interest which has been the subject of a notice in the register at any time since the coming into force of this section.

(4)   Where the grant of a leasehold estate in land out of a registered estate does not involve a registrable disposition, this section has effect as if –
  (a)   the grant involved such a disposition, and
  (b)   the disposition were registered at the time of the grant.

30   Effect of registered dispositions: charges
(1)   If a registrable disposition of a registered charge is made for valuable consideration, completion of the disposition by registration has the effect of

postponing to the interest under the disposition any interest affecting the charge immediately before the disposition whose priority is not protected at the time of registration.

(2)   For the purposes of subsection (1), the priority of an interest is protected –
    (a)   in any case, if the interest –
        (i)   is a registered charge or the subject of a notice in the register,
        (ii)   falls within any of the paragraphs of Schedule 3, or
        (iii)   appears from the register to be excepted from the effect of registration, and
    (b)   in the case of a disposition of a charge which relates to a leasehold estate, if the burden of the interest is incident to the estate.

(3)   Subsection (2)(a)(ii) does not apply to an interest which has been the subject of a notice in the register at any time since the coming into force of this section.

31   Inland Revenue charges

The effect of a disposition of a registered estate or charge on a charge under section 237 of the Inheritance Tax Act 1984 (charge for unpaid tax) is to be determined, not in accordance with sections 28 to 30 above, but in accordance with sections 237(6) and 238 of that Act (under which a purchaser in good faith for money or money's worth takes free from the charge in the absence of registration).

PART 4
Notices and Restrictions

Notices

32   Nature and effect

(1)   A notice is an entry in the register in respect of the burden of an interest affecting a registered estate or charge.

(2)   The entry of a notice is to be made in relation to the registered estate or charge affected by the interest concerned.

(3)   The fact that an interest is the subject of a notice does not necessarily mean that the interest is valid, but does mean that the priority of the interest, if valid, is protected for the purposes of sections 29 and 30.

33   Excluded interests

No notice may be entered in the register in respect of any of the following –
    (a)   an interest under –
        (i)   a trust of land, or
        (ii)   a settlement under the Settled Land Act 1925,
    (b)   a leasehold estate in land which –
        (i)   is granted for a term of years of three years or less from the date of the grant, and
        (ii)   is not required to be registered,

(c) a restrictive covenant made between a lessor and lessee, so far as relating to the demised premises,

(d) an interest which is capable of being registered under the Commons Registration Act 1965, and

(e) an interest in any coal or coal mine, the rights attached to any such interest and the rights of any person under section 38, 49 or 51 of the Coal Industry Act 1994.

34 Entry on application

(1) A person who claims to be entitled to the benefit of an interest affecting a registered estate or charge may, if the interest is not excluded by section 33, apply to the registrar for the entry in the register of a notice in respect of the interest.

(2) Subject to rules, an application under this section may be for –
(a) an agreed notice, or
(b) a unilateral notice.

(3) The registrar may only approve an application for an agreed notice if –
(a) the applicant is the relevant registered proprietor, or a person entitled to be registered as such proprietor,
(b) the relevant registered proprietor, or a person entitled to be registered as such proprietor, consents to the entry of the notice, or
(c) the registrar is satisfied as to the validity of the applicant's claim.

(4) In subsection (3), references to the relevant registered proprietor are to the proprietor of the registered estate or charge affected by the interest to which the application relates.

35 Unilateral notices

(1) If the registrar enters a notice in the register in pursuance of an application under section 34(2)(b) ('a unilateral notice'), he must give notice of the entry to –
(a) the proprietor of the registered estate or charge to which it relates, and
(b) such other persons as rules may provide.

(2) A unilateral notice must –
(a) indicate that it is such a notice, and
(b) identify who is the beneficiary of the notice.

(3) The person shown in the register as the beneficiary of a unilateral notice, or such other person as rules may provide, may apply to the registrar for the removal of the notice from the register.

36 Cancellation of unilateral notices

(1) A person may apply to the registrar for the cancellation of a unilateral notice if he is –
(a) the registered proprietor of the estate or charge to which the notice relates, or
(b) a person entitled to be registered as the proprietor of that estate or charge.

(2)   Where an application is made under subsection (1), the registrar must give the beneficiary of the notice notice of the application and of the effect of subsection (3).

(3)   If the beneficiary of the notice does not exercise his right to object to the application before the end of such period as rules may provide, the registrar must cancel the notice.

(4)   In this section –
'beneficiary', in relation to a unilateral notice, means the person shown in the register as the beneficiary of the notice, or such other person as rules may provide;
'unilateral notice' means a notice entered in the register in pursuance of an application under section 34(2)(b).

37   Unregistered interests
(1)   If it appears to the registrar that a registered estate is subject to an unregistered interest which –
      (a)   falls within any of the paragraphs of Schedule 1, and
      (b)   is not excluded by section 33,
he may enter a notice in the register in respect of the interest.

(2)   The registrar must give notice of an entry under this section to such persons as rules may provide.

38   Registrable dispositions
Where a person is entered in the register as the proprietor of an interest under a disposition falling within section 27(2)(b) to (e), the registrar must also enter a notice in the register in respect of that interest.

39   Supplementary
Rules may make provision about the form and content of notices in the register.

Restrictions

40   Nature
(1)   A restriction is an entry in the register regulating the circumstances in which a disposition of a registered estate or charge may be the subject of an entry in the register.

(2)   A restriction may, in particular –
      (a)   prohibit the making of an entry in respect of any disposition, or a disposition of a kind specified in the restriction;
      (b)   prohibit the making of an entry –
            (i)   indefinitely,
            (ii)   for a period specified in the restriction, or
            (iii) until the occurrence of an event so specified.

(3)   Without prejudice to the generality of subsection (2)(b)(iii), the events which may be specified include –

    (a)   the giving of notice,
    (b)   the obtaining of consent, and
    (c)   the making of an order by the court or registrar.

(4)   The entry of a restriction is to be made in relation to the registered estate or charge to which it relates.

41   Effect

(1)   Where a restriction is entered in the register, no entry in respect of a disposition to which the restriction applies may be made in the register otherwise than in accordance with the terms of the restriction, subject to any order under subsection (2).

(2)   The registrar may by order –
    (a)   disapply a restriction in relation to a disposition specified in the order or dispositions of a kind so specified, or
    (b)   provide that a restriction has effect, in relation to a disposition specified in the order or dispositions of a kind so specified, with modifications so specified.

(3)   The power under subsection (2) is exercisable only on the application of a person who appears to the registrar to have a sufficient interest in the restriction.

42   Power of registrar to enter

(1)   The registrar may enter a restriction in the register if it appears to him that it is necessary or desirable to do so for the purpose of –
    (a)   preventing invalidity or unlawfulness in relation to dispositions of a registered estate or charge,
    (b)   securing that interests which are capable of being overreached on a disposition of a registered estate or charge are overreached, or
    (c)   protecting a right or claim in relation to a registered estate or charge.

(2)   No restriction may be entered under subsection (1)(c) for the purpose of protecting the priority of an interest which is, or could be, the subject of a notice.

(3)   The registrar must give notice of any entry made under this section to the proprietor of the registered estate or charge concerned, except where the entry is made in pursuance of an application under section 43.

(4)   For the purposes of subsection (1)(c), a person entitled to the benefit of a charging order relating to an interest under a trust shall be treated as having a right or claim in relation to the trust property.

43   Applications

(1)   A person may apply to the registrar for the entry of a restriction under section 42(1) if –
    (a)   he is the relevant registered proprietor, or a person entitled to be registered as such proprietor,

    (b)   the relevant registered proprietor, or a person entitled to be registered as such proprietor, consents to the application, or

    (c)   he otherwise has a sufficient interest in the making of the entry.

(2)   Rules may –

    (a)   require the making of an application under subsection (1) in such circumstances, and by such person, as the rules may provide;

    (b)   make provision about the form of consent for the purposes of sub-section (1)(b);

    (c)   provide for classes of person to be regarded as included in sub-section (1)(c);

    (d)   specify standard forms of restriction.

(3)   If an application under subsection (1) is made for the entry of a restriction which is not in a form specified under subsection (2)(d), the registrar may only approve the application if it appears to him –

    (a)   that the terms of the proposed restriction are reasonable, and

    (b)   that applying the proposed restriction would –

        (i)   be straightforward, and

        (ii)   not place an unreasonable burden on him.

(4)   In subsection (1), references to the relevant registered proprietor are to the proprietor of the registered estate or charge to which the application relates.

44   Obligatory restrictions

(1)   If the registrar enters two or more persons in the register as the proprietor of a registered estate in land, he must also enter in the register such restrictions as rules may provide for the purpose of securing that interests which are capable of being overreached on a disposition of the estate are overreached.

(2)   Where under any enactment the registrar is required to enter a restriction without application, the form of the restriction shall be such as rules may provide.

45   Notifiable applications

(1)   Where an application under section 43(1) is notifiable, the registrar must give notice of the application, and of the right to object to it, to –

    (a)   the proprietor of the registered estate or charge to which it relates, and

    (b)   such other persons as rules may provide.

(2)   The registrar may not determine an application to which subsection (1) applies before the end of such period as rules may provide, unless the person, or each of the persons, notified under that subsection has exercised his right to object to the application or given the registrar notice that he does not intend to do so.

(3)   For the purposes of this section, an application under section 43(1) is notifiable unless it is –

(a) made by or with the consent of the proprietor of the registered estate or charge to which the application relates, or a person entitled to be registered as such proprietor,

(b) made in pursuance of rules under section 43(2)(a), or

(c) an application for the entry of a restriction reflecting a limitation under an order of the court or registrar, or an undertaking given in place of such an order.

46 Power of court to order entry

(1) If it appears to the court that it is necessary or desirable to do so for the purpose of protecting a right or claim in relation to a registered estate or charge, it may make an order requiring the registrar to enter a restriction in the register.

(2) No order under this section may be made for the purpose of protecting the priority of an interest which is, or could be, the subject of a notice.

(3) The court may include in an order under this section a direction that an entry made in pursuance of the order is to have overriding priority.

(4) If an order under this section includes a direction under subsection (3), the registrar must make such entry in the register as rules may provide.

(5) The court may make the exercise of its power under subsection (3) subject to such terms and conditions as it thinks fit.

47 Withdrawal

A person may apply to the registrar for the withdrawal of a restriction if –

(a) the restriction was entered in such circumstances as rules may provide, and

(b) he is of such a description as rules may provide.

PART 5
Charges

Relative priority

48 Registered charges

(1) Registered charges on the same registered estate, or on the same registered charge, are to be taken to rank as between themselves in the order shown in the register.

(2) Rules may make provision about –

(a) how the priority of registered charges as between themselves is to be shown in the register, and

(b) applications for registration of the priority of registered charges as between themselves.

49 Tacking and further advances

(1) The proprietor of a registered charge may make a further advance on the

security of the charge ranking in priority to a subsequent charge if he has not received from the subsequent chargee notice of the creation of the subsequent charge.

(2)   Notice given for the purposes of subsection (1) shall be treated as received at the time when, in accordance with rules, it ought to have been received.

(3)   The proprietor of a registered charge may also make a further advance on the security of the charge ranking in priority to a subsequent charge if –
   (a)   the advance is made in pursuance of an obligation, and
   (b)   at the time of the creation of the subsequent charge the obligation was entered in the register in accordance with rules.

(4)   The proprietor of a registered charge may also make a further advance on the security of the charge ranking in priority to a subsequent charge if –
   (a)   the parties to the prior charge have agreed a maximum amount for which the charge is security, and
   (b)   at the time of the creation of the subsequent charge the agreement was entered in the register in accordance with rules.

(5)   Rules may–
   (a)   disapply subsection (4) in relation to charges of a description specified in the rules, or
   (b)   provide for the application of that subsection to be subject, in the case of charges of a description so specified, to compliance with such conditions as may be so specified.

(6)   Except as provided by this section, tacking in relation to a charge over registered land is only possible with the agreement of the subsequent chargee.

50   Overriding statutory charges: duty of notification
If the registrar enters a person in the register as the proprietor of a charge which –
   (a)   is created by or under an enactment, and
   (b)   has effect to postpone a charge which at the time of registration of the statutory charge is –
      (i)   entered in the register, or
      (ii)   the basis for an entry in the register,
he must in accordance with rules give notice of the creation of the statutory charge to such person as rules may provide.

Powers as chargee

51   Effect of completion by registration
On completion of the relevant registration requirements, a charge created by means of a registrable disposition of a registered estate has effect, if it would not otherwise do so, as a charge by deed by way of legal mortgage.

52   Protection of disponees
(1)   Subject to any entry in the register to the contrary, the proprietor of a registered

charge is to be taken to have, in relation to the property subject to the charge, the powers of disposition conferred by law on the owner of a legal mortgage.

(2)   Subsection (1) has effect only for the purpose of preventing the title of a disponee being questioned (and so does not affect the lawfulness of a disposition).

53   Powers as sub-chargee

The registered proprietor of a sub-charge has, in relation to the property subject to the principal charge or any intermediate charge, the same powers as the sub-chargor.

Realisation of security

54   Proceeds of sale: chargee's duty

For the purposes of section 105 of the Law of Property Act 1925 (mortgagee's duties in relation to application of proceeds of sale), in its application to the proceeds of sale of registered land, a person shall be taken to have notice of anything in the register immediately before the disposition on sale.

55   Local land charges

A charge over registered land which is a local land charge may only be realised if the title to the charge is registered.

Miscellaneous

56   Receipt in case of joint proprietors

Where a charge is registered in the name of two or more proprietors, a valid receipt for the money secured by the charge may be given by –

    (a)   the registered proprietors,

    (b)   the survivors or survivor of the registered proprietors, or

    (c)   the personal representative of the last survivor of the registered proprietors.

57   Entry of right of consolidation

Rules may make provision about entry in the register of a right of consolidation in relation to a registered charge.

PART 6
Registration: General

Registration as proprietor

58   Conclusiveness

(1)   If, on the entry of a person in the register as the proprietor of a legal estate, the legal estate would not otherwise be vested in him, it shall be deemed to be vested in him as a result of the registration.

(2)   Subsection (1) does not apply where the entry is made in pursuance of a registrable disposition in relation to which some other registration requirement remains to be met.

59 Dependent estates

(1) The entry of a person in the register as the proprietor of a legal estate which subsists for the benefit of a registered estate must be made in relation to the registered estate.

(2) The entry of a person in the register as the proprietor of a charge on a registered estate must be made in relation to that estate.

(3) The entry of a person in the register as the proprietor of a sub-charge on a registered charge must be made in relation to that charge.

Boundaries

60 Boundaries

(1) The boundary of a registered estate as shown for the purposes of the register is a general boundary, unless shown as determined under this section.

(2) A general boundary does not determine the exact line of the boundary.

(3) Rules may make provision enabling or requiring the exact line of the boundary of a registered estate to be determined and may, in particular, make provision about –
  (a) the circumstances in which the exact line of a boundary may or must be determined,
  (b) how the exact line of a boundary may be determined,
  (c) procedure in relation to applications for determination, and
  (d) the recording of the fact of determination in the register or the index maintained under section 68.

(4) Rules under this section must provide for applications for determination to be made to the registrar.

61 Accretion and diluvion

(1) The fact that a registered estate in land is shown in the register as having a particular boundary does not affect the operation of accretion or diluvion.

(2) An agreement about the operation of accretion or diluvion in relation to a registered estate in land has effect only if registered in accordance with rules.

Quality of title

62 Power to upgrade title

(1) Where the title to a freehold estate is entered in the register as possessory or qualified, the registrar may enter it as absolute if he is satisfied as to the title to the estate.

(2) Where the title to a leasehold estate is entered in the register as good leasehold, the registrar may enter it as absolute if he is satisfied as to the superior title.

(3)   Where the title to a leasehold estate is entered in the register as possessory or qualified the registrar may –
    (a)   enter it as good leasehold if he is satisfied as to the title to the estate, and
    (b)   enter it as absolute if he is satisfied both as to the title to the estate and as to the superior title.

(4)   Where the title to a freehold estate in land has been entered in the register as possessory for at least twelve years, the registrar may enter it as absolute if he is satisfied that the proprietor is in possession of the land.

(5)   Where the title to a leasehold estate in land has been entered in the register as possessory for at least twelve years, the registrar may enter it as good leasehold if he is satisfied that the proprietor is in possession of the land.

(6)   None of the powers under subsections (1) to (5) is exercisable if there is outstanding any claim adverse to the title of the registered proprietor which is made by virtue of an estate, right or interest whose enforceability is preserved by virtue of the existing entry about the class of title.

(7)   The only persons who may apply to the registrar for the exercise of any of the powers under subsections (1) to (5) are –
    (a)   the proprietor of the estate to which the application relates,
    (b)   a person entitled to be registered as the proprietor of that estate,
    (c)   the proprietor of a registered charge affecting that estate, and
    (d)   a person interested in a registered estate which derives from that estate.

(8)   In determining for the purposes of this section whether he is satisfied as to any title, the registrar is to apply the same standards as those which apply under section 9 or 10 to first registration of title.

(9)   The Lord Chancellor may by order amend subsection (4) or (5) by substituting for the number of years for the time being specified in that subsection such number of years as the order may provide.

63   Effect of upgrading title
(1)   On the title to a registered freehold or leasehold estate being entered under section 62 as absolute, the proprietor ceases to hold the estate subject to any estate, right or interest whose enforceability was preserved by virtue of the previous entry about the class of title.

(2)   Subsection (1) also applies on the title to a registered leasehold estate being entered under section 62 as good leasehold, except that the entry does not affect or prejudice the enforcement of any estate, right or interest affecting, or in derogation of, the title of the lessor to grant the lease.

64   Use of register to record defects in title
(1)   If it appears to the registrar that a right to determine a registered estate in land is exercisable, he may enter the fact in the register.

(2)   Rules may make provision about entries under subsection (1) and may, in particular, make provision about –

    (a)   the circumstances in which there is a duty to exercise the power conferred by that subsection,

    (b)   how entries under that subsection are to be made, and

    (c)   the removal of such entries.

Alteration of register

65   Alteration of register
Schedule 4 (which makes provision about alteration of the register) has effect.

Information etc

66   Inspection of the registers etc
(1)   Any person may inspect and make copies of, or of any part of –

    (a)   the register of title,

    (b)   any document kept by the registrar which is referred to in the register of title,

    (c)   any other document kept by the registrar which relates to an application to him, or

    (d)   the register of cautions against first registration.

(2)   The right under subsection (1) is subject to rules which may, in particular –

    (a)   provide for exceptions to the right, and

    (b)   impose conditions on its exercise, including conditions requiring the payment of fees.

67   Official copies of the registers etc
(1)   An official copy of, or of a part of –

    (a)   the register of title,

    (b)   any document which is referred to in the register of title and kept by the registrar,

    (c)   any other document kept by the registrar which relates to an application to him, or

    (d)   the register of cautions against first registration,

is admissible in evidence to the same extent as the original.

(2)   A person who relies on an official copy in which there is a mistake is not liable for loss suffered by another by reason of the mistake.

(3)   Rules may make provision for the issue of official copies and may, in particular, make provision about –

    (a)   the form of official copies,

    (b)   who may issue official copies,

    (c)   applications for official copies, and

    (d)   the conditions to be met by applicants for official copies, including conditions requiring the payment of fees.

68 Index

(1) The registrar must keep an index for the purpose of enabling the following matters to be ascertained in relation to any parcel of land –
  (a) whether any registered estate relates to the land,
  (b) how any registered estate which relates to the land is identified for the purposes of the register,
  (c) whether the land is affected by any, and, if so what, caution against first registration, and
  (d) such other matters as rules may provide.

(2) Rules may –
  (a) make provision about how the index is to be kept and may, in particular, make provision about –
    (i) the information to be included in the index,
    (ii) the form in which information included in the index is to be kept, and
    (iii) the arrangement of that information;
  (b) make provision about official searches of the index.

69 Historical information

(1) The registrar may on application provide information about the history of a registered title.

(2) Rules may make provision about applications for the exercise of the power conferred by subsection (1).

(3) The registrar may –
  (a) arrange for the provision of information about the history of registered titles, and
  (b) authorise anyone who has the function of providing information under paragraph (a) to have access on such terms as the registrar thinks fit to any relevant information kept by him.

70 Official searches

Rules may make provision for official searches of the register, including searches of pending applications for first registration, and may, in particular, make provision about –
  (a) the form of applications for searches,
  (b) the manner in which such applications may be made,
  (c) the form of official search certificates, and
  (d) the manner in which such certificates may be issued.

Applications

71 Duty to disclose unregistered interests

Where rules so provide –
  (a) a person applying for registration under Chapter 1 of Part 2 must provide

to the registrar such information as the rules may provide about any
interest affecting the estate to which the application relates which –
  (i)   falls within any of the paragraphs of Schedule 1, and
  (ii)   is of a description specified by the rules;
  (b)   a person applying to register a registrable disposition of a registered estate
         must provide to the registrar such information as the rules may provide
         about any unregistered interest affecting the estate which –
  (i)   falls within any of the paragraphs of Schedule 3, and
  (ii)   is of description specified by the rules.

72   Priority protection

(1)   For the purposes of this section, an application for an entry in the register is
protected if –
  (a)   it is one to which a priority period relates, and
  (b)   it is made before the end of that period.

(2)   Where an application for an entry in the register is protected, any entry made in
the register during the priority period relating to the application is postponed to any
entry made in pursuance of it.

(3)   Subsection (2) does not apply if –
  (a)   the earlier entry was made in pursuance of a protected application, and
  (b)   the priority period relating to that application ranks ahead of the one
         relating to the application for the other entry.

(4)   Subsection (2) does not apply if the earlier entry is one to which a direction
under section 46(3) applies.

(5)   The registrar may defer dealing with an application for an entry in the register if
it appears to him that subsection (2) might apply to the entry were he to make it.

(6)   Rules may –
  (a)   make provision for priority periods in connection with –
  (i)   official searches of the register, including searches of pending
          applications for first registration, or
  (ii)   the noting in the register of a contract for the making of a registrable
          disposition of a registered estate or charge;
  (b)   make provision for the keeping of records in relation to priority periods
         and the inspection of such records.

(7)   Rules under subsection (6)(a) may, in particular, make provision about –
  (a)   the commencement and length of a priority period,
  (b)   the applications for registration to which such a period relates,
  (c)   the order in which competing priority periods rank, and
  (d)   the application of subsections (2) and (3) in cases where more than one
         priority period relates to the same application.

73   Objections

(1)   Subject to subsections (2) and (3), anyone may object to an application to the registrar.

(2)   In the case of an application under section 18, only the person who lodged the caution to which the application relates, or such other person as rules may provide, may object.

(3)   In the case of an application under section 36, only the person shown in the register as the beneficiary of the notice to which the application relates, or such other person as rules may provide, may object.

(4)   The right to object under this section is subject to rules.

(5)   Where an objection is made under this section, the registrar –
  (a)   must give notice of the objection to the applicant, and
  (b)   may not determine the application until the objection has been disposed of.

(6)   Subsection (5) does not apply if the objection is one which the registrar is satisfied is groundless.

(7)   If it is not possible to dispose by agreement of an objection to which sub-section (5) applies, the registrar must refer the matter to the adjudicator.

(8)   Rules may make provision about references under subsection (7).

74   Effective date of registration
An entry made in the register in pursuance of –
  (a)   an application for registration of an unregistered legal estate, or
  (b)   an application for registration in relation to a disposition required to be completed by registration,
has effect from the time of the making of the application.

Proceedings before the registrar

75   Production of documents

(1)   The registrar may require a person to produce a document for the purposes of proceedings before him.

(2)   The power under subsection (1) is subject to rules.

(3)   A requirement under subsection (1) shall be enforceable as an order of the court.

(4)   A person aggrieved by a requirement under subsection (1) may appeal to a county court, which may make any order which appears appropriate.

76   Costs
(1)   The registrar may make orders about costs in relation to proceedings before him.

(2)   The power under subsection (1) is subject to rules which may, in particular, make provision about –
   (a)   who may be required to pay costs,
   (b)   whose costs a person may be required to pay,
   (c)   the kind of costs which a person may be required to pay, and
   (d)   the assessment of costs.

(3)   Without prejudice to the generality of subsection (2), rules under that subsection may include provision about –
   (a)   costs of the registrar, and
   (b)   liability for costs thrown away as the result of neglect or delay by a legal representative of a party to proceedings.

(4)   An order under subsection (1) shall be enforceable as an order of the court.

(5)   A person aggrieved by an order under subsection (1) may appeal to a county court, which may make any order which appears appropriate.

Miscellaneous

77   Duty to act reasonably
(1)   A person must not exercise any of the following rights without reasonable cause –
   (a)   the right to lodge a caution under section 15,
   (b)   the right to apply for the entry of a notice or restriction, and
   (c)   the right to object to an application to the registrar.

(2)   The duty under this section is owed to any person who suffers damage in consequence of its breach.

78   Notice of trust not to affect registrar
The registrar shall not be affected with notice of a trust.

PART 7
Special Cases

The Crown

79   Voluntary registration of demesne land
(1)   Her Majesty may grant an estate in fee simple absolute in possession out of demesne land to Herself.

(2)   The grant of an estate under subsection (1) is to be regarded as not having been

made unless an application under section 3 is made in respect of the estate before the end of the period for registration.

(3)   The period for registration is two months beginning with the date of the grant, or such longer period as the registrar may provide under subsection (4).

(4)   If on the application of Her Majesty the registrar is satisfied that there is a good reason for doing so, he may by order provide that the period for registration ends on such later date as he may specify in the order.

(5)   If an order under subsection (4) is made in a case where subsection (2) has already applied, that application of the subsection is to be treated as not having occurred.

80   Compulsory registration of grants out of demesne land
(1)   Section 4(1) shall apply as if the following were included among the events listed –
   (a)   the grant by Her Majesty out of demesne land of an estate in fee simple absolute in possession, otherwise than under section 79;
   (b)   the grant by Her Majesty out of demesne land of an estate in land –
      (i)   for a term of years absolute of more than seven years from the date of the grant, and
      (ii)   for valuable or other consideration, by way of gift or in pursuance of an order of any court.

(2)   In subsection (1)(b)(ii), the reference to grant by way of gift includes grant for the purpose of constituting a trust under which Her Majesty does not retain the whole of the beneficial interest.

(3)   Subsection (1) does not apply to the grant of an estate in mines and minerals held apart from the surface.

(4)   The Lord Chancellor may by order –
   (a)   amend this section so as to add to the events in subsection (1) such events relating to demesne land as he may specify in the order, and
   (b)   make such consequential amendments of any provision of, or having effect under, any Act as he thinks appropriate.

(5)   In its application by virtue of subsection (1), section 7 has effect with the substitution for subsection (2) of –
   '(2) On the application of subsection (1), the grant has effect as a contract made for valuable consideration to grant the legal estate concerned'.

81   Demesne land: cautions against first registration
(1)   Section 15 shall apply as if demesne land were held by Her Majesty for an unregistered estate in fee simple absolute in possession.

(2)   The provisions of this Act relating to cautions against first registration shall, in

relation to cautions lodged by virtue of subsection (1), have effect subject to such modifications as rules may provide.

82   Escheat etc
(1)   Rules may make provision about –
    (a)   the determination of a registered freehold estate in land, and
    (b)   the registration of an unregistered freehold legal estate in land in respect of land to which a former registered freehold estate in land related.

(2)   Rules under this section may, in particular –

    (a)   make provision for determination to be dependent on the meeting of such registration requirements as the rules may specify;
    (b)   make provision for entries relating to a freehold estate in land to continue in the register, notwithstanding determination, for such time as the rules may provide;
    (c)   make provision for the making in the register in relation to a former freehold estate in land of such entries as the rules may provide;
    (d)   make provision imposing requirements to be met in connection with an application for the registration of such an unregistered estate as is mentioned in subsection (1)(b).

83   Crown and Duchy land: representation
(1)   With respect to a Crown or Duchy interest, the appropriate authority –
    (a)   may represent the owner of the interest for all purposes of this Act,
    (b)   is entitled to receive such notice as that person is entitled to receive under this Act, and
    (c)   may make such applications and do such other acts as that person is entitled to make or do under this Act.

(2)   In this section –
'the appropriate authority' means –
    (a)   in relation to an interest belonging to Her Majesty in right of the Crown and forming part of the Crown Estate, the Crown Estate Commissioners;
    (b)   in relation to any other interest belonging to Her Majesty in right of the Crown, the government department having the management of the interest or, if there is no such department, such person as Her Majesty may appoint in writing under the Royal Sign Manual;
    (c)   in relation to an interest belonging to Her Majesty in right of the Duchy of Lancaster, the Chancellor of the Duchy;
    (d)   in relation to an interest belonging to the Duchy of Cornwall, such person as the Duke of Cornwall, or the possessor for the time being of the Duchy of Cornwall, appoints;
    (e)   in relation to an interest belonging to a government department, or held in trust for Her Majesty for the purposes of a government department, that department;

'Crown interest' means an interest belonging to Her Majesty in right of the Crown, or belonging to a government department, or held in trust for Her Majesty for the purposes of a government department;

'Duchy interest' means an interest belonging to Her Majesty in right of the Duchy of Lancaster, or belonging to the Duchy of Cornwall;

'interest' means any estate, interest or charge in or over land and any right or claim in relation to land.

84   Disapplication of requirements relating to Duchy land

Nothing in any enactment relating to the Duchy of Lancaster or the Duchy of Cornwall shall have effect to impose any requirement with respect to formalities or enrolment in relation to a disposition by a registered proprietor.

85   Bona vacantia

Rules may make provision about how the passing of a registered estate or charge as bona vacantia is to be dealt with for the purposes of this Act.

Pending actions etc

86   Bankruptcy

(1)   In this Act, references to an interest affecting an estate or charge do not include a petition in bankruptcy or bankruptcy order.

(2)   As soon as practicable after registration of a petition in bankruptcy as a pending action under the Land Charges Act 1972, the registrar must enter in the register in relation to any registered estate or charge which appears to him to be affected a notice in respect of the pending action.

(3)   Unless cancelled by the registrar in such manner as rules may provide, a notice entered under subsection (2) continues in force until –
  (a)   a restriction is entered in the register under subsection (4), or
  (b)   the trustee in bankruptcy is registered as proprietor.

(4)   As soon as practicable after registration of a bankruptcy order under the Land Charges Act 1972, the registrar must, in relation to any registered estate or charge which appears to him to be affected by the order, enter in the register a restriction reflecting the effect of the Insolvency Act 1986.

(5)   Where the proprietor of a registered estate or charge is adjudged bankrupt, the title of his trustee in bankruptcy is void as against a person to whom a registrable disposition of the estate or charge is made if –
  (a)   the disposition is made for valuable consideration,
  (b)   the person to whom the disposition is made acts in good faith, and
  (c)   at the time of the disposition–
    (i)   no notice or restriction is entered under this section in relation to the registered estate or charge, and
    (ii)   the person to whom the disposition is made has no notice of the bankruptcy petition or the adjudication.

(6)   Subsection (5) only applies if the relevant registration requirements are met in relation to the disposition, but, when they are met, has effect as from the date of the disposition.

(7)   Nothing in this section requires a person to whom a registrable disposition is made to make any search under the Land Charges Act 1972.

87   Pending land actions, writs, orders and deeds of arrangement
(1)   Subject to the following provisions, references in this Act to an interest affecting an estate or charge include –
> (a)   a pending land action within the meaning of the Land Charges Act 1972,
> (b)   a writ or order of the kind mentioned in section 6(1)(a) of that Act (writ or order affecting land issued or made by any court for the purposes of enforcing a judgment or recognisance),
> (c)   an order appointing a receiver or sequestrator, and
> (d)   a deed of arrangement.

(2)   No notice may be entered in the register in respect of –
> (a)   an order appointing a receiver or sequestrator, or
> (b)   a deed of arrangement.

(3)   None of the matters mentioned in subsection (1) shall be capable of falling within paragraph 2 of Schedule 1 or 3.

(4)   In its application to any of the matters mentioned in subsection (1), this Act shall have effect subject to such modifications as rules may provide.

(5)   In this section, 'deed of arrangement' has the same meaning as in the Deeds of Arrangement Act 1914.

Miscellaneous

88   Incorporeal hereditaments
In its application to –
> (a)   rentcharges,
> (b)   franchises,
> (c)   profits a prendre in gross, or
> (d)   manors,
this Act shall have effect subject to such modification as rules may provide.

89   Settlements
(1)   Rules may make provision for the purposes of this Act in relation to the application to registered land of the enactments relating to settlements under the Settled Land Act 1925.

(2)   Rules under this section may include provision modifying any of those enactments in its application to registered land.

(3)   In this section, 'registered land' means an interest the title to which is, or is required to be, registered.

90   PPP leases relating to transport in London
(1)   No application for registration under section 3 may be made in respect of a leasehold estate in land under a PPP lease.

(2)   The requirement of registration does not apply on the grant or transfer of a leasehold estate in land under a PPP lease.

(3)   For the purposes of section 27, the following are not dispositions requiring to be completed by registration –
- (a)   the grant of a term of years absolute under a PPP lease;
- (b)   the express grant of an interest falling within section 1(2) of the Law of Property Act 1925, where the interest is created for the benefit of a leasehold estate in land under a PPP lease.

(4)   No notice may be entered in the register in respect of an interest under a PPP lease.

(5)   Schedules 1 and 3 have effect as if they included a paragraph referring to a PPP lease.

(6)   In this section, 'PPP lease' has the meaning given by section 218 of the Greater London Authority Act 1999 (which makes provision about leases created for public-private partnerships relating to transport in London).

PART 8
Electronic Conveyancing

91   Electronic dispositions: formalities
(1)   This section applies to a document in electronic form where –
- (a)   the document purports to effect a disposition which falls within sub-section (2), and
- (b)   the conditions in subsection (3) are met.

(2)   A disposition falls within this subsection if it is –
- (a)   a disposition of a registered estate or charge,
- (b)   a disposition of an interest which is the subject of a notice in the register, or
- (c)   a disposition which triggers the requirement of registration,
which is of a kind specified by rules.

(3)   The conditions referred to above are that –
- (a)   the document makes provision for the time and date when it takes effect,
- (b)   the document has the electronic signature of each person by whom it purports to be authenticated,
- (c)   each electronic signature is certified, and

(d)   such other conditions as rules may provide are met.

(4)   A document to which this section applies is to be regarded as –
(a)   in writing, and
(b)   signed by each individual, and sealed by each corporation, whose electronic signature it has.

(5)   A document to which this section applies is to be regarded for the purposes of any enactment as a deed.

(6)   If a document to which this section applies is authenticated by a person as agent, it is to be regarded for the purposes of any enactment as authenticated by him under the written authority of his principal.

(7)   If notice of an assignment made by means of a document to which this section applies is given in electronic form in accordance with rules, it is to be regarded for the purposes of any enactment as given in writing.

(8)   The right conferred by section 75 of the Law of Property Act 1925 (purchaser's right to have the execution of a conveyance attested) does not apply to a document to which this section applies.

(9)   If subsection (4) of section 36A of the Companies Act 1985 (execution of documents) applies to a document because of subsection (4) above, subsection (6) of that section (presumption of due execution) shall have effect in relation to the document with the substitution of 'authenticated' for 'signed'.

(10)   In this section, references to an electronic signature and to the certification of such a signature are to be read in accordance with section 7(2) and (3) of the Electronic Communications Act 2000.

92   Land registry network

(1)   The registrar may provide, or arrange for the provision of, an electronic communications network for use for such purposes as he thinks fit relating to registration or the carrying on of transactions which –
(a)   involve registration, and
(b)   are capable of being effected electronically.

(2)   Schedule 5 (which makes provision in connection with a network provided under subsection (1) and transactions carried on by means of such a network) has effect.

93   Power to require simultaneous registration

(1)   This section applies to a disposition of –
(a)   a registered estate or charge, or
(b)   an interest which is the subject of a notice in the register,
where the disposition is of a description specified by rules.

(2)   A disposition to which this section applies, or a contract to make such a disposition, only has effect if it is made by means of a document in electronic form and if, when the document purports to take effect –

(a)   it is electronically communicated to the registrar, and

(b)   the relevant registration requirements are met.

(3)   For the purposes of subsection (2)(b), the relevant registration requirements are –

(a)   in the case of a registrable disposition, the requirements under Schedule 2, and

(b)   in the case of any other disposition, or a contract, such requirements as rules may provide.

(4)   Section 27(1) does not apply to a disposition to which this section applies.

(5)   Before making rules under this section the Lord Chancellor must consult such persons as he considers appropriate.

(6)   In this section, 'disposition', in relation to a registered charge, includes postponement.

94   Electronic settlement

The registrar may take such steps as he thinks fit for the purpose of securing the provision of a system of electronic settlement in relation to transactions involving registration.

95   Supplementary

Rules may –

(a)   make provision about the communication of documents in electronic form to the registrar;

(b)   make provision about the electronic storage of documents communicated to the registrar in electronic form.

PART 9
Adverse Possession

96   Disapplication of periods of limitation

(1)   No period of limitation under section 15 of the Limitation Act 1980 (time limits in relation to recovery of land) shall run against any person, other than a chargee, in relation to an estate in land or rentcharge the title to which is registered.

(2)   No period of limitation under section 16 of that Act (time limits in relation to redemption of land) shall run against any person in relation to such an estate in land or rentcharge.

(3)   Accordingly, section 17 of that Act (extinction of title on expiry of time limit) does not operate to extinguish the title of any person where, by virtue of this section, a period of limitation does not run against him.

97   Registration of adverse possessor
Schedule 6 (which makes provision about the registration of an adverse possessor of an estate in land or rentcharge) has effect.

98   Defences
(1)   A person has a defence to an action for possession of land if –
   (a)   on the day immediately preceding that on which the action was brought he was entitled to make an application under paragraph 1 of Schedule 6 to be registered as the proprietor of an estate in the land, and
   (b)   had he made such an application on that day, the condition in paragraph 5(4) of that Schedule would have been satisfied.

(2)   A judgment for possession of land ceases to be enforceable at the end of the period of two years beginning with the date of the judgment if the proceedings in which the judgment is given were commenced against a person who was at that time entitled to make an application under paragraph 1 of Schedule 6.

(3)   A person has a defence to an action for possession of land if on the day immediately preceding that on which the action was brought he was entitled to make an application under paragraph 6 of Schedule 6 to be registered as the proprietor of an estate in the land.

(4)   A judgment for possession of land ceases to be enforceable at the end of the period of two years beginning with the date of the judgment if, at the end of that period, the person against whom the judgment was given is entitled to make an application under paragraph 6 of Schedule 6 to be registered as the proprietor of an estate in the land.

(5)   Where in any proceedings a court determines that –
   (a)   a person is entitled to a defence under this section, or
   (b)   a judgment for possession has ceased to be enforceable against a person by virtue of subsection (4),
the court must order the registrar to register him as the proprietor of the estate in relation to which he is entitled to make an application under Schedule 6.

(6)   The defences under this section are additional to any other defences a person may have.

(7)   Rules may make provision to prohibit the recovery of rent due under a rentcharge from a person who has been in adverse possession of the rentcharge.

PART 10
Land Registry

Administration

99   The land registry
(1)   There is to continue to be an office called Her Majesty's Land Registry which is to deal with the business of registration under this Act.

(2)   The land registry is to consist of –
  (a)   the Chief Land Registrar, who is its head, and
  (b)   the staff appointed by him;
and references in this Act to a member of the land registry are to be read accordingly.

(3)   The Lord Chancellor shall appoint a person to be the Chief Land Registrar.

(4)   Schedule 7 (which makes further provision about the land registry) has effect.

100   Conduct of business

(1)   Any function of the registrar may be carried out by any member of the land registry who is authorised for the purpose by the registrar.

(2)   The Lord Chancellor may by regulations make provision about the carrying out of functions during any vacancy in the office of registrar.

(3)   The Lord Chancellor may by order designate a particular office of the land registry as the proper office for the receipt of applications or a specified description of application.

(4)   The registrar may prepare and publish such forms and directions as he considers necessary or desirable for facilitating the conduct of the business of registration under this Act.

101   Annual report

(1)   The registrar must make an annual report on the business of the land registry to the Lord Chancellor.

(2)   The registrar must publish every report under this section and may do so in such manner as he thinks fit.

(3)   The Lord Chancellor must lay copies of every report under this section before Parliament.

Fees and indemnities

102   Fee orders

The Lord Chancellor may with the advice and assistance of the body referred to in section 127(2) (the Rule Committee), and the consent of the Treasury, by order –
  (a)   prescribe fees to be paid in respect of dealings with the land registry, except under section 69(3)(b) or 105;
  (b)   make provision about the payment of prescribed fees.

103   Indemnities

Schedule 8 (which makes provision for the payment of indemnities by the registrar) has effect.

Miscellaneous

104   General information about land
The registrar may publish information about land in England and Wales if it appears
to him to be information in which there is legitimate public interest.

105   Consultancy and advisory services
(1)   The registrar may provide, or arrange for the provision of, consultancy or
advisory services about the registration of land in England and Wales or elsewhere.

(2)   The terms on which services are provided under this section by the registrar, in
particular terms as to payment, shall be such as he thinks fit.

106   Incidental powers: companies
(1)   If the registrar considers it expedient to do so in connection with his functions
under section 69(3)(a), 92(1), 94 or 105(1) or paragraph 10 of Schedule 5, he may–
    (a)   form, or participate in the formation of, a company, or
    (b)   purchase, or invest in, a company.

(2)   In this section –
'company' means a company within the meaning of the Companies Act 1985;
'invest' means invest in any way (whether by acquiring assets, securities or rights or
    otherwise).

(3)   This section is without prejudice to any powers of the registrar exercisable
otherwise than by virtue of this section.

PART 11
Adjudication

107   The adjudicator
(1)   The Lord Chancellor shall appoint a person to be the Adjudicator to Her
Majesty's Land Registry.

(2)   To be qualified for appointment under subsection (1), a person must have a 10
year general qualification (within the meaning of section 71 of the Courts and Legal
Services Act 1990).

(3)   Schedule 9 (which makes further provision about the adjudicator) has effect.

108   Jurisdiction
(1)   The adjudicator has the following functions –
    (a)   determining matters referred to him under section 73(7), and
    (b)   determining appeals under paragraph 4 of Schedule 5.

(2)   Also, the adjudicator may, on application, make any order which the High Court
could make for the rectification or setting aside of a document which –
    (a)   effects a qualifying disposition of a registered estate or charge,

(b)   is a contract to make such a disposition, or

(c)   effects a transfer of an interest which is the subject of a notice in the register.

(3)   For the purposes of subsection (2)(a), a qualifying disposition is –

(a)   a registrable disposition, or

(b)   a disposition which creates an interest which may be the subject of a notice in the register.

(4)   The general law about the effect of an order of the High Court for the rectification or setting aside of a document shall apply to an order under this section.

109   Procedure

(1)   Hearings before the adjudicator shall be held in public, except where he is satisfied that exclusion of the public is just and reasonable.

(2)   Subject to that, rules may regulate the practice and procedure to be followed with respect to proceedings before the adjudicator and matters incidental to or consequential on such proceedings.

(3)   Rules under subsection (2) may, in particular, make provision about –

(a)   when hearings are to be held,

(b)   requiring persons to attend hearings to give evidence or to produce documents,

(c)   the form in which any decision of the adjudicator is to be given,

(d)   payment of costs of a party to proceedings by another party to the proceedings, and

(e)   liability for costs thrown away as the result of neglect or delay by a legal representative of a party to proceedings.

110   Functions in relation to disputes

(1)   In proceedings on a reference under section 73(7), the adjudicator may, instead of deciding a matter himself, direct a party to the proceedings to commence proceedings within a specified time in the court for the purpose of obtaining the court's decision on the matter.

(2)   Rules may make provision about the reference under subsection (1) of matters to the court and may, in particular, make provision about –

(a)   adjournment of the proceedings before the adjudicator pending the outcome of the proceedings before the court, and

(b)   the powers of the adjudicator in the event of failure to comply with a direction under subsection (1).

(3)   Rules may make provision about the functions of the adjudicator in consequence of a decision on a reference under section 73(7) and may, in particular, make provision enabling the adjudicator to determine, or give directions about the determination of –

(a)   the application to which the reference relates, or

(b)   such other present or future application to the registrar as the rules may provide.

(4)   If, in the case of a reference under section 73(7) relating to an application under paragraph 1 of Schedule 6, the adjudicator determines that it would be unconscionable because of an equity by estoppel for the registered proprietor to seek to dispossess the applicant, but that the circumstances are not such that the applicant ought to be registered as proprietor, the adjudicator –

(a)   must determine how the equity due to the applicant is to be satisfied, and
(b)   may for that purpose make any order that the High Court could make in the exercise of its equitable jurisdiction.

111   Appeals

(1)   Subject to subsection (2), a person aggrieved by a decision of the adjudicator may appeal to the High Court.

(2)   In the case of a decision on an appeal under paragraph 4 of Schedule 5, only appeal on a point of law is possible.

(3)   If on an appeal under this section relating to an application under paragraph 1 of Schedule 6 the court determines that it would be unconscionable because of an equity by estoppel for the registered proprietor to seek to dispossess the applicant, but that the circumstances are not such that the applicant ought to be registered as proprietor, the court must determine how the equity due to the applicant is to be satisfied.

112   Enforcement of orders etc

A requirement of the adjudicator shall be enforceable as an order of the court.

113   Fees

The Lord Chancellor may by order –
(a)   prescribe fees to be paid in respect of proceedings before the adjudicator;
(b)   make provision about the payment of prescribed fees.

114   Supplementary

Power to make rules under this Part is exercisable by the Lord Chancellor.

PART 12
Miscellaneous and General

Miscellaneous

115   Rights of pre-emption

(1)   A right of pre-emption in relation to registered land has effect from the time of creation as an interest capable of binding successors in title (subject to the rules about the effect of dispositions on priority).

(2)   This section has effect in relation to rights of pre-emption created on or after the day on which this section comes into force.

116   Proprietary estoppel and mere equities
It is hereby declared for the avoidance of doubt that, in relation to registered land, each of the following –
(a)   an equity by estoppel, and
(b)   a mere equity,
has effect from the time the equity arises as an interest capable of binding successors in title (subject to the rules about the effect of dispositions on priority).

117   Reduction in unregistered interests with automatic protection
(1)   Paragraphs 10 to 14 of Schedules 1 and 3 shall cease to have effect at the end of the period of ten years beginning with the day on which those Schedules come into force.

(2)   If made before the end of the period mentioned in subsection (1), no fee may be charged for –
(a)   an application to lodge a caution against first registration by virtue of an interest falling within any of paragraphs 10 to 14 of Schedule 1, or
(b)   an application for the entry in the register of a notice in respect of an interest falling within any of paragraphs 10 to 14 of Schedule 3.

118   Power to reduce qualifying term
(1)   The Lord Chancellor may by order substitute for the term specified in any of the following provisions –
(a)   section 3(3),
(b)   section 4(1)(c)(i) and (2)(b),
(c)   section 15(3)(a)(ii),
(d)   section 27(2)(b)(i),
(e)   section 80(1)(b)(i),
(f)   paragraph 1 of Schedule 1,
(g)   paragraphs 4(1), 5(1) and 6(1) of Schedule 2, and
(h)   paragraph 1 of Schedule 3,
such shorter term as he thinks fit.

(2)   An order under this section may contain such transitional provision as the Lord Chancellor thinks fit.

(3)   Before making an order under this section, the Lord Chancellor must consult such persons as he considers appropriate.

119   Power to deregister manors
On the application of the proprietor of a registered manor, the registrar may remove the title to the manor from the register.

120   Conclusiveness of filed copies etc
(1)   This section applies where –

(a) a disposition relates to land to which a registered estate relates, and

(b) an entry in the register relating to the registered estate refers to a document kept by the registrar which is not an original.

(2) As between the parties to the disposition, the document kept by the registrar is to be taken –

(a) to be correct, and

(b) to contain all the material parts of the original document.

(3) No party to the disposition may require production of the original document.

(4) No party to the disposition is to be affected by any provision of the original document which is not contained in the document kept by the registrar.

121 Forwarding of applications to registrar of companies

The Lord Chancellor may by rules make provision about the transmission by the registrar to the registrar of companies (within the meaning of the Companies Act 1985) of applications under –

(a) Part 12 of that Act (registration of charges), or

(b) Chapter 3 of Part 23 of that Act (corresponding provision for oversea companies).

122 Repeal of Land Registry Act 1862

(1) The Land Registry Act 1862 shall cease to have effect.

(2) The registrar shall have custody of records of title made under that Act.

(3) The registrar may discharge his duty under subsection (2) by keeping the relevant information in electronic form.

(4) The registrar may on application provide a copy of any information included in a record of title made under that Act.

(5) Rules may make provision about applications for the exercise of the power conferred by subsection (4).

Offences etc

123 Suppression of information

(1) A person commits an offence if in the course of proceedings relating to registration under this Act he suppresses information with the intention of –

(a) concealing a person's right or claim, or

(b) substantiating a false claim.

(2) A person guilty of an offence under this section is liable –

(a) on conviction on indictment, to imprisonment for a term not exceeding two years or to a fine;

(b)   on summary conviction, to imprisonment for a term not exceeding six months or to a fine not exceeding the statutory maximum, or to both.

124 Improper alteration of the registers

(1)   A person commits an offence if he dishonestly induces another –
  (a)   to change the register of title or cautions register, or
  (b)   to authorise the making of such a change.

(2)   A person commits an offence if he intentionally or recklessly makes an unauthorised change in the register of title or cautions register.

(3)   A person guilty of an offence under this section is liable –
  (a)   on conviction on indictment, to imprisonment for a term not exceeding 2 years or to a fine;
  (b)   on summary conviction, to imprisonment for a term not exceeding six months or to a fine not exceeding the statutory maximum, or to both.

(4)   In this section, references to changing the register of title include changing a document referred to in it.

125 Privilege against self-incrimination

(1)   The privilege against self-incrimination, so far as relating to offences under this Act, shall not entitle a person to refuse to answer any question or produce any document or thing in any legal proceedings other than criminal proceedings.

(2)   No evidence obtained under subsection (1) shall be admissible in any criminal proceedings under this Act against the person from whom it was obtained or that person's spouse.

Land registration rules

126 Miscellaneous and general powers

Schedule 10 (which contains miscellaneous and general land registration rule-making powers) has effect.

127 Exercise of powers

(1)   Power to make land registration rules is exercisable by the Lord Chancellor with the advice and assistance of the Rule Committee.

(2)   The Rule Committee is a body consisting of –
  (a)   a judge of the Chancery Division of the High Court nominated by the Lord Chancellor,
  (b)   the registrar,
  (c)   a person nominated by the General Council of the Bar,
  (d)   a person nominated by the Council of the Law Society,
  (e)   a person nominated by the Council of Mortgage Lenders,
  (f)   a person nominated by the Council of Licensed Conveyancers,
  (g)   a person nominated by the Royal Institution of Chartered Surveyors,

(h)   a person with experience in, and knowledge of, consumer affairs, and

(i)   any person nominated under subsection (3).

(3)   The Lord Chancellor may nominate to be a member of the Rule Committee any person who appears to him to have qualifications or experience which would be of value to the committee in considering any matter with which it is concerned.

Supplementary

128 Rules, regulations and orders

(1)   Any power of the Lord Chancellor to make rules, regulations or orders under this Act includes power to make different provision for different cases.

(2)   Any power of the Lord Chancellor to make rules, regulations or orders under this Act is exercisable by statutory instrument.

(3)   A statutory instrument containing –
  (a)   regulations under section 100(2), or
  (b)   an order under section 100(3), 102 or 113,
is to be laid before Parliament after being made.

(4)   A statutory instrument containing –
  (a)   land registration rules,
  (b)   rules under Part 11 or section 121,
  (c)   regulations under paragraph 5 of Schedule 9, or
  (d)   an order under section 5(1), 62(9), 80(4), 118(1) or 130,
is subject to annulment in pursuance of a resolution of either House of Parliament.

(5)   Rules under section 93 or paragraph 1, 2 or 3 of Schedule 5 shall not be made unless a draft of the rules has been laid before and approved by resolution of each House of Parliament.

129 Crown application

This Act binds the Crown.

130 Application to internal waters

This Act applies to land covered by internal waters of the United Kingdom which are –
  (a)   within England or Wales, or
  (b)   adjacent to England or Wales and specified for the purposes of this section by order made by the Lord Chancellor.

131 'Proprietor in possession'

(1)   For the purposes of this Act, land is in the possession of the proprietor of a registered estate in land if it is physically in his possession, or in that of a person who is entitled to be registered as the proprietor of the registered estate.

(2)   In the case of the following relationships, land which is (or is treated as being) in

the possession of the second-mentioned person is to be treated for the purposes of subsection (1) as in the possession of the first-mentioned person –

(a)　landlord and tenant;

(b)　mortgagor and mortgagee;

(c)　licensor and licensee;

(d)　trustee and beneficiary.

(3)　In subsection (1), the reference to entitlement does not include entitlement under Schedule 6.

132　General interpretation

(1)　In this Act –

'adjudicator' means the Adjudicator to Her Majesty's Land Registry;

'caution against first registration' means a caution lodged under section 15;

'cautions register' means the register kept under section 19(1);

'charge' means any mortgage, charge or lien for securing money or money's worth;

'demesne land' means land belonging to Her Majesty in right of the Crown which is not held for an estate in fee simple absolute in possession;

'land' includes –

(a)　buildings and other structures,

(b)　land covered with water, and

(c)　mines and minerals, whether or not held with the surface;

'land registration rules' means any rules under this Act, other than rules under section 93, Part 11, section 121 or paragraph 1, 2 or 3 of Schedule 5;

'legal estate' has the same meaning as in the Law of Property Act 1925;

'legal mortgage' has the same meaning as in the Law of Property Act 1925;

'mines and minerals' includes any strata or seam of minerals or substances in or under any land, and powers of working and getting any such minerals or substances;

'registrar' means the Chief Land Registrar;

'register' means the register of title, except in the context of cautions against first registration;

'registered' means entered in the register;

'registered charge' means a charge the title to which is entered in the register;

'registered estate' means a legal estate the title to which is entered in the register, other than a registered charge;

'registered land' means a registered estate or registered charge;

'registrable disposition' means a disposition which is required to be completed by registration under section 27;

'requirement of registration' means the requirement of registration under section 4;

'sub-charge' means a charge under section 23(2)(b);

'term of years absolute' has the same meaning as in the Law of Property Act 1925;

'valuable consideration' does not include marriage consideration or a nominal consideration in money.

(2)　In subsection (1), in the definition of 'demesne land', the reference to land belonging to Her Majesty does not include land in relation to which a freehold estate in land has determined, but in relation to which there has been no act of entry or management by the Crown.

(3)   In this Act –
    (a)   references to the court are to the High Court or a county court,
    (b)   references to an interest affecting an estate or charge are to an adverse
        right affecting the title to the estate or charge, and
    (c)   references to the right to object to an application to the registrar are to the
        right under section 73.

Final provisions

133   Minor and consequential amendments

Schedule 11 (which makes minor and consequential amendments) has effect.

134   Transition

(1)   The Lord Chancellor may by order make such transitional provisions and savings as he thinks fit in connection with the coming into force of any of the provisions of this Act.

(2)   Schedule 12 (which makes transitional provisions and savings) has effect.

(3)   Nothing in Schedule 12 affects the power to make transitional provisions and savings under subsection (1); and an order under that subsection may modify any provision made by that Schedule.

135   Repeals

The enactments specified in Schedule 13 (which include certain provisions which are already spent) are hereby repealed to the extent specified there.

136   Short title, commencement and extent

(1)   This Act may be cited as the Land Registration Act 2002.

(2)   This Act shall come into force on such day as the Lord Chancellor may by order appoint, and different days may be so appointed for different purposes.

(3)   Subject to subsection (4), this Act extends to England and Wales only.

(4)   Any amendment or repeal by this Act of an existing enactment, other than –
    (a)   section 37 of the Requisitioned Land and War Works Act 1945, and
    (b)   Schedule 2A to the Building Societies Act 1986,
has the same extent as the enactment amended or repealed.

SCHEDULE 1
Unregistered Interests which Override First Registration

Leasehold estates in land

1   A leasehold estate in land granted for a term not exceeding seven years from the date of the grant, except for a lease the grant of which falls within section 4(1) (d), (e) or (f).

Interests of persons in actual occupation

2   An interest belonging to a person in actual occupation, so far as relating to land of which he is in actual occupation, except for an interest under a settlement under the Settled Land Act 1925.

Easements and profits a prendre

3   A legal easement or profit a prendre.

Customary and public rights

4   A customary right.

5   A public right.

Local land charges

6   A local land charge.

Mines and minerals

7   An interest in any coal or coal mine, the rights attached to any such interest and the rights of any person under section 38, 49 or 51 of the Coal Industry Act 1994.

8   In the case of land to which title was registered before 1898, rights to mines and minerals (and incidental rights) created before 1898.

9   In the case of land to which title was registered between 1898 and 1925 inclusive, rights to mines and minerals (and incidental rights) created before the date of registration of the title.

Miscellaneous

10   A franchise.

11   A manorial right.

12   A right to rent which was reserved to the Crown on the granting of any freehold estate (whether or not the right is still vested in the Crown).

13   A non-statutory right in respect of an embankment or sea or river wall.

14   A right to payment in lieu of tithe.

SCHEDULE 2
Registrable Dispositions: Registration Requirements

PART 1
Registered Estates

Introductory

1   This Part deals with the registration requirements relating to those dispositions of registered estates which are required to be completed by registration.

Transfer

2—(1)   In the case of a transfer of whole or part, the transferee, or his successor in title, must be entered in the register as the proprietor.

(2)   In the case of a transfer of part, such details of the transfer as rules may provide must be entered in the register in relation to the registered estate out of which the transfer is made.

Lease of estate in land

3—(1)   This paragraph applies to a disposition consisting of the grant out of an estate in land of a term of years absolute.

(2)   In the case of a disposition to which this paragraph applies –
    (a)   the grantee, or his successor in title, must be entered in the register as the proprietor of the lease, and
    (b)   a notice in respect of the lease must be entered in the register.

Lease of franchise or manor

4—(1)   This paragraph applies to a disposition consisting of the grant out of a franchise or manor of a lease for a term of more than seven years from the date of the grant.

(2)   In the case of a disposition to which this paragraph applies –
    (a)   the grantee, or his successor in title, must be entered in the register as the proprietor of the lease, and
    (b)   a notice in respect of the lease must be entered in the register.

5—(1)   This paragraph applies to a disposition consisting of the grant out of a franchise or manor of a lease for a term not exceeding seven years from the date of the grant.

(2)   In the case of a disposition to which this paragraph applies, a notice in respect of the lease must be entered in the register.

Creation of independently registrable legal interest

6—(1)   This paragraph applies to a disposition consisting of the creation of a legal rentcharge or profit a prendre in gross, other than one created for, or for an interest equivalent to, a term of years absolute not exceeding seven years from the date of creation.

(2)   In the case of a disposition to which this paragraph applies –
    (a)   the grantee, or his successor in title, must be entered in the register as the proprietor of the interest created, and
    (b)   a notice in respect of the interest created must be entered in the register.

(3)   In sub-paragraph (1), the reference to a legal rentcharge or profit a prendre in gross is to one falling within section 1(2) of the Law of Property Act 1925.

Creation of other legal interest

7—(1)   This paragraph applies to a disposition which –

    (a)   consists of the creation of an interest of a kind falling within section 1(2)(a), (b) or (e) of the Law of Property Act 1925, and

    (b)   is not a disposition to which paragraph 4, 5 or 6 applies.

(2)   In the case of a disposition to which this paragraph applies –

    (a)   a notice in respect of the interest created must be entered in the register, and

    (b)   if the interest is created for the benefit of a registered estate, the proprietor of the registered estate must be entered in the register as its proprietor.

(3)   Rules may provide for sub-paragraph (2) to have effect with modifications in relation to a right of entry over or in respect of a term of years absolute.

Creation of legal charge

8   In the case of the creation of a charge, the chargee, or his successor in title, must be entered in the register as the proprietor of the charge.

PART 2
Registered Charges

Introductory

9   This Part deals with the registration requirements relating to those dispositions of registered charges which are required to be completed by registration.

Transfer

10   In the case of a transfer, the transferee, or his successor in title, must be entered in the register as the proprietor.

Creation of sub-charge

11   In the case of the creation of a sub-charge, the sub-chargee, or his successor in title, must be entered in the register as the proprietor of the sub-charge.

SCHEDULE 3
Unregistered Interests Which Override Registered Dispositions

Leasehold estates in land

1   A leasehold estate in land granted for a term not exceeding seven years from the date of the grant, except for –

    (a)   a lease the grant of which falls within section 4(1)(d), (e) or (f);

    (b)   a lease the grant of which constitutes a registrable disposition.

Interests of persons in actual occupation

2   An interest belonging at the time of the disposition to a person in actual occupation, so far as relating to land of which he is in actual occupation, except for –

    (a)   an interest under a settlement under the Settled Land Act 1925;

(b)   an interest of a person of whom inquiry was made before the disposition
       and who failed to disclose the right when he could reasonably have been
       expected to do so;

(c)   an interest –
       (i)   which belongs to a person whose occupation would not have been
              obvious on a reasonably careful inspection of the land at the time of
              the disposition, and
       (ii)   of which the person to whom the disposition is made does not have
              actual knowledge at that time;

(d)   a leasehold estate in land granted to take effect in possession after the end
       of the period of three months beginning with the date of the grant and
       which has not taken effect in possession at the time of the disposition.

Easements and profits a prendre

3—(1)   A legal easement or profit a prendre, except for an easement, or a profit a
prendre which is not registered under the Commons Registration Act 1965, which at
the time of the disposition –

(a)   is not within the actual knowledge of the person to whom the disposition
       is made, and

(b)   would not have been obvious on a reasonably careful inspection of the
       land over which the easement or profit is exercisable.

(2)   The exception in sub-paragraph (1) does not apply if the person entitled to the
easement or profit proves that it has been exercised in the period of one year ending
with the day of the disposition.

Customary and public rights

4   A customary right.

5   A public right.

Local land charges

6   A local land charge.

Mines and minerals

7   An interest in any coal or coal mine, the rights attached to any such interest and
the rights of any person under section 38, 49 or 51 of the Coal Industry Act 1994.

8   In the case of land to which title was registered before 1898, rights to mines and
minerals (and incidental rights) created before 1898.

9   In the case of land to which title was registered between 1898 and 1925
inclusive, rights to mines and minerals (and incidental rights) created before the date
of registration of the title.

Miscellaneous

10   A franchise.

11   A manorial right.

12   A right to rent which was reserved to the Crown on the granting of any freehold estate (whether or not the right is still vested in the Crown).

13   A non-statutory right in respect of an embankment or sea or river wall.

14   A right to payment in lieu of tithe.

SCHEDULE 4
Alteration of the Register

Introductory

1   In this Schedule, references to rectification, in relation to alteration of the register, are to alteration which –
   (a)   involves the correction of a mistake, and
   (b)   prejudicially affects the title of a registered proprietor.

Alteration pursuant to a court order

2—(1)   The court may make an order for alteration of the register for the purpose of –
   (a)   correcting a mistake,
   (b)   bringing the register up to date, or
   (c)   giving effect to any estate, right or interest excepted from the effect of registration.

(2)   An order under this paragraph has effect when served on the registrar to impose a duty on him to give effect to it.

3—(1)   This paragraph applies to the power under paragraph 2, so far as relating to rectification.

(2)   If alteration affects the title of the proprietor of a registered estate in land, no order may be made under paragraph 2 without the proprietor's consent in relation to land in his possession unless –
   (a)   he has by fraud or lack of proper care caused or substantially contributed to the mistake, or
   (b)   it would for any other reason be unjust for the alteration not to be made.

(3)   If in any proceedings the court has power to make an order under paragraph 2, it must do so, unless there are exceptional circumstances which justify its not doing so.

(4)   In sub-paragraph (2), the reference to the title of the proprietor of a registered estate in land includes his title to any registered estate which subsists for the benefit of the estate in land.

4   Rules may –

(a)   make provision about the circumstances in which there is a duty to exercise the power under paragraph 2, so far as not relating to rectification;

(b)   make provision about the form of an order under paragraph 2;

(c)   make provision about service of such an order.

Alteration otherwise than pursuant to a court order

5   The registrar may alter the register for the purpose of –

(a)   correcting a mistake,

(b)   bringing the register up to date,

(c)   giving effect to any estate, right or interest excepted from the effect of registration, or

(d)   removing a superfluous entry.

6—(1)   This paragraph applies to the power under paragraph 5, so far as relating to rectification.

(2)   No alteration affecting the title of the proprietor of a registered estate in land may be made under paragraph 5 without the proprietor's consent in relation to land in his possession unless –

(a)   he has by fraud or lack of proper care caused or substantially contributed to the mistake, or

(b)   it would for any other reason be unjust for the alteration not to be made.

(3)   If on an application for alteration under paragraph 5 the registrar has power to make the alteration, the application must be approved, unless there are exceptional circumstances which justify not making the alteration.

(4)   In sub-paragraph (2), the reference to the title of the proprietor of a registered estate in land includes his title to any registered estate which subsists for the benefit of the estate in land.

7   Rules may –

(a)   make provision about the circumstances in which there is a duty to exercise the power under paragraph 5, so far as not relating to rectification;

(b)   make provision about how the register is to be altered in exercise of that power;

(c)   make provision about applications for alteration under that paragraph, including provision requiring the making of such applications;

(d)   make provision about procedure in relation to the exercise of that power, whether on application or otherwise.

Rectification and derivative interests

8   The powers under this Schedule to alter the register, so far as relating to rectification, extend to changing for the future the priority of any interest affecting the registered estate or charge concerned.

Costs in non-rectification cases

9—(1)   If the register is altered under this Schedule in a case not involving rectification, the registrar may pay such amount as he thinks fit in respect of any costs or expenses reasonably incurred by a person in connection with the alteration which have been incurred with the consent of the registrar.

(2) The registrar may make a payment under sub-paragraph (1) notwithstanding the absence of consent if –

    (a) it appears to him –

        (i) that the costs or expenses had to be incurred urgently, and

        (ii) that it was not reasonably practicable to apply for his consent, or

    (b) he has subsequently approved the incurring of the costs or expenses.

SCHEDULE 5
Land Registry Network

Access to network

1—(1) A person who is not a member of the land registry may only have access to a land registry network under authority conferred by means of an agreement with the registrar.

(2) An agreement for the purposes of sub-paragraph (1) ('network access agreement') may authorise access for –

    (a) the communication, posting or retrieval of information,

    (b) the making of changes to the register of title or cautions register,

    (c) the issue of official search certificates,

    (d) the issue of official copies, or

    (e) such other conveyancing purposes as the registrar thinks fit.

(3) Rules may regulate the use of network access agreements to confer authority to carry out functions of the registrar.

(4) The registrar must, on application, enter into a network access agreement with the applicant if the applicant meets such criteria as rules may provide.

Terms of access

2—(1) The terms on which access to a land registry network is authorised shall be such as the registrar thinks fit, subject to sub-paragraphs (3) and (4), and may, in particular, include charges for access.

(2) The power under sub-paragraph (1) may be used, not only for the purpose of regulating the use of the network, but also for –

    (a) securing that the person granted access uses the network to carry on such qualifying transactions as may be specified in, or under, the agreement,

    (b) such other purpose relating to the carrying on of qualifying transactions as rules may provide, or

    (c) enabling network transactions to be monitored.

(3) It shall be a condition of a network access agreement which enables the person

granted access to use the network to carry on qualifying transactions that he must comply with any rules for the time being in force under paragraph 5.

(4)   Rules may regulate the terms on which access to a land registry network is authorised.

Termination of access

3—(1)   The person granted access by a network access agreement may terminate the agreement at any time by notice to the registrar.

(2)   Rules may make provision about the termination of a network access agreement by the registrar and may, in particular, make provision about –
   (a)   the grounds of termination,
   (b)   the procedure to be followed in relation to termination, and
   (c)   the suspension of termination pending appeal.

(3)   Without prejudice to the generality of sub-paragraph (2)(a), rules under that provision may authorise the registrar to terminate a network access agreement if the person granted access –
   (a)   fails to comply with the terms of the agreement,
   (b)   ceases to be a person with whom the registrar would be required to enter into a network access agreement conferring the authority which the agreement confers, or
   (c)   does not meet such conditions as the rules may provide.

Appeals

4—(1)   A person who is aggrieved by a decision of the registrar with respect to entry into, or termination of, a network access agreement may appeal against the decision to the adjudicator.

(2)   On determining an appeal under this paragraph, the adjudicator may give such directions as he considers appropriate to give effect to his determination.

(3)   Rules may make provision about appeals under this paragraph.

Network transaction rules

5—(1)   Rules may make provision about how to go about network transactions.

(2)   Rules under sub-paragraph (1) may, in particular, make provision about dealings with the land registry, including provision about –
   (a)   the procedure to be followed, and
   (b)   the supply of information (including information about unregistered interests).

Overriding nature of network access obligations

6   To the extent that an obligation not owed under a network access agreement conflicts with an obligation owed under such an agreement by the person granted access, the obligation not owed under the agreement is discharged.

Do-it-yourself conveyancing

7—(1)   If there is a land registry network, the registrar has a duty to provide such assistance as he thinks appropriate for the purpose of enabling persons engaged in qualifying transactions who wish to do their own conveyancing to do so by means of the network.

(2)   The duty under sub-paragraph (1) does not extend to the provision of legal advice.

Presumption of authority

8   Where –
  (a)   a person who is authorised under a network access agreement to do so uses the network for the making of a disposition or contract, and
  (b)   the document which purports to effect the disposition or to be the contract –
      (i)   purports to be authenticated by him as agent, and
      (ii)   contains a statement to the effect that he is acting under the authority of his principal,
he shall be deemed, in favour of any other party, to be so acting.

Management of network transactions

9—(1)   The registrar may use monitoring information for the purpose of managing network transactions and may, in particular, disclose such information to persons authorised to use the network, and authorise the further disclosure of information so disclosed, if he considers it is necessary or desirable to do so.

(2)   The registrar may delegate his functions under sub-paragraph (1), subject to such conditions as he thinks fit.

(3)   In sub-paragraph (1), 'monitoring information' means information provided in pursuance of provision in a network access agreement included under paragraph 2(2)(c).

Supplementary

10   The registrar may provide, or arrange for the provision of, education and training in relation to the use of a land registry network.

11—(1)   Power to make rules under paragraph 1, 2 or 3 is exercisable by the Lord Chancellor.

(2)   Before making such rules, the Lord Chancellor must consult such persons as he considers appropriate.

(3)   In making rules under paragraph 1 or 3(2)(a), the Lord Chancellor must have regard, in particular, to the need to secure –
  (a)   the confidentiality of private information kept on the network,
  (b)   competence in relation to the use of the network (in particular for the purpose of making changes), and

(c)   the adequate insurance of potential liabilities in connection with use of the network.

12   In this Schedule –

'land registry network' means a network provided under section 92(1);

'network access agreement' has the meaning given by paragraph 1(2);

'network transaction' means a transaction carried on by means of a land registry network;

'qualifying transaction' means a transaction which –
  (a)   involves registration, and
  (b)   is capable of being effected electronically.

SCHEDULE 6
Registration of Adverse Possessor

Right to apply for registration

1—(1)   A person may apply to the registrar to be registered as the proprietor of a registered estate in land if he has been in adverse possession of the estate for the period of ten years ending on the date of the application.

(2)   A person may also apply to the registrar to be registered as the proprietor of a registered estate in land if –
  (a)   he has in the period of six months ending on the date of the application ceased to be in adverse possession of the estate because of eviction by the registered proprietor, or a person claiming under the registered proprietor,
  (b)   on the day before his eviction he was entitled to make an application under sub-paragraph (1), and
  (c)   the eviction was not pursuant to a judgment for possession.

(3)   However, a person may not make an application under this paragraph if –
  (a)   he is a defendant in proceedings which involve asserting a right to possession of the land, or
  (b)   judgment for possession of the land has been given against him in the last two years.

(4)   For the purposes of sub-paragraph (1), the estate need not have been registered throughout the period of adverse possession.

Notification of application

2—(1)   The registrar must give notice of an application under paragraph 1 to –
  (a)   the proprietor of the estate to which the application relates,
  (b)   the proprietor of any registered charge on the estate,
  (c)   where the estate is leasehold, the proprietor of any superior registered estate,
  (d)   any person who is registered in accordance with rules as a person to be notified under this paragraph, and
  (e)   such other persons as rules may provide.

(2)   Notice under this paragraph shall include notice of the effect of paragraph 4.

Treatment of application
3—(1)   A person given notice under paragraph 2 may require that the application to which the notice relates be dealt with under paragraph 5.

(2)   The right under this paragraph is exercisable by notice to the registrar given before the end of such period as rules may provide.

4   If an application under paragraph 1 is not required to be dealt with under paragraph 5, the applicant is entitled to be entered in the register as the new proprietor of the estate.

5—(1)   If an application under paragraph 1 is required to be dealt with under this paragraph, the applicant is only entitled to be registered as the new proprietor of the estate if any of the following conditions is met.

(2)   The first condition is that –
(a)   it would be unconscionable because of an equity by estoppel for the registered proprietor to seek to dispossess the applicant, and
(b)   the circumstances are such that the applicant ought to be registered as the proprietor.

(3)   The second condition is that the applicant is for some other reason entitled to be registered as the proprietor of the estate.

(4)   The third condition is that –
(a)   the land to which the application relates is adjacent to land belonging to the applicant,
(b)   the exact line of the boundary between the two has not been determined under rules under section 60,
(c)   for at least ten years of the period of adverse possession ending on the date of the application, the applicant (or any predecessor in title) reasonably believed that the land to which the application relates belonged to him, and
(d)   the estate to which the application relates was registered more than one year prior to the date of the application.

(5)   In relation to an application under paragraph 1(2), this paragraph has effect as if the reference in sub-paragraph (4)(c) to the date of the application were to the day before the date of the applicant's eviction.

Right to make further application for registration
6—(1)   Where a person's application under paragraph 1 is rejected, he may make a further application to be registered as the proprietor of the estate if he is in adverse possession of the estate from the date of the application until the last day of the period of two years beginning with the date of its rejection.

(2)   However, a person may not make an application under this paragraph if –

(a)   he is a defendant in proceedings which involve asserting a right to possession of the land,

(b)   judgment for possession of the land has been given against him in the last two years, or

(c)   he has been evicted from the land pursuant to a judgment for possession.

7   If a person makes an application under paragraph 6, he is entitled to be entered in the register as the new proprietor of the estate.

Restriction on applications

8—(1)   No one may apply under this Schedule to be registered as the proprietor of an estate in land during, or before the end of twelve months after the end of, any period in which the existing registered proprietor is for the purposes of the Limitation (Enemies and War Prisoners) Act 1945 –

(a)   an enemy, or

(b)   detained in enemy territory.

(2)   No-one may apply under this Schedule to be registered as the proprietor of an estate in land during any period in which the existing registered proprietor is –

(a)   unable because of mental disability to make decisions about issues of the kind to which such an application would give rise, or

(b)   unable to communicate such decisions because of mental disability or physical impairment.

(3)   For the purposes of sub-paragraph (2), 'mental disability' means a disability or disorder of the mind or brain, whether permanent or temporary, which results in an impairment or disturbance of mental functioning.

(4)   Where it appears to the registrar that sub-paragraph (1) or (2) applies in relation to an estate in land, he may include a note to that effect in the register.

Effect of registration

9—(1)   Where a person is registered as the proprietor of an estate in land in pursuance of an application under this Schedule, the title by virtue of adverse possession which he had at the time of the application is extinguished.

(2)   Subject to sub-paragraph (3), the registration of a person under this Schedule as the proprietor of an estate in land does not affect the priority of any interest affecting the estate.

(3)   Subject to sub-paragraph (4), where a person is registered under this Schedule as the proprietor of an estate, the estate is vested in him free of any registered charge affecting the estate immediately before his registration.

(4)   Sub-paragraph (3) does not apply where registration as proprietor is in pursuance of an application determined by reference to whether any of the conditions in paragraph 5 applies.

Apportionment and discharge of charges

10—(1) Where –

  (a)   a registered estate continues to be subject to a charge notwithstanding the registration of a person under this Schedule as the proprietor, and

  (b)   the charge affects property other than the estate,

the proprietor of the estate may require the chargee to apportion the amount secured by the charge at that time between the estate and the other property on the basis of their respective values.

(2)   The person requiring the apportionment is entitled to a discharge of his estate from the charge on payment of –

  (a)   the amount apportioned to the estate, and

  (b)   the costs incurred by the chargee as a result of the apportionment.

(3)   On a discharge under this paragraph, the liability of the chargor to the chargee is reduced by the amount apportioned to the estate.

(4)   Rules may make provision about apportionment under this paragraph, in particular, provision about –

  (a)   procedure,

  (b)   valuation,

  (c)   calculation of costs payable under sub-paragraph (2)(b), and

  (d)   payment of the costs of the chargor.

Meaning of 'adverse possession'

11—(1) A person is in adverse possession of an estate in land for the purposes of this Schedule if, but for section 96, a period of limitation under section 15 of the Limitation Act 1980 would run in his favour in relation to the estate.

(2)   A person is also to be regarded for those purposes as having been in adverse possession of an estate in land –

  (a)   where he is the successor in title to an estate in the land, during any period of adverse possession by a predecessor in title to that estate, or

  (b)   during any period of adverse possession by another person which comes between, and is continuous with, periods of adverse possession of his own.

(3)   In determining whether for the purposes of this paragraph a period of limitation would run under section 15 of the Limitation Act 1980, there are to be disregarded –

  (a)   the commencement of any legal proceedings, and

  (b)   paragraph 6 of Schedule 1 to that Act.

Trusts

12   A person is not to be regarded as being in adverse possession of an estate for the purposes of this Schedule at any time when the estate is subject to a trust, unless the interest of each of the beneficiaries in the estate is an interest in possession.

Crown foreshore

13—(1) Where –

(a)   a person is in adverse possession of an estate in land,
(b)   the estate belongs to Her Majesty in right of the Crown or the Duchy of Lancaster or to the Duchy of Cornwall, and
(c)   the land consists of foreshore,

paragraph 1(1) is to have effect as if the reference to ten years were to sixty years.

(2)   For the purposes of sub-paragraph (1), land is to be treated as foreshore if it has been foreshore at any time in the previous ten years.

(3)   In this paragraph, 'foreshore' means the shore and bed of the sea and of any tidal water, below the line of the medium high tide between the spring and neap tides.

Rentcharges
14   Rules must make provision to apply the preceding provisions of this Schedule to registered rentcharges, subject to such modifications and exceptions as the rules may provide.

Procedure
15   Rules may make provision about the procedure to be followed pursuant to an application under this Schedule.

SCHEDULE 7
The Land Registry

Holding of office by Chief Land Registrar
1—(1)   The registrar may at any time resign his office by written notice to the Lord Chancellor.

(2)   The Lord Chancellor may remove the registrar from office if he is unable or unfit to discharge the functions of office.

(3)   Subject to the above, a person appointed to be the registrar is to hold and vacate office in accordance with the terms of his appointment and, on ceasing to hold office, is eligible for reappointment.

Remuneration etc of Chief Land Registrar
2—(1)   The Lord Chancellor shall pay the registrar such remuneration, and such travelling and other allowances, as the Lord Chancellor may determine.

(2)   The Lord Chancellor shall –
(a)   pay such pension, allowances or gratuities as he may determine to or in respect of a person who is or has been the registrar, or
(b)   make such payments as he may determine towards provision for the payment of a pension, allowances or gratuities to or in respect of such a person.

(3)   If, when a person ceases to be the registrar, the Lord Chancellor determines that there are special circumstances which make it right that the person should receive

compensation, the Lord Chancellor may pay to the person by way of compensation a sum of such amount as he may determine.

Staff
3—(1)   The registrar may appoint such staff as he thinks fit.

(2)   The terms and conditions of appointments under this paragraph shall be such as the registrar, with the approval of the Minister for the Civil Service, thinks fit.

Indemnity for members

4   No member of the land registry is to be liable in damages for anything done or omitted in the discharge or purported discharge of any function relating to land registration, unless it is shown that the act or omission was in bad faith.

Seal

5   The land registry is to continue to have a seal and any document purporting to be sealed with it is to be admissible in evidence without any further or other proof.

Documentary evidence

6   The Documentary Evidence Act 1868 has effect as if–
   (a)   the registrar were included in the first column of the Schedule to that Act,
   (b)   the registrar and any person authorised to act on his behalf were mentioned in the second column of that Schedule, and
   (c)   the regulations referred to in that Act included any form or direction issued by the registrar or by any such person.

Parliamentary disqualification

7   In Part 3 of Schedule 1 to the House of Commons Disqualification Act 1975 (other disqualifying offices), there is inserted at the appropriate place –
'Chief Land Registrar.';
and a corresponding amendment is made in Part 3 of Schedule 1 to the Northern Ireland Assembly Disqualification Act 1975.

SCHEDULE 8
Indemnities

Entitlement
1—(1)   A person is entitled to be indemnified by the registrar if he suffers loss by reason of –
   (a)   rectification of the register,
   (b)   a mistake whose correction would involve rectification of the register,
   (c)   a mistake in an official search,
   (d)   a mistake in an official copy,
   (e)   a mistake in a document kept by the registrar which is not an original and is referred to in the register,
   (f)   the loss or destruction of a document lodged at the registry for inspection or safe custody,
   (g)   a mistake in the cautions register, or

(h)   failure by the registrar to perform his duty under section 50.

(2)   For the purposes of sub-paragraph (1)(a) –

(a)   any person who suffers loss by reason of the change of title under section 62 is to be regarded as having suffered loss by reason of rectification of the register, and

(b)   the proprietor of a registered estate or charge claiming in good faith under a forged disposition is, where the register is rectified, to be regarded as having suffered loss by reason of such rectification as if the disposition had not been forged.

(3)   No indemnity under sub-paragraph (1)(b) is payable until a decision has been made about whether to alter the register for the purpose of correcting the mistake; and the loss suffered by reason of the mistake is to be determined in the light of that decision.

Mines and minerals
2   No indemnity is payable under this Schedule on account of –

(a)   any mines or minerals, or

(b)   the existence of any right to work or get mines or minerals,

unless it is noted in the register that the title to the registered estate concerned includes the mines or minerals.

Costs
3—(1)   In respect of loss consisting of costs or expenses incurred by the claimant in relation to the matter, an indemnity under this Schedule is payable only on account of costs or expenses reasonably incurred by the claimant with the consent of the registrar.

(2)   The requirement of consent does not apply where –

(a)   the costs or expenses must be incurred by the claimant urgently, and

(b)   it is not reasonably practicable to apply for the registrar's consent.

(3)   If the registrar approves the incurring of costs or expenses after they have been incurred, they shall be treated for the purposes of this paragraph as having been incurred with his consent.

4—(1)   If no indemnity is payable to a claimant under this Schedule, the registrar may pay such amount as he thinks fit in respect of any costs or expenses reasonably incurred by the claimant in connection with the claim which have been incurred with the consent of the registrar.

(2)   The registrar may make a payment under sub-paragraph (1) notwithstanding the absence of consent if –

(a)   it appears to him –

(i)   that the costs or expenses had to be incurred urgently, and

(ii)   that it was not reasonably practicable to apply for his consent, or

(b)   he has subsequently approved the incurring of the costs or expenses.

Claimant's fraud or lack of care

5—(1)   No indemnity is payable under this Schedule on account of any loss suffered by a claimant –

    (a)   wholly or partly as a result of his own fraud, or

    (b)   wholly as a result of his own lack of proper care.

(2)   Where any loss is suffered by a claimant partly as a result of his own lack of proper care, any indemnity payable to him is to be reduced to such extent as is fair having regard to his share in the responsibility for the loss.

(3)   For the purposes of this paragraph any fraud or lack of care on the part of a person from whom the claimant derives title (otherwise than under a disposition for valuable consideration which is registered or protected by an entry in the register) is to be treated as if it were fraud or lack of care on the part of the claimant.

Valuation of estates etc

6   Where an indemnity is payable in respect of the loss of an estate, interest or charge, the value of the estate, interest or charge for the purposes of the indemnity is to be regarded as not exceeding –

    (a)   in the case of an indemnity under paragraph 1(1)(a), its value immediately before rectification of the register (but as if there were to be no rectification), and

    (b)   in the case of an indemnity under paragraph 1(1)(b), its value at the time when the mistake which caused the loss was made.

Determination of indemnity by court

7—(1)   A person may apply to the court for the determination of any question as to –

    (a)   whether he is entitled to an indemnity under this Schedule, or

    (b)   the amount of such an indemnity.

(2)   Paragraph 3(1) does not apply to the costs of an application to the court under this paragraph or of any legal proceedings arising out of such an application.

Time limits

8   For the purposes of the Limitation Act 1980 –

    (a)   a liability to pay an indemnity under this Schedule is a simple contract debt, and

    (b)   the cause of action arises at the time when the claimant knows, or but for his own default might have known, of the existence of his claim.

Interest

9   Rules may make provision about the payment of interest on an indemnity under this Schedule, including –

    (a)   the circumstances in which interest is payable, and

    (b)   the periods for and rates at which it is payable.

Recovery of indemnity by registrar

10—(1)   Where an indemnity under this Schedule is paid to a claimant in respect of any loss, the registrar is entitled (without prejudice to any other rights he may have) –

(a)   to recover the amount paid from any person who caused or substantially contributed to the loss by his fraud, or

(b)   for the purpose of recovering the amount paid, to enforce the rights of action referred to in sub-paragraph (2).

(2)   Those rights of action are –

(a)   any right of action (of whatever nature and however arising) which the claimant would have been entitled to enforce had the indemnity not been paid, and

(b)   where the register has been rectified, any right of action (of whatever nature and however arising) which the person in whose favour the register has been rectified would have been entitled to enforce had it not been rectified.

(3)   References in this paragraph to an indemnity include interest paid on an indemnity under rules under paragraph 9.

Interpretation

11—(1)   For the purposes of this Schedule, references to a mistake in something include anything mistakenly omitted from it as well as anything mistakenly included in it.

(2)   In this Schedule, references to rectification of the register are to alteration of the register which –

(a)   involves the correction of a mistake, and

(b)   prejudicially affects the title of a registered proprietor.

SCHEDULE 9
The Adjudicator

Holding of office

1—(1)   The adjudicator may at any time resign his office by written notice to the Lord Chancellor.

(2)   The Lord Chancellor may remove the adjudicator from office on the ground of incapacity or misbehaviour.

(3)   Section 26 of the Judicial Pensions and Retirement Act 1993 (compulsory retirement at 70, subject to the possibility of annual extension up to 75) applies to the adjudicator.

(4)   Subject to the above, a person appointed to be the adjudicator is to hold and vacate office in accordance with the terms of his appointment and, on ceasing to hold office, is eligible for reappointment.

Remuneration

2—(1)   The Lord Chancellor shall pay the adjudicator such remuneration, and such other allowances, as the Lord Chancellor may determine.

(2)   The Lord Chancellor shall –
  (a)   pay such pension, allowances or gratuities as he may determine to or in respect of a person who is or has been the adjudicator, or
  (b)   make such payments as he may determine towards provision for the payment of a pension, allowances or gratuities to or in respect of such a person.

(3)   Sub-paragraph (2) does not apply if the office of adjudicator is a qualifying judicial office within the meaning of the Judicial Pensions and Retirement Act 1993.

(4)   If, when a person ceases to be the adjudicator, the Lord Chancellor determines that there are special circumstances which make it right that the person should receive compensation, the Lord Chancellor may pay to the person by way of compensation a sum of such amount as he may determine.

Staff

3—(1)   The adjudicator may appoint such staff as he thinks fit.

(2)   The terms and conditions of appointments under this paragraph shall be such as the adjudicator, with the approval of the Minister for the Civil Service, thinks fit.

Conduct of business

4—(1)   Subject to sub-paragraph (2), any function of the adjudicator may be carried out by any member of his staff who is authorised by him for the purpose.

(2)   In the case of functions which are not of an administrative character, sub-paragraph (1) only applies if the member of staff has a 10 year general qualification (within the meaning of section 71 of the Courts and Legal Services Act 1990).

5   The Lord Chancellor may by regulations make provision about the carrying out of functions during any vacancy in the office of adjudicator.

Finances

6   The Lord Chancellor shall be liable to reimburse expenditure incurred by the adjudicator in the discharge of his functions.

7   The Lord Chancellor may require the registrar to make payments towards expenses of the Lord Chancellor under this Schedule.

Application of Tribunals and Inquiries Act 1992

8   In Schedule 1 to the Tribunal and Inquiries Act 1992 (tribunals under the supervision of the Council on Tribunals), after paragraph 27 there is inserted –

| 'Land Registration | 27B The Adjudicator to Her Majesty's Land Registry.' |

Parliamentary disqualification

9   In Part 1 of Schedule 1 to the House of Commons Disqualification Act 1975 (judicial offices), there is inserted at the end –

'Adjudicator to Her Majesty's Land Registry.';

and a corresponding amendment is made in Part 1 of Schedule 1 to the Northern Ireland Assembly Disqualification Act 1975.

SCHEDULE 10
Miscellaneous and General Powers

PART 1
Miscellaneous

Dealings with estates subject to compulsory first registration

1—(1)   Rules may make provision–
   (a)   applying this Act to a pre-registration dealing with a registrable legal estate as if the dealing had taken place after the date of first registration of the estate, and
   (b)   about the date on which registration of the dealing is effective.

(2)   For the purposes of sub-paragraph (1) –
   (a)   a legal estate is registrable if a person is subject to a duty under section 6 to make an application to be registered as the proprietor of it, and
   (b)   a pre-registration dealing is one which takes place before the making of such an application.

Regulation of title matters between sellers and buyers

2—(1)   Rules may make provision about the obligations with respect to –
   (a)   proof of title, or
   (b)   perfection of title,
of the seller under a contract for the transfer, or other disposition, for valuable consideration of a registered estate or charge.

(2)   Rules under this paragraph may be expressed to have effect notwithstanding any stipulation to the contrary.

Implied covenants

3   Rules may –
   (a)   make provision about the form of provisions extending or limiting any covenant implied by virtue of Part 1 of the Law of Property (Miscellaneous Provisions) Act 1994 (implied covenants for title) on a registrable disposition;
   (b)   make provision about the application of section 77 of the Law of Property Act 1925 (implied covenants in conveyance subject to rents) to transfers of registered estates;

(c) make provision about reference in the register to implied covenants, including provision for the state of the register to be conclusive in relation to whether covenants have been implied.

Land certificates

4 Rules may make provision about –
   (a) when a certificate of registration of title to a legal estate may be issued,
   (b) the form and content of such a certificate, and
   (c) when such a certificate must be produced or surrendered to the registrar.

PART 2
General

Notice

5—(1) Rules may make provision about the form, content and service of notice under this Act.

(2) Rules under this paragraph about the service of notice may, in particular –
   (a) make provision requiring the supply of an address for service and about the entry of addresses for service in the register;
   (b) make provision about –
      (i) the time for service,
      (ii) the mode of service, and
      (iii) when service is to be regarded as having taken place.

Applications

6 Rules may –
   (a) make provision about the form and content of applications under this Act;
   (b) make provision requiring applications under this Act to be supported by such evidence as the rules may provide;
   (c) make provision about when an application under this Act is to be taken as made;
   (d) make provision about the order in which competing applications are to be taken to rank;
   (e) make provision for an alteration made by the registrar for the purpose of correcting a mistake in an application or accompanying document to have effect in such circumstances as the rules may provide as if made by the applicant or other interested party or parties.

Statutory statements

7 Rules may make provision about the form of any statement required under an enactment to be included in an instrument effecting a registrable disposition or a disposition which triggers the requirement of registration.

Residual power

8 Rules may make any other provision which it is expedient to make for the purposes of carrying this Act into effect, whether similar or not to any provision which may be made under the other powers to make land registration rules.

SCHEDULE 11
Minor and Consequential Amendments

Settled Land Act 1925
1   Section 119(3) of the Settled Land Act 1925 ceases to have effect.

Law of Property Act 1925
2—(1)   The Law of Property Act 1925 is amended as follows.

(2)   In section 44, after subsection (4) there is inserted –
'(4A)   Subsections (2) and (4) of this section do not apply to a contract to grant
a term of years if the grant will be an event within section 4(1) of the Land
Registration Act 2002 (events which trigger compulsory first registration of
title).'

(3)   In that section, in subsection (5), for 'the last three preceding subsections' there
is substituted 'subsections (2) to (4) of this section'.

(4)   In that section, at the end there is inserted –
'(12) Nothing in this section applies in relation to registered land or to a term of
years to be derived out of registered land.'

(5)   In section 84(8), the words from ', but' to the end are omitted.

(6)   In section 85(3), for the words from the beginning to the second 'or' there is
substituted 'Subsection (2) does not apply to registered land, but, subject to that, this
section applies whether or not the land is registered land and whether or not'.

(7)   In section 86(3), for the words from the beginning to the second 'or' there is
substituted 'Subsection (2) does not apply to registered land, but, subject to that, this
section applies whether or not the land is registered land and whether or not'.

(8)   In section 87, at the end there is inserted –
'(4)   Subsection (1) of this section shall not be taken to be affected by section
23(1)(a) of the Land Registration Act 2002 (under which owner's powers in
relation to a registered estate do not include power to mortgage by demise or
sub-demise).'

(9)   In section 94(4), for the words from 'registered' to the end there is substituted
'on registered land'.

(10) In section 97, for 'Land Registration Act 1925' there is substituted 'Land
Registration Act 2002'.

(11) In section 115(10), for the words from 'charge' to the end there is substituted
'registered charge (within the meaning of the Land Registration Act 2002)'.

(12) In section 125(2), for the words from '(not being' to '1925)' there is substituted '(not being registered land)'.

(13) In section 205(1)(xxii) –
  (a) for 'Land Registration Act 1925' there is substituted 'Land Registration Act 2002;', and
  (b) the words from ', and' to the end are omitted.

Administration of Estates Act 1925
3   In section 43(2) of the Administration of Estates Act 1925, for 'Land Registration Act 1925' there is substituted 'Land Registration Act 2002'.

Requisitioned Land and War Works Act 1945
4—(1)   Section 37 of the Requisitioned Land and War Works Act 1945 is amended as follows.

(2)   In subsection (2), for 'Land Registration Act 1925' there is substituted 'Land Registration Act 2002'.

(3)   Subsection (3) ceases to have effect.

Law of Property (Joint Tenants) Act 1964
5   In section 3 of the Law of Property (Joint Tenants) Act 1964, for the words from 'any land' to the end there is substituted 'registered land'.

Gas Act 1965
6—(1)   The Gas Act 1965 is amended as follows.

(2)   In section 12(3), for 'Land Registration Act 1925' there is substituted 'Land Registration Act 2002'.

(3)   In sections 12(4) and 13(6), for the words from 'be deemed' to the end there is substituted–
  '(a) for the purposes of the Land Charges Act 1925, be deemed to be a charge affecting land falling within Class D(iii), and
  (b) for the purposes of the Land Registration Act 2002, be deemed to be an equitable easement.'

Commons Registration Act 1965
7—(1)   The Commons Registration Act 1965 is amended as follows.

(2)   In sections 1(1), (2) and (3), 4(3) and 8(1), for 'under the Land Registration Acts 1925 and 1936' there is substituted 'in the register of title'.

(3)   In section 9, for 'the Land Registration Acts 1925 and 1936' there is substituted 'in the register of title'.

(4)   In section 12 (in both places), for 'under the Land Registration Acts 1925 and 1936' there is substituted 'in the register of title'.

(5)   In section 22, in subsection (1), there is inserted at the appropriate place–
    '"register of title" means the register kept under section 1 of the Land Registration Act 2002;'.

(6)   In that section, in subsection (2), for 'under the Land Registration Acts 1925 and 1936' there is substituted 'in the register of title'.

Leasehold Reform Act 1967
8—(1)   The Leasehold Reform Act 1967 is amended as follows.

(2)   In section 5(5) –
    (a)   for 'an overriding interest within the meaning of the Land Registration Act 1925' there is substituted 'regarded for the purposes of the Land Registration Act 2002 as an interest falling within any of the paragraphs of Schedule 1 or 3 to that Act', and
    (b)   for 'or caution under the Land Registration Act 1925' there is substituted 'under the Land Registration Act 2002'.

(3)   In Schedule 4, in paragraph 1(3) –
    (a)   for paragraph (a) there is substituted –
        '(a)   the covenant may be the subject of a notice in the register of title kept under the Land Registration Act 2002, if apart from this subsection it would not be capable of being the subject of such a notice; and', and
    (b)   in paragraph (b), for 'notice of the covenant has been so registered, the covenant' there is substituted 'a notice in respect of the covenant has been entered in that register, it'.

Law of Property Act 1969
9   In section 24(1) of the Law of Property Act 1969, for 'Land Registration Act 1925' there is substituted 'Land Registration Act 2002'.

Land Charges Act 1972
10—(1)   The Land Charges Act 1972 is amended as follows.

(2)   In section 14(1), for the words from 'Land Registration' to the end there is substituted 'Land Registration Act 2002'.

(3)   In section 14(3) –
    (a)   for the words from 'section 123A' to 'register)' there is substituted 'section 7 of the Land Registration Act 2002 (effect of failure to comply with requirement of registration)', and
    (b)   for 'that section' there is substituted 'section 6 of that Act'.

(4)   In section 17(1), in the definition of 'registered land', for 'Land Registration Act 1925' there is substituted 'Land Registration Act 2002'.

Consumer Credit Act 1974
11   In section 177(1) and (6) of the Consumer Credit Act 1974, for 'Land Registration Act 1925' there is substituted 'Land Registration Act 2002'.

Solicitors Act 1974
12—(1)   The Solicitors Act 1974 is amended as follows.

(2)   In sections 22(1) and 56(1)(f), for 'Land Registration Act 1925' there is substituted 'Land Registration Act 2002'.

(3)   Section 75(b) ceases to have effect.

Local Land Charges Act 1975
13   In section 10(3)(b)(ii) of the Local Land Charges Act 1975, for 'under the Land Registration Act 1925' there is substituted 'in the register of title kept under the Land Registration Act 2002'.

Rent Act 1977
14   In section 136(b) of the Rent Act 1977, for the words from 'charge' to the end there is substituted 'registered charge (within the meaning of the Land Registration Act 2002)'.

Charging Orders Act 1979
15   In section 3(2) and (6) of the Charging Orders Act 1979, for 'Land Registration Act 1925' there is substituted 'Land Registration Act 2002'.

Highways Act 1980
16   Section 251(5) of the Highways Act 1980 ceases to have effect.

Inheritance Tax Act 1984
17   In section 238(3) of the Inheritance Tax Act 1984, for paragraph (a) there is substituted –
    '(a)   in relation to registered land–
        (i)   if the disposition is required to be completed by registration, the time of registration, and
        (ii)   otherwise, the time of completion,'.

Housing Act 1985
18—(1)   The Housing Act 1985 is amended as follows.

(2)   In section 37(5), for the words from 'and' to the end there is substituted –
    '(5A)   Where the Chief Land Registrar approves an application for registration of –
        (a)   a disposition of registered land, or
        (b)   the disponee's title under a disposition of unregistered land,

and the instrument effecting the disposition contains a covenant of the kind mentioned in subsection (1), he must enter in the register a restriction reflecting the limitation imposed by the covenant'.

(3)   In section 154(5), for 'Land Registration Acts 1925 to 1971' there is substituted 'Land Registration Act 2002'.

(4)   In section 157(7), for the words from 'the appropriate' to the end there is substituted 'a restriction in the register of title reflecting the limitation'.

(5)   In section 165(6), for 'section 83 of the Land Registration Act 1925' there is substituted 'Schedule 8 to the Land Registration Act 2002'.

(6)   In Schedule 9A, in paragraph 2(2), for the words from the beginning to 'the disponor' there is substituted 'Where on a qualifying disposal the disponor's title to the dwelling-house is not registered, the disponor'.

(7)   In that Schedule, for paragraph 4 there is substituted –
     '4—(1)   This paragraph applies where the Chief Land Registrar approves an application for registration of –
          (a)   a disposition of registered land, or
          (b)   the disponee's title under a disposition of unregistered land,
          and the instrument effecting the disposition contains the statement required by paragraph 1.
       (2)   The Chief Land Registrar must enter in the register –
          (a)   a notice in respect of the rights of qualifying persons under this Part in relation to dwelling-houses comprised in the disposal, and
          (b)   a restriction reflecting the limitation under section 171D(2) on subsequent disposal.'

(8)   In that Schedule, for paragraph 5(2) there is substituted –
     '(2)   If the landlord's title is registered, the landlord shall apply for the entry in the register of –
          (a)   a notice in respect of the rights of the qualifying person or persons under the provisions of this Part, and
          (b)   a restriction reflecting the limitation under section 171D(2) on subsequent disposal.'

(9)   In that Schedule, paragraph 5(3) ceases to have effect.

(10)   In that Schedule, in paragraph 6, for sub-paragraph (1) there is substituted –
     '(1)   The rights of a qualifying person under this Part in relation to the qualifying dwelling house shall not be regarded as falling within Schedule 3 to the Land Registration Act 2002 (and so are liable to be postponed under section 29 of that Act, unless protected by means of a notice in the register).'

(11)   In that Schedule, in paragraph 9(2), for 'Land Registration Acts 1925 to 1986'

there is substituted 'Land Registration Act 2002'.

(12) In Schedule 17, in paragraph 2(2), for 'Land Registration Acts 1925 to 1971' there is substituted 'Land Registration Act 2002'.

(13) In Schedule 20, in paragraph 17(2), for 'Land Registration Acts 1925 to 1986' there is substituted 'Land Registration Act 2002'.

Building Societies Act 1986
19—(1) In Schedule 2A to the Building Societies Act 1986, paragraph 1 is amended as follows.

(2) In sub-paragraph (2), for 'charge or incumbrance registered under the Land Registration Act 1925' there is substituted 'registered charge (within the meaning of the Land Registration Act 2002)'.

(3) Sub-paragraph (4) ceases to have effect.

(4) In sub-paragraph (5), the definition of 'registered land' and the preceding 'and' cease to have effect.

Landlord and Tenant Act 1987
20 In sections 24(8) and (9), 28(5), 30(6) and 34(9) of the Landlord and Tenant Act 1987, for 'Land Registration Act 1925' there is substituted 'Land Registration Act 2002'.

Diplomatic and Consular Premises Act 1987
21—(1) The Diplomatic and Consular Premises Act 1987 is amended as follows.

(2) In section 5, after the definition of the expression 'diplomatic premises' there is inserted –
    '"land" includes buildings and other structures, land covered with water and any estate, interest, easement, servitude or right in or over land,'.

(3) In Schedule 1, in paragraph 1 –
    (a) before the definition of the expression 'the registrar' there is inserted –
        '"registered land" has the same meaning as in the Land Registration Act 2002;', and
    (b) the words from 'and expressions' to the end are omitted.

Criminal Justice Act 1988
22—(1) The Criminal Justice Act 1988 is amended as follows.

(2) In section 77(12) –
    (a) for 'Land Registration Act 1925' there is substituted 'Land Registration Act 2002', and
    (b) in paragraph (a), at the end there is inserted ', except that no notice may be

entered in the register of title under the Land Registration Act 2002 in respect of such orders'.

(3)   In section 79(1) and (4), for 'Land Registration Act 1925' there is substituted 'Land Registration Act 2002'.

Housing Act 1988
23—(1)   The Housing Act 1988 is amended as follows.

(2)   In section 81, in subsection (9)(c), for 'Land Registration Acts 1925 to 1986' there is substituted 'Land Registration Act 2002'.

(3)   In that section, for subsection (10) there is substituted –
'(10) Where the Chief Land Registrar approves an application for registration of –
      (a) a disposition of registered land, or
      (b) the approved person's title under a disposition of unregistered land,
and the instrument effecting the disposition contains the statement required by subsection (1) above, he shall enter in the register a restriction reflecting the limitation under this section on subsequent disposal.'

(4)   In section 90(4), for 'Land Registration Act 1925' there is substituted 'Land Registration Act 2002'.

(5)   In section 133, in subsection (8) –
  (a)   for the words 'conveyance, grant or assignment' there is substituted 'transfer or grant',
  (b)   for the words 'section 123 of the Land Registration Act 1925' there is substituted 'section 4 of the Land Registration Act 2002', and
  (c)   in paragraph (c), for 'Land Registration Acts 1925 to 1986' there is substituted 'Land Registration Act 2002'.

(6)   In that section, for subsection (9) there is substituted –
'(9) Where the Chief Land Registrar approves an application for registration of –
      (a)   a disposition of registered land, or
      (b)   a person's title under a disposition of unregistered land,
and the instrument effecting the original disposal contains the statement required by subsection (3)(d) above, he shall enter in the register a restriction reflecting the limitation under this section on subsequent disposal.'

Local Government and Housing Act 1989
24—(1)   Section 173 of the Local Government and Housing Act 1989 is amended as follows.

(2)   In subsection (8) –
  (a)   for the words 'conveyance, grant or assignment' there is substituted 'transfer or grant',

(b)   for the words 'section 123 of the Land Registration Act 1925' there is substituted 'section 4 of the Land Registration Act 2002', and

(c)   in paragraph (c), for 'Land Registration Acts 1925 to 1986' there is substituted 'Land Registration Act 2002'.

(3)   For subsection (9) there is substituted –

'(9)   Where the Chief Land Registrar approves an application for registration of –

(a)   a disposition of registered land, or

(b)   a person's title under a disposition of unregistered land,

and the instrument effecting the initial transfer contains the statement required by subsection (3) above, he shall enter in the register a restriction reflecting the limitation under this section on subsequent disposal.'

Water Resources Act 1991
25—(1)   Section 158 of the Water Resources Act 1991 is amended as follows.

(2)   In subsection (5) –

(a)   for paragraphs (a) and (b) there is substituted –

'(a)   the agreement may be the subject of a notice in the register of title under the Land Registration Act 2002 as if it were an interest affecting the registered land;

(b)   the provisions of sections 28 to 30 of that Act (effect of dispositions of registered land on priority of adverse interests) shall apply as if the agreement were such an interest;', and

(b)   in paragraph (c), for 'where notice of the agreement has been so registered,' there is substituted 'subject to the provisions of those sections,'.

(3)   In subsection (6), for 'Land Registration Act 1925' there is substituted 'Land Registration Act 2002'.

Access to Neighbouring Land Act 1992
26—(1)   The Access to Neighbouring Land Act 1992 is amended as follows.

(2)   In section 4(1), for 'Land Registration Act 1925' there is substituted 'Land Registration Act 2002'.

(3)   In section 5, in subsection (4) –

(a)   in paragraph (b), for 'notice or caution under the Land Registration Act 1925' there is substituted 'notice under the Land Registration Act 2002', and

(b)   for 'entry, notice or caution' there is substituted 'entry or notice'.

(4)   In that section, for subsection (5) there is substituted –

'(5)   The rights conferred on a person by or under an access order shall not be capable of falling within paragraph 2 of Schedule 1 or 3 to the Land Registration Act 2002 (overriding status of interest of person in actual occupation).'

(5)   In that section, in subsection (6), for 'Land Registration Act 1925' there is substituted 'Land Registration Act 2002'.

Further and Higher Education Act 1992
27   In Schedule 5 to the Further and Higher Education Act 1992, in paragraph 6(1) –
    (a)   for 'Land Registration Acts 1925 to 1986' there is substituted 'Land Registration Act 2002', and
    (b)   for 'those Acts' there is substituted 'that Act'.

Judicial Pensions and Retirement Act 1993
28   In Schedule 5 to the Judicial Pensions and Retirement Act 1993, there is inserted at the end –
    'Adjudicator to Her Majesty's Land Registry'

Charities Act 1993
29—(1)   The Charities Act 1993 is amended as follows.

(2)   In section 37, for subsections (7) and (8) there is substituted –
'(7)   Where the disposition to be effected by any such instrument as is mentioned in subsection (1)(b) or (5)(b) above will be –
    (a)   a registrable disposition, or
    (b)   a disposition which triggers the requirement of registration,
the statement which, by virtue of subsection (1) or (5) above, is to be contained in the instrument shall be in such form as may be prescribed by land registration rules.

(8)   Where the registrar approves an application for registration of –
    (a)   a disposition of registered land, or
    (b)   a person's title under a disposition of unregistered land,
and the instrument effecting the disposition contains a statement complying with subsections (5) and (7) above, he shall enter in the register a restriction reflecting the limitation under section 36 above on subsequent disposal.'

(3)   In that section, in subsection (9) –
    (a)   for 'the restriction to be withdrawn' there is substituted 'the removal of the entry', and
    (b)   for 'withdraw the restriction' there is substituted 'remove the entry'.

(4)   In that section, in subsection (11), for 'Land Registration Act 1925' there is substituted 'Land Registration Act 2002'.

(5)   In section 39, in subsection (1), at the end there is inserted 'by land registration rules'.

(6)   In that section, for subsections (1A) and (1B) there is substituted –
'(1A)   Where any such mortgage will be one to which section 4(1)(g) of the Land Registration Act 2002 applies –

(a) the statement required by subsection (1) above shall be in such form as may be prescribed by land registration rules; and

(b) if the charity is not an exempt charity, the mortgage shall also contain a statement, in such form as may be prescribed by land registration rules, that the restrictions on disposition imposed by section 36 above apply to the land (subject to subsection (9) of that section).

(1B)   Where –

(a) the registrar approves an application for registration of a person's title

to land in connection with such a mortgage as is mentioned in subsection (1A) above,

(b) the mortgage contains statements complying with subsections (1) and (1A) above, and

(c) the charity is not an exempt charity,

the registrar shall enter in the register a restriction reflecting the limitation under section 36 above on subsequent disposal.

(1C)   Section 37(9) above shall apply in relation to any restriction entered under subsection (1B) as it applies in relation to any restriction entered under section 37(8).'

(7)   In that section, in subsection (6), for the words from 'and subsections' to the end there is substituted 'and subsections (1) to (1B) above shall be construed as one with the Land Registration Act 2002'.

Leasehold Reform, Housing and Urban Development Act 1993
30—(1) The Leasehold Reform, Housing and Urban Development Act 1993 is amended as follows.

(2)   In sections 34(10) and 57(11), for the words from 'rules' to the end there is substituted 'land registration rules under the Land Registration Act 2002'.

(3)   In section 97, in subsection (1) –
(a)   for 'an overriding interest within the meaning of the Land Registration Act 1925' there is substituted 'capable of falling within paragraph 2 of Schedule 1 or 3 to the Land Registration Act 2002', and
(b)   for 'or caution under the Land Registration Act 1925' there is substituted 'under the Land Registration Act 2002'.

(4)   In that section, in subsection (2), for 'Land Registration Act 1925' there is substituted 'Land Registration Act 2002'.

Law of Property (Miscellaneous Provisions) Act 1994
31—(1) The Law of Property (Miscellaneous Provisions) Act 1994 is amended as follows.

(2)   In section 6 (cases in which there is no liability under covenants implied by virtue of Part 1 of that Act), at the end there is inserted –

'(4) Moreover, where the disposition is of an interest the title to which is registered under the Land Registration Act 2002, that person is not liable under any of those covenants for anything (not falling within subsection (1) or (2)) which at the time of the disposition was entered in relation to that interest in the register of title under that Act.'

(3) In section 17(3) –
    (a) in paragraph (c), for the words from 'any' to the end there is substituted 'the Adjudicator to Her Majesty's Land Registry', and

    (b) for 'section 144 of the Land Registration Act 1925' there is substituted 'the Land Registration Act 2002'.

Drug Trafficking Act 1994
32—(1) The Drug Trafficking Act 1994 is amended as follows.

(2) In section 26(12) –
    (a) for 'Land Registration Act 1925' there is substituted 'Land Registration Act 2002', and
    (b) in paragraph (a), at the end there is inserted ', except that no notice may be entered in the register of title under the Land Registration Act 2002 in respect of such orders'.

(3) In section 28(1) and (4), for 'Land Registration Act 1925' there is substituted 'Land Registration Act 2002'.

Landlord and Tenant (Covenants) Act 1995
33—(1) The Landlord and Tenant (Covenants) Act 1995 is amended as follows.

(2) In sections 3(6) and 15(5)(b), for 'Land Registration Act 1925' there is substituted 'Land Registration Act 2002'.

(3) In section 20, in subsection (2), for the words from 'rules' to the end there is substituted 'land registration rules under the Land Registration Act 2002'.

(4) In that section, in subsection (6) –
    (a) for 'an overriding interest within the meaning of the Land Registration Act 1925' there is substituted 'capable of falling within paragraph 2 of Schedule 1 or 3 to the Land Registration Act 2002', and
    (b) for 'or caution under the Land Registration Act 1925' there is substituted 'under the Land Registration Act 2002'.

Family Law Act 1996
34—(1) The Family Law Act 1996 is amended as follows.

(2) In section 31(10) –
    (a) for 'Land Registration Act 1925' there is substituted 'Land Registration Act 2002', and

(b) for paragraph (b) there is substituted –

'(b) a spouse's matrimonial home rights are not to be capable of falling within paragraph 2 of Schedule 1 or 3 to that Act.'

(3) In Schedule 4, in paragraph 4(6), for 'section 144 of the Land Registration Act 1925' there is substituted 'by land registration rules under the Land Registration Act 2002'.

Housing Act 1996
35 In section 13(5) of the Housing Act 1996, for the words from 'if' to the end there is substituted 'if the first disposal involves registration under the Land Registration Act 2002, the Chief Land Registrar shall enter in the register of title a restriction reflecting the limitation'.

Education Act 1996
36 In Schedule 7 to the Education Act 1996, in paragraph 11 –
(a) in sub-paragraph (a), for 'Land Registration Acts 1925 to 1986' there is substituted 'Land Registration Act 2002', and
(b) in sub-paragraphs (b) and (c), for 'those Acts' there is substituted 'that Act'.

School Standards and Framework Act 1998
37 In Schedule 22 to the School Standards and Framework Act 1998, in paragraph 9(1) –
(a) in paragraph (a), for 'Land Registration Acts 1925 to 1986' there is substituted 'Land Registration Act 2002', and
(b) in paragraphs (b) and (c), for 'those Acts' there is substituted 'that Act'.

Terrorism Act 2000
38 In Schedule 4 to the Terrorism Act 2000, in paragraph 8(1)–
(a) for 'Land Registration Act 1925' there is substituted 'Land Registration Act 2002', and
(b) in paragraph (a), at the end there is inserted ', except that no notice may be entered in the register of title under the Land Registration Act 2002 in respect of such orders'.

Finance Act 2000
39 In section 128 of the Finance Act 2000 –
(a) in subsection (2), for the words from 'rule' to the end there is substituted 'land registration rules under the Land Registration Act 2002', and
(b) in subsection (8)(a), for 'Land Registration Act 1925' there is substituted 'Land Registration Act 2002'.

International Criminal Court Act 2001
40 In Schedule 6 to the International Criminal Court Act 2001, in paragraph 7(1) –
(a) for 'Land Registration Act 1925' there is substituted 'Land Registration Act 2002', and
(b) in paragraph (a), at the end there is inserted ', except that no notice may be

entered in the register of title under the Land Registration Act 2002 in respect of such orders'.

SCHEDULE 12
Transition

Existing entries in the register

1   Nothing in the repeals made by this Act affects the validity of any entry in the register.

2—(1)   This Act applies to notices entered under the Land Registration Act 1925 as it applies to notices entered in pursuance of an application under section 34(2)(a).

(2)   This Act applies to restrictions and inhibitions entered under the Land Registration Act 1925 as it applies to restrictions entered under this Act.

(3)   Notwithstanding their repeal by this Act, sections 55 and 56 of the Land Registration Act 1925 shall continue to have effect so far as relating to cautions against dealings lodged under that Act.

(4)   Rules may make provision about cautions against dealings entered under the Land Registration Act 1925.

(5)   In this paragraph, references to the Land Registration Act 1925 include a reference to any enactment replaced (directly or indirectly) by that Act.

3   An entry in the register which, immediately before the repeal of section 144(1)(xi) of the Land Registration Act 1925, operated by virtue of rule 239 of the Land Registration Rules (SI 1925/1093) as a caution under section 54 of that Act shall continue to operate as such a caution.

Existing cautions against first registration

4   Notwithstanding the repeal of section 56(3) of the Land Registration Act 1925, that provision shall continue to have effect in relation to cautions against first registration lodged under that Act, or any enactment replaced (directly or indirectly) by that Act.

Pending applications

5   Notwithstanding the repeal of the Land Registration Act 1925, that Act shall continue to have effect in relation to an application for the entry in the register of a notice, restriction, inhibition or caution against dealings which is pending immediately before the repeal of the provision under which the application is made.

6   Notwithstanding the repeal of section 53 of the Land Registration Act 1925, subsections (1) and (2) of that section shall continue to have effect in relation to an application to lodge a caution against first registration which is pending immediately before the repeal of those provisions.

Former overriding interests

7   For the period of three years beginning with the day on which Schedule 1 comes into force, it has effect with the insertion after paragraph 14 of –

'15   A right acquired under the Limitation Act 1980 before the coming into force of this Schedule.'

8   Schedule 3 has effect with the insertion after paragraph 2 of –

'2A—(1)   An interest which, immediately before the coming into force of this Schedule, was an overriding interest under section 70(1)(g) of the Land Registration Act 1925 by virtue of a person's receipt of rents and profits, except for an interest of a person of whom inquiry was made before the disposition and who failed to disclose the right when he could reasonably have been expected to do so.

(2)   Sub-paragraph (1) does not apply to an interest if at any time since the coming into force of this Schedule it has been an interest which, had the Land Registration Act 1925 continued in force, would not have been an overriding interest under section 70(1)(g) of that Act by virtue of a person's receipt of rents and profits.'

9—(1)   This paragraph applies to an easement or profit a prendre which was an overriding interest in relation to a registered estate immediately before the coming into force of Schedule 3, but which would not fall within paragraph 3 of that Schedule if created after the coming into force of that Schedule.

(2)   In relation to an interest to which this paragraph applies, Schedule 3 has effect as if the interest were not excluded from paragraph 3.

10   For the period of three years beginning with the day on which Schedule 3 comes into force, paragraph 3 of the Schedule has effect with the omission of the exception.

11   For the period of three years beginning with the day on which Schedule 3 comes into force, it has effect with the insertion after paragraph 14 of –

'15   A right under paragraph 18(1) of Schedule 12.'

12   Paragraph 1 of each of Schedules 1 and 3 shall be taken to include an interest which immediately before the coming into force of the Schedule was an overriding interest under section 70(1)(k) of the Land Registration Act 1925.

13   Paragraph 6 of each of Schedules 1 and 3 shall be taken to include an interest which immediately before the coming into force of the Schedule was an overriding interest under section 70(1)(i) of the Land Registration Act 1925 and whose status as such was preserved by section 19(3) of the Local Land Charges Act 1975 (transitional provision in relation to change in definition of 'local land charge').

Cautions against first registration

14—(1)   For the period of two years beginning with the day on which section 15 comes into force, it has effect with the following omissions –

(a)   in subsection (1), the words 'Subject to subsection (3),', and
(b)   subsection (3).

(2)   Any caution lodged by virtue of sub-paragraph (1) which is in force immediately before the end of the period mentioned in that sub-paragraph shall cease to have effect at the end of that period, except in relation to applications for registration made before the end of that period.

(3)   This paragraph does not apply to section 15 as applied by section 81.

15—(1) As applied by section 81, section 15 has effect for the period of ten years beginning with the day on which it comes into force, or such longer period as rules may provide, with the omission of subsection (3)(a)(i).

(2)   Any caution lodged by virtue of sub-paragraph (1) which is in force immediately before the end of the period mentioned in that sub-paragraph shall cease to have effect at the end of that period, except in relation to applications for registration made before the end of that period.

16   This Act shall apply as if the definition of 'caution against first registration' in section 132 included cautions lodged under section 53 of the Land Registration Act 1925.

Applications under section 34 or 43 by cautioners
17   Where a caution under section 54 of the Land Registration Act 1925 is lodged in respect of a person's estate, right, interest or claim, he may only make an application under section 34 or 43 above in respect of that estate, right, interest or claim if he also applies to the registrar for the withdrawal of the caution.

Adverse possession
18—(1) Where a registered estate in land is held in trust for a person by virtue of section 75(1) of the Land Registration Act 1925 immediately before the coming into force of section 97, he is entitled to be registered as the proprietor of the estate.

(2)   A person has a defence to any action for the possession of land (in addition to any other defence he may have) if he is entitled under this paragraph to be registered as the proprietor of an estate in the land.

(3)   Where in an action for possession of land a court determines that a person is entitled to a defence under this paragraph, the court must order the registrar to register him as the proprietor of the estate in relation to which he is entitled under this paragraph to be registered.

(4)   Entitlement under this paragraph shall be disregarded for the purposes of section 131(1).

(5)   Rules may make transitional provision for cases where a rentcharge is held in

trust under section 75(1) of the Land Registration Act 1925 immediately before the coming into force of section 97.

Indemnities
19—(1) Schedule 8 applies in relation to claims made before the commencement of that Schedule which have not been settled by agreement or finally determined by that time (as well as to claims for indemnity made after the commencement of that Schedule).

(2) But paragraph 3(1) of that Schedule does not apply in relation to costs and expenses incurred in respect of proceedings, negotiations or other matters begun before 27 April 1997.

Implied indemnity covenants on transfers of pre-1996 leases
20—(1) On a disposition of a registered leasehold estate by way of transfer, the following covenants are implied in the instrument effecting the disposition, unless the contrary intention is expressed –
    (a)   in the case of a transfer of the whole of the land comprised in the registered lease, the covenant in sub-paragraph (2), and
    (b)   in the case of a transfer of part of the land comprised in the lease –
        (i)   the covenant in sub-paragraph (3), and
        (ii)   where the transferor continues to hold land under the lease, the covenant in sub-paragraph (4).

(2) The transferee covenants with the transferor that during the residue of the term granted by the registered lease the transferee and the persons deriving title under him will –
    (a)   pay the rent reserved by the lease,
    (b)   comply with the covenants and conditions contained in the lease, and
    (c)   keep the transferor and the persons deriving title under him indemnified against all actions, expenses and claims on account of any failure to comply with paragraphs (a) and (b).

(3) The transferee covenants with the transferor that during the residue of the term granted by the registered lease the transferee and the persons deriving title under him will –
    (a)   where the rent reserved by the lease is apportioned, pay the rent apportioned to the part transferred,
    (b)   comply with the covenants and conditions contained in the lease so far as affecting the part transferred, and
    (c)   keep the transferor and the persons deriving title under him indemnified against all actions, expenses and claims on account of any failure to comply with paragraphs (a) and (b).

(4) The transferor covenants with the transferee that during the residue of the term granted by the registered lease the transferor and the persons deriving title under him will –

(a)   where the rent reserved by the lease is apportioned, pay the rent apportioned to the part retained,

(b)   comply with the covenants and conditions contained in the lease so far as affecting the part retained, and

(c)   keep the transferee and the persons deriving title under him indemnified against all actions, expenses and claims on account of any failure to comply with paragraphs (a) and (b).

(5)   This paragraph does not apply to a lease which is a new tenancy for the purposes of section 1 of the Landlord and Tenant (Covenants) Act 1995.

SCHEDULE 13
Repeals

Short title and chapter	*Extent of repeal*
Land Registry Act 1862	The whole Act
Settled Land Act 1925	Section 119(3)
Law of Property Act 1925	In section 84(8), the words from ', but' to the end In section 205(1)(xxii), the words from ', and' to the end
Land Registration Act 1925	The whole Act
Law of Property (Amendment) Act 1926	Section 5
Land Registration Act 1936	The whole Act
Requisitioned Land and War Works Act 1945	Section 37(3)
Mental Health Act 1959	In Schedule 7, the entry relating to the Land Registration Act 1925
Charities Act 1960	In Schedule 6, the entry relating to the Land Registration Act 1925
Civil Evidence Act 1968	In the Schedule, the entry relating to the Land Registration Act 1925
Post Office Act 1969	In Schedule 4, paragraph 27
Law of Property Act 1969	Section 28(7)
Land Registration and Land Charges Act 1971	The whole Act
Superannuation Act 1972	In Schedule 6, paragraph 16
Local Government Act 1972	In Schedule 29, paragraph 26
Solicitors Act 1974	Section 75(b)
Finance Act 1975	In Schedule 12, paragraph 5

Short title and chapter	Extent of repeal
Local Land Charges Act 1975	Section 19(3) In Schedule 1, the entry relating to the Land Registration Act 1925
Endowments and Glebe Measure 1976 (No 4)	In Schedule 5, paragraph 1
Administration of Justice Act 1977	Sections 24 and 26
Charging Orders Act 1979	Section 3(3) Section 7(4)
Limitation Act 1980	In section 17, paragraph (b) and the preceding 'and'
Highways Act 1980	Section 251(5)
Matrimonial Homes and Property Act 1981	Section 4
Administration of Justice Act 1982	Sections 66 and 67 and Schedule 5
Mental Health Act 1983	In Schedule 4, paragraph 6
Capital Transfer Tax Act 1984	In Schedule 8, paragraph 1
Administration of Justice Act 1985	In section 34, in subsection (1), paragraph (b) and the preceding 'and' and, in subsection (2), paragraph (b) In Schedule 2, paragraph 37(b)
Insolvency Act 1985	In Schedule 8, paragraph 5
Housing Act 1985	Section 36(3) Section 154(1), (6) and (7) Section 156(3) Section 168(5) In Schedule 9A, paragraphs 2(1), 3 and 5(3)
Land Registration Act 1986	Sections 1 to 4
Insolvency Act 1986	In Schedule 14, the entry relating to the Land Registration Act 1925
Building Societies Act 1986	In Schedule 2A, in paragraph 1, sub-paragraph (4) and, in sub-paragraph (5), the definition of 'registered land' and the preceding 'and' In Schedule 18, paragraph 2 In Schedule 21, paragraph 9(b)
Patronage (Benefices) Measure 1986 (No 3)	Section 6
Landlord and Tenant Act 1987	Section 28(6) In Schedule 4, paragraphs 1 and 2
Diplomatic and Consular Premises Act 1987	In Schedule 1, in paragraph 1, the words from 'and expressions' to the end

Short title and chapter	*Extent of repeal*
Land Registration Act 1988	The whole Act
Criminal Justice Act 1988	Section 77(13) In Schedule 15, paragraphs 6 and 7
Housing Act 1988	In Schedule 11, paragraph 2(3)
Finance Act 1989	Sections 178(2)(e) and 179(1)(a)(iv)
Courts and Legal Services Act 1990	In Schedule 10, paragraph 3 In Schedule 17, paragraph 2
Access to Neighbouring Land Act 1992	Section 5(2) and (3)
Leasehold Reform, Housing and Urban Development Act 1993	Section 97(3) In Schedule 21, paragraph 1
Coal Industry Act 1994	In Schedule 9, paragraph 1
Law of Property (Miscellaneous Provisions) Act 1994	In Schedule 1, paragraph 2
Drug Trafficking Act 1994	Section 26(13) In Schedule 1, paragraph 1
Family Law Act 1996	Section 31(11) In Schedule 8, paragraph 45
Trusts of Land and Appointment of Trustees Act 1996	In Schedule 3, paragraph 5
Housing Act 1996	Section 11(4)
Housing Grants, Construction and Regeneration Act 1996	Section 138(3)
Land Registration Act 1997	Sections 1 to 3 and 5(4) and (5) In Schedule 1, paragraphs 1 to 6
Greater London Authority Act 1999	Section 219
Terrorism Act 2000	In Schedule 4, paragraph 8(2) and (3)
Trustee Act 2000	In Schedule 2, paragraph 26
International Criminal Court Act 2001	In Schedule 6, paragraph 7(2)

INDEX

Equitable interest/mere equity
    charge, see Charge
    priority issues, *see* Priority
Escheated land   2.61, 3.112
Estate contract   5.34, 7.32, 7.53
Estate in land
    compulsory first registration, triggers for   2.11
      'qualifying estate'   2.57
    registrable disposition   3.12, *see also* Registrable disposition
    voluntary first registration, categories for   2.3, 2.5
Estate, registered
    electronic disposition   7.11, 7.53, 7.54
    recovery action, *see* Adverse possession
Estoppel, equity arising by   3.40
Estoppel, proprietary   2.41
    adverse possession condition   8.31–8.83
      adjudicator's discretion, and appeal from   8.33, 9.20, 9.23
      court discretion   8.32
      facts to be proved   8.31
      possession proceedings defence   8.58
Estuary, *see* River
Evidence
    self-incrimination privilege   9.30
Execution
    company, by, *see* Company/corporation
    signature, electronic, *see* Electronic conveyancing
Expenses, *see* Costs

Fees   5.19, 7.57, 9.15, 10.11
Fee simple absolute in possession
    registration   2.5, 3.12
First registration   2.1 et seq
    application   5.36
    caution against, *see* Caution against first registration
    changes made by Act (summary)   2.1, 2.2
    classes of title, *see* Title
    compulsory, *see* Compulsory first registration
    effect   2.1, 2.2, 2.35–2.52
      priorities   2.35, 2.47
    interests overriding, *see* Easement; Lease; Occupation; Profit à prendre;
      Unregistered interests
    rule-making powers   2.53
    voluntary, *see* Voluntary first registration
Fishing rights   2.8
Forged transfer   5.3
Franchise
    lease of   3.17
    overriding nature of   2.48, 3.93
      phasing out of   2.50, 3.93
    'qualifying estate'   2.57
    registrable disposition   3.12, 3.17
    voluntary registration   2.3, 2.7, 2.8
Fraud
    electronic system, and   7.4, 7.49
    indemnity, and, *see* Indemnity
    proprietor's protection lost by   5.55